The Tenth Muse:
Classical Drama
In Translation

The Tenth Muse: Classical Drama In Translation

edited with an introduction by

Charles Doria

SWALLOW PRESS

OHIO UNIVERSITY PRESS
Chicago   Athens, Ohio   London

Published by
OHIO UNIVERSITY PRESS

Library of Congress Cataloging in Publication Data
Main entry under title:

The Tenth muse.

1. Classical drama--Translations into
English. 2. English drama--Translations from
classical languages. I. Doria, Charles.
PA3626.A2D74   882'.01'08   77-88695
ISBN 0-8040-0781-0
ISBN 0-8040-0813-2 (pbk.)

Portions of the following translations have appeared in these magazines: Emily Hilburn's *Prometheus Bound,* Douglass Parker's *Thyestes* and Tim Reynolds' *Peace* in *Arion* (University of Texas at Austin); George Economou's *The Cyclops* and Armand Schwerner's *Philoctetes* in *The Sun* (New York City). In addition Mr. Schwerner's translation has been recorded on cassette tape and is commercially available as: *Philoctetes,* NY. the New Wilderness Audiographics Series, 1976 #NW-76-16, 365 West End Avenue, New York City.

Table of Contents

*For All the Muses
and Their Interpreters*

Editor's Introduction

I thought, rather than writing the usual sort of introduction to an anthology of classical plays in translation, that it would be useful for me instead to go into some of the reasons that led me to assemble this collection in the first place. Some of the questions that I'd been asking myself when I first started thinking about this book: why another anthology of plays in translation? how can I make the one I have in mind interesting and appealing? and bring people into the enterprise who under the usual circumstances that obtain in the ever-shrinking world of Classical Philology would never have dreamed or been asked to become involved? Even to begin answering these questions (assuming, that is, it's my obligation) involves me in two other areas: the nature of classical drama and the art of translation. These are matters of recurring interest; they concern more than myself and the contributors to this volume. So in that sense they do deserve some attempt at explanation. Yet I find myself almost unable to believe that by doing this I've even begun exploring and mapping out the central concerns and patterns of this anthology. Certain things, I'm convinced, will make themselves evident, if they're at all well-done (as I believe the translations in this volume are) or else not at all. Yet my hope is that by supplying even partial answers to these questions, I will leave myself and my readers in some way better off: better informed about what we're both getting into in this book.

To make a beginning: Anyone, especially if he or she has read an ancient play or two has an idea what it is—a poem for the theater, with long speeches; quirky, weighted repartee formally exhanged between the principal characters and/or the chorus; very little action on-stage, hardly any business to speak of, most important events in the plot taking place off-stage or before the drama opens. These formal, oratorio-like conventions are traditionally interspersed by long choral movements that sometimes introduce the main characters, comment on their actions and motives, bring in mythological and historical parallels by way of oblique analogy, and often include in their musing moral and philosophical reflections that seem to have at times only the most tangential bearing on the principal foci of the play in which they, the chorus, supposedly form an integral part. Their lives, we are often led to suppose, are vitally affected by the fate the title characters in their plays either elect ("character is destiny," says Heraclitus) or else befalls them by way of compelling circumstance. The net effect of all this is that the reader is very likely left with the impression that Classical Drama is a very intricate and obscure art form, involving notions and traditions about theater, poetry, music, dance, to say nothing of hieratic and mythic expression, that seem as impenetrable as they are irrecoverable—or at best difficult to establish and experience in terms of our own contemporaneity. In short I think Classical Drama could become a kind of Endangered Species: just another slightly dusty cultural artifact in the over-large museum of the modern imagination. For it does seem to me sometimes that Antiquity's notions of drama and our own are quite separate and nearly impossible to bridge.

To discover, as scholars have, that both Comedy and Tragedy grow from a common root, the Mysteries of Dionysos, from whose cult ritual scenarios, now no longer extant, have been hypothesized in which the procreative (roughly 'the comic') and destructive (similarly the 'tragic') aspects of Nature are celebrated only complicates matters further. For except for Euripides' *Bacchai* no surviving play actually deals with these themes in a literal way. When Aristotle in his *Poetics* calls the plots (and the word he uses here is *mythos*) of Tragedy "slices from the Homeric banquet" this has the unfortunate side-effect of isolating key elements of ancient drama inside the now permanently lost world of classical mythology.

For unlike the Bible the religions of the Greeks and Romans no longer have the power of summoning belief, no matter how vestigial. This means

2

any chance we might have of experiencing the Ancients' drama in the way people in the Middle Ages did their Mystery Plays is just about nil. As for classical drama as art: What does that mean if we have no anchoring point for it inside ourselves, particularly now when we are happily engaged in breaking down the artificial and constricting barriers between the 'popular' and the 'serious,' between the 'natural' and the 'sophisticated,' between the so-called 'civilized and urbane' and the 'primitive'? What matters in notating the effect any discrete experience has on our spirit is how, as the medieval John of Salisbury among others knew, it moves, delights and instructs, how it quickens us and breaks down the limits dividing self and world, narrow community and what lies beyond. So I think it will be on something like these terms that Classical Drama, if it is to have any valid claim at all towards energizing the soul, will take effect. To re-construct it carefully and painfully through philology, linguistics, history, numismatics, archaeology and the other learned hobbies, as if we were attempting to repair and restore a shattered Athenian amphora (and sometimes ancient texts are as battered as that), is an exercise in futility of the first order if what we really intend is to bring the play back as drama, as act. In fact 'drama' in Greek means precisely that: "a deed, act."

So this was one of the first things I looked for in assembling this collection: how well each translation functioned as a performable play in our language along the lines I've just set forth; how well as a text independent of its Latin or Greek original it communicates the enlivening power we rightfully expect from effective theater, even if, as is the case with most of us these days, what precisely the ancients' theater was all about still eludes us.

Classical scholarship, which is quite necessary for the mechanical preservation of ancient texts, as I see it, plays no part in this. In fact at times the attitudes of official philology have become positive hindrances. It should be remembered that the texts of most classical plays (the only important exception I think to this involves Menander, whose plays are still coming to light in whole or part in papyri newly discovered in the sands of Egypt) have been pretty well established since the late Renaissance. Classicists, however, not content with having performed this major task towards maintaining European cultural continuity and identity, have in time-honored bureaucratic tradition persisted with ever-increasing obscurantism and industrious perversity in analyzing and dissecting the corpus of Classical Drama with the mechanical and unreflective tools of their craft to such an extent that it now requires a long specialist education to become conversant with the ancient stage in ways these professional antiquarians can understand and respect. Pound's setting the classicists in hell because they "obscured the text with philology" has probably never been more true than at present. And I think it is precisely these parochial and self-serving attitudes on the part of these self-appointed guardians of our Classical Tradition that are largely responsible for the present low esteem the old languages today enjoy and the sparse and still-decreasing enrollments in Greek and Latin at all levels of education in this country. For a people who like to think that the major and enduring portion of its heritage as well as its principal point of origin are preserved in the writings of the Romans and Greeks this is indeed a depressing situation and not one likely to improve in the near future, since its remedy lies elsewhere than in the hands of those responsible for creating it over the years.

Another barrier between us and ancient drama, as I indicated earlier, is classical mythology, which we read for the most part as entertaining fiction, not important records of history, religion and collective observation of self and nature. We no longer take story and story-telling as something pure and simple, 'logical' as from *logos*, binding us and our world under its spell. For us the universe is not literal as it once was; the heavens and the earth no longer declare the majesty of the gods. Story (in Greek once more the word is *mythos*) for us must be either true or false, verifiable or 'created' and original—as if considerations of this sort really mattered to or even entered the minds of the ancient story teller, the shaman, those who danced the stories and rites, those who sung them. We seem unable to cultivate within ourselves, even artificially and deliberately, that state of mind we patronizingly call 'innocent' or 'primitive' which would allow us to do so and thereby provide re-entry into the living past of our ancestors and their psychic reality. Sometimes, I think, it must appear to that fabled observer from Mars as if we live our lives and think our thoughts in self-imposed ignorance and isolation from ourselves and our history, imitating at great cost and unacknowledged pain (in the face of overwhelming evidence that it would be in our best interests as well as our

4

planet's for us not to go on any further in the present mode) the three brazen monkeys whose hands cover eyes, ears and mouth. At one time we believed, just as many people still on earth do, that Nature was divine, the whole world was alive with *numen,* and that those who inhabit the layers of the cosmos, the birds, the animals, the fish, the worms, the stars, to say nothing of our own bifurcated ambiguity, were all likewise divine, sharing and co-operating inside the divine soul present everywhere. And so the stories told about what happens in the world and the things of the world were not subject to our canons, our standards of accuracy and record-keeping but instead were the human mental and verbal extensions of the numinous presence of Nature and all her aspects. But what has happened? We call attitudes like this 'primitive,' 'atavistic.' Those addicted to theology have even gone so far as to label it pantheistic and therefore heretical. Our scientists and others of the righteously rational ilk (like the classicists discussed earlier) think Nature dead and by so doing objectify her at the same time as they dehumanize themselves. I attribute this sorry state of affairs— which the moral as well as the ecological condition of the world amply demonstrates—to dame philosophy and her ignorant son, science, who still denies his parentage. For philosophy, originally Plato's trifle, selectively exploits the soul by dividing its unities into appetites which are gratified or not according to plan and not natural impulse, into will which is exercised where it is proper and profitable to do so, and into intellect which by capricious fiat needs to be in constant search of new knowledge, new facts, to glut a newly awakened cerebral hunger whose appeasement is imperative to all else. How many of us remember that Wisdom/Achamoth (whose true birth lies in fear of the divine) is not set forth in Aristotle's encyclopedia and its epigones but springs like Athena from the mind of god and married to it brings the cosmos, the visible world, Nature, to birth. As for science it develops and colonizes outside in the same ways philosophy decreed for the soul while seeking to impose on the primary human spirit. Science, selectively manipulating and stripping those elements deemed of principal benefit to mankind (this is sometimes mockingly called 'humanism') to the principal exclusion and detriment of all else resident there, like a mad necrophiliac defiles the corpse of the world that Doctor Philosophy signed both death warrant and certificate for.

These two, panders to all that is worst and most selfish in us, have so coarsened the soul that it is no wonder that mythology, tales from the Book of Nature, is closed for the present. Until the mythological sense and respect for the divine in all things (*tabu*—that word that rings so archaically but needfully in the ear) are brought back, and true philosophy and science re-invented, we will continue having a hard time getting to the heart of the drama in the ancient theater (admittedly a minor matter in this context), and more importantly in returning us and our dishonored world back to ourselves and Nature, back to the ancient view we find of this in these plays possibly more intensely so than anywhere else.

This then in essence is what I hoped to accomplish in this anthology: to do something towards restoring the sense of myth to modern consciousness and allow the contributors presented here an opportunity to do so each in their own way. I also wanted to remove the act of translation as far as possible from the hands of the specialists, the classicists, who, as I've tried to show, have been content merely to act as preservers and propagators of what is salvageable from the wreck of Antiquity. Therefore I think I can safely say that one unique aspect of this book is that it unites classicists (who simply as bearers of the great names of the past are valuable), translators and poets in a single shared enterprise. In addition this anthology contains at least one example of every known type of Classical Drama: Greek tragedy (Aeschylus' *The Suppliants* and *Prometheus Bound*, Sophocles' *Philoctetes*, and Euripides' *The Bacchai;* satyr play (Euripides' *The Cyclops*—which is also the sole survivor of this genre); Greek ("Old") Comedy (Aristophanes' *Peace*); Latin ("New") Comedy (Plautus' *The Rope*); and Latin chamber tragedy (Seneca's *Thyestes*). My hope was that these varied bases and personal contrasts would produce not some seamless and harmonized ('homogenized') view of classical drama, but one instead that reflected all its individual differences and multiplicities and oppositions, and above all the contributors' earnest and intense efforts to render the old mythology, the Mediterranean experience, in as close and unartificial way as possible.

In this way, for example, Richard Caldwell made use of his own researches into mythology and psychology in his translation of *The Suppliants;* in fact he originally conceived of the play as the collective dream of the chorus, the Suppliants themselves. Emily Hilburn first began her *Prometheus Bound* as a project in pure translation under former *Arion* editors,

James Hynd and Douglass Parker, and only later chose to focus on the dramatic contrast between Prometheus and Io, twin poles of suffering in that play. Armand Schwerner provides a radical revision of the *Philoctetes* for the contemporary stage, drawing on his experience with such theater and music groups as Charlie Morrow's New Wilderness Preservation Band as well as his work with the oral literatures of many 'primitive' cultures. George Economou, hewing closely to the Greek line for line, gives *The Cylcops* a witty and stylish English transparency. I attempted to endow my *Bacchai* with the same qualities I felt were present when a class of mine several years ago staged it as a semi-spontaneous impromptu. Tim Reynolds' *Peace* originally appeared as a musical (with songs by Al Carmines) at St. Mark's in New York in 1968/9 and was later recorded. However the version published here more closely reflects Aristophanes' original. W. Thomas MacCary offers a densely compacted reading of *The Rope*, one that in its layerings reflects his study of the Greek erotic novella and its survivals in Boccaccio and Chaucer, of Shakespeare's late romances such as *The Tempest* (for which *The Rope* is a probable source), as well as of European comic opera and American musical comedy. Douglass Parker, who is perhaps best known for his translations of Aristophanes, in his *Thyestes* attempts to recreate in English the swell and thunder of Seneca's rhetoric, something our theater hasn't known since the Elizabethans translated and staged the philosopher's pocket dramas.

As far as my editorial policy is concerned, there is none. Each translator speaks his own language as he or she derives it from dialog with self and text. This is because I believe any attempt on my part to alter the final form of these translations would be a falsification and betrayal of the talent and work of each contributor, and would also constitute an effort to introduce by the back door those very strivings towards centralism, dogmatism and codification (rule-making as an end in itself) that I condemn elsewhere and see as harmful in our present cultural condition. Finally I consider permissiveness in all senses of the word as the quintessential of any law-abiding community and as absolutely necessary if we are ever to get our stricken nation back on its feet again in a world once new that can be (and underneath it all, I'm sure, still is) as beautiful and nurturing as the one our ancestors knew.

In attempting to construct such a vision of the whole out of separate

7

parts that do not cohere and must not be made to on the procrustean bed of our awkward sciences and ungainly philosophies, I was heartened by these words of Robert Duncan in his essay "Rites of Participation," which point a way towards a community of that permissive openness and strenuousness I would like to see come into being:

> The intense yearning, the desire for something else, of which we too have only a dark and doubtful presentiment remains, but our *arete*, our ideal of vital being, rises not in our identification in a hierarchy of higher forms but in our identification with the universe. To compose such a symposium of the whole, such a totality, all the old excluded orders must be included. The female, the proletariat, the foreign; the animal and vegetative; the unconscious and the unknown; the criminal and failure—all that has been outcast and vagabond must return to be admitted in the creation of what we consider we are.

So to return these plays in their fullness and offer them as mirrors both of the ancients and ourselves: that is the aim, perhaps overly ambitious, of this anthology. But I hope at least some of these expectations and their possible fulfillment are not entirely in vain.

Charles Doria

The Suppliants

Aeschylus

translated by

Richard Caldwell

10

Introduction

Aeschylus' *Suppliants* "is generally regarded as the earliest of extant Greek plays. It is certainly the most primitive, and perhaps, in the common opinion of scholars, the most stiff, helpless, and unintelligible."[1] This statement of Gilbert Murray, made in 1930, would still be valid today were it not for the publication in 1952 of a papyrus fragment which showed that the play was produced after 467 B.C., probably in 463, only seven years before Aeschylus' death. The new dating, however, has provided no new solutions to the old problems of the play's meaning; it has merely eliminated the one old solution, which used early dating to explain "primitive unintelligibility" and "primitive unintelligibility" to prove early dating.

The chief problems are these: the Danaids' aversion to marriage, the characterization of Danaos, the role of Pelasgos, the significance of Zeus, the emphasis on Io and her tortured wanderings, the parthenogenesis of Epaphos, and the role of the Danaids as both chorus and protagonist. I would like to suggest that a coherent and unified approach to these problems can be developed in terms of the following hypothesis:

1. *The Suppliants* is a complex elaboration in dramatic form of two common mythical situations: the father who denies prospective suitors access to his desirable daughter, and the maiden who flees in fear from any sexual encounter.

2. Because of their incestuous attachment to their father, the Danaids are unable to love other men and view potential usurpers of Danaos' position as violent rapists.

11

3. The incestuous fantasy is concealed (and managed) by the Danaids through a series of substitutions in which Danaos is replaced by Pelasgos and Zeus, the play's two figures of paternal power and dominance (just as myths and cultures regularly project the father's authority onto kings and gods).

4. Just as the father is replaced, ultimately, by Zeus in the Danaids' fantasy, so their unnamed mothers are replaced by their ancestress Io, whom Zeus loved, whom the Danaids refer to as mother, and with whom they identify.

To return now to the seven problems mentioned earlier:

1. The Danaids' aversion to marriage is not caused by the violence and repulsiveness of the sons of Aigyptos, but is itself the cause for the mixture of fear and hatred with which they regard their cousins. The aversion itself is doubly determined: on one hand, they are saving themselves for the father they love; on the other hand, their hysterical fear of sex is a common attribute of the ravished maidens of antiquity and has its modern counterpart in the typical anxieties which prospective sexual activity produces in an adolescent girl, who "has difficulty in perceiving vaginal sex as pleasurable and confounds sex with blood, mutilation, pain, penetration, and pregnancy."[2]

2. Critics have uniformly complained of the "wooden" characterization of Danaos, especially his long awkward silences, his inept advice, his abrupt departure when the Egyptians appear. While the play was thought to be primitive, these faults could be explained by reference to Aeschylus' inexperience in handling a second actor, but such explanations will no longer do. In my view, these are not faults at all. Danaos is a father who has been replaced by Pelasgos and Zeus in his daughters' fantasy; his silence or absence while the Danaids argue with Pelasgos or pray to Zeus is a sign that he has been replaced, whereas his presence, required to reveal the core of the fantasy, is nevertheless an embarrassment (i.e., source of conflict) to his daughters. His fatuous speeches are a reminder of the infantile nature of the fantasy, and his jealous concern for his daughters' virginity indicates his complicity in their fixation (psychoanalytically, his "counter-oedipal complex").[3]

3. The absolute authority which the Danaids attribute to Pelasgos, at variance with his actual role as a constitutional monarch who needs the

12

consent of his people, nevertheless conforms with his status in the Danaids' fantasy, a replacement for the omnipotence of the oedipal father.

4. Of all Greek tragedies, the *Suppliants* contains the most expansive and absolute statements of the omnipotence and omniscience of Zeus. This is not, as some have thought, an Akhenaton-like theological statement by Aeschylus; it is a statement by the Danaids of the qualities invested in the father of childhood and now transferred to the supreme deity. The replacement of Danaos by Zeus is an unconscious effort by the Danaids to maintain their oedipal fixation while at the same time suppressing its incestuous aspect. Dodds could have been thinking of the Danaids when he wrote, "It was natural to project on to the heavenly Father those curious mixed feelings about the human one which the child dared not acknowledge even to himself."[4]

5. Although Io is their great-great-great-grandmother, the Danaids clearly identify her both with their mother(s) and with themselves. They repeatedly call her mother, but they also find in her a double of themselves, both actually and wishfully. The situation is clearly contradictory: they view Io both as a woman who, like them, renounced sexuality in the face of threatening masculinity, but also as a mother who enjoyed a sexual relationship with the father. But such contradictions are the ordinary discourse of the unconscious. Io's tortured wanderings, then, are both her punishment for keeping the father to herself and a projection by the Danaids of their own incestuous guilt feelings.

6. The conception of Epaphos, not from ordinary sexual intercourse but from the breath and touch of Zeus, follows from the roles of Io and Zeus as fantasied mother and father. The Danaids deny authentic sexuality to this relationship because they wish to have the father for themselves and to deny to the mother sexual access to the father; at the same time they strengthen their own identification with Io by assigning her to a state of quasi-virginity. This is the female counterpart of the phenomenon of immaculate conception commonly found in myth (e.g., the Christian myth of Jesus and the Aztec myth of Quetzalcoatl, conceived by the breath and touch of the sky-god Tonacatecutli on the virgin Chimalma).[5]

7. Why is the protagonist of the *Suppliants* an undifferentiated group? If we turn the question around and ask why the Danaids have not achieved individuation, a possible answer is that they do not possess the power of

independent choice. Bound to a compulsive repetition of the past and an obsessive attachment to their father (an attachment which can only be intensified by the series of substitutions it goes through), the Danaids exemplify the group's members' abdication of individual will to an all-powerful leader. The necessary step to individuality and maturity (a step taken later in the myth by Hypermnestra) is a sexual initiative, the transformation of a girl in love with her father into a woman able to love other men. One of Freud's earliest metapsychological statements would seem to describe well this aspect of the Danaids' situation:

At the same time as these plainly incestuous fantasies are overcome and repudiated, one of the most significant, but also one of the most painful psychical achievements of the pubertal period is completed: detachment from parental authority, a process that alone makes possible the opposition, which is so important for the progress of civilization, between the new generation and the old. At every stage in the course of development through which all human beings ought by rights to pass, a certain number are held back; so there are some who have never got over their parents' authority and have withdrawn their affection from them either very incompletely or not at all. They are mostly girls, who, to the delight of their parents, have persisted in all their childish love far beyond puberty. It is most instructive to find that it is precisely these girls who in their later marriage lack the capacity to give their husbands what is due to them: they make cold wives and remain sexually anaesthetic.[6]

Finally, how might the *Suppliants* be played? My one suggestion would be that whatever happens on stage be set in flickering and ineffectual opposition to an overpowering atmosphere, that dreamlike darkness where desire and fear are at last indistinguishable.

Richard Caldwell

NOTES

1 G. Murray, *Aeschylus: The Suppliant Women* (London 1930) 7.
2 J. Bardwick, *Psychology of Women: A Study of Bio-Cultural Conflicts* (New York 1971) 52.
3 D. Kouretas, "Application de la psychanalyse à la mythologie: la névrose sexuelle des Danaides d'après les 'Suppliantes' d'Eschyle," *Revue Française de Psychanalyse* 21 (1957) 597-602.
4 E. R. Dodds, *The Greeks and the Irrational* (Berkeley 1951) 48.
5 E. Jones, "The Madonna's Conception through the Ear" in his *Essays in Applied Psychoanalysis* (London 1923) 357.
6 S. Freud, "Three Essays on the Theory of Sexuality" (1905) *Standard Edition* VII, 226-227.

CHARACTERS

DANAOS, King of Libya *(garrulous, officious paternalist)*

THE DANAIDS, his daughters* *(single -minded virgins, often hysterical)*

PELASGOS, King of Argos *(authoritative constitutional lawyer)*

EGYPTIAN HERALD *(bad-tempered barbarian, speaks Greek/English badly)*

ARGIVE ATTENDANTS

Non-speaking characters (slave girls, attendants, Egyptian and Argive soldiers) appear as indicated in stage directions.

*The traditional number of Danaids is 50, but the part could be played by any number from 2 to 50. The Danaids speak one at a time (unless otherwise indicated). Any of them may speak, or there may be a spokeswoman. In longer choral passages, change in speaker is indicated by successive numbering.

15

SCENE

Greece, between Argos and the sea. The stage is a sacred grove with several statues of Greek gods (Zeus, Poseidon, Apollo, Hermes, et. al.) in the center. The city of Argos is off-stage right, the sea is off-stage left and can be seen from a slight rise stage left.

(Danaos enters from the left, leading his daughters and their slave girls; all wear flowing and exotic eastern clothing; the Danaids are veiled from head to waist. They appear fatigued and unsure until Danaos sees the group of statues and points them out to his daughters. Responding to his gestures, they move quickly to the statues and stand before them with outstretched arms. Each speaks in turn.)

DANAIDS:

1 Is this our journey's end?

2 Zeus, you kept us safe,
   watched over our sailing
   from the Nile delta,

3 guarded us ever since
   we escaped your land,

4 running away
   like murderers or exiles
   but you know why:

5 we don't want to marry
   our cousins, Aigyptos' sons.

6 We always hated men:
   what they do to women
   sickens us.

7 Zeus, protect us.

And Danaos, father and lord,
stay with us.

8   You saved us before,
sending us by sea
back to Argos where we began,

9   where Io turned cow in heat,
dancing to the god-fly's sting
as she learned the perfect love of Zeus—
his gentle hand,
his soft breath.

10   He hardly touched her.

11   What better than our motherland
to run to!
Holding weapons of the helpless:
sharp sticks impaling
woolen tufts.

12   City,
earth,
clear water,

13   gods above,
paingods waiting below,
Zeus who watches and holds
the house of the pure—

14   we beg you:
take us
to the land's chaste breath,

15   keep us
from swarming men,

16   drown them,
smash their boat,

oars stabbing the sea;

17 make the wind whirl
thunder blaze
ocean rage
kill them!

18 before they mount their cousins
and force from us
what we will never give.

19 Our song begins
in a meadow across the sea.
A strange creature waited:
a cow,
but so delicate and milkwhite,
somehow beautiful,
she made you think of a
girl looking for flowers.
Her god appeared,
breathed on her,
touched her.
Epaphos ("Touch") was born.
Our mother's calf
will make men sorry
if they touch us.

20 When I remember
Epaphos and our mother
I seem to walk the meadow of her love,
I see the flowers and the pain.

21 Is it a dream?
Will someone finally believe?

22 If anyone hears us cry
he'll think he hears
the nightingale's fear,

that sobbing melody
the hawk-chased wife of Tereus sings.

23   She's like us.
They drove her
from all she knew.

24   They changed her love to hate.
Her bitter song accuses
maleness that made her
kill her son
and lose her woman shape.

25   The only thing I love is pain—
the sounds grief makes
drawing blood on my soft cheek.

26   Let others gather flowers,
we have our sorrow.

27   Our fear of men who loved us
drove us from the land of mist:
can we trust
the man who helps us?

28   The heat that rises in men never cools,
but our gods will stop them.
They know there's
no justice in marriage:
they will listen and hate.

29   God acts when nothing's left,
they feed when war starves:
they'll help us fight.

30   Zeus will see us through:
his thought an overgrown
tangled forest,

31   his desire a swelling river
rushing past eye,
somehow someway
getting what he wants.

32   Zeus bows his head,
the pieces fall in place:
sudden blaze
in blackest night,
dark disorder
in clear day.

33   Zeus cuts down men's towers,
strips off their weapons,
gets what he wants
without even leaving his throne.

34   Zeus knows
a tree chopped down
grows straight up again.

35   That's the way it is with men:
a ceaseless whip
drives them mad
to rape women and call it marriage.

36   Our song is pain
and tears of misery:
how does our life
differ from death?

37   Familiar earth,
cow land of Apis,
you know what my words conceal:
watch me
tear off these linen veils!

(Some of the Danaids take off their veils, putting them on and

*around the gods' statues. From the waist up they wear loose thin
shirts which expose their shoulders and the upper part of their breasts.)*

38   Blind gifts rise
     to those who cannot die,
     from those who are afraid to:
     who knows where
     the indifferent wave falls?

39   Land we know,
     cow land of Apis,
     you know what my words hide:
     take away these veils,
     rip them apart!

40   I remember other cloth,
     our boat's sail,
     kept whole in wind's gentle breath.
     I remember the heavy beating oars
     pushing back the greedy sea.
     All-seeing father,
     make our maiden voyage
     end in happiness!

41   We honor
     our holy mother:
     no man will ever touch us,
     marry us,
     tame us!

42   Zeus' chaste daughter,
     a virgin like us,
     wants what we want:
     to keep sacred walls intact.
     Our pursuers will learn
     her strength and anger.

43　We honor
our mother:
no man will touch us,
marry us,
break us!

44　If we don't win
the gods above,
we'll hang ourselves
and go beneath earth

45　where darkness welcomes,

46　where Zeus,
Lord of the Dead,
can embrace us.

47　He made Io learn
gods' anger
finds its victim.
I too know his wife's jealousy:
storms rise from passion's breath.

48　Blame even Zeus
if he dishonors the cow's child,
his own child,

49　and turns away
from our tears
in our need.

50　He taught Io
that gods' anger
finds its victim.
I too know Hera's anger:
the storm that follows passion's breath.

(As Danaos speaks, he orates, rambles, preaches, emphasizes his concern by touching his daughters, putting his arm around them, etc.)

DANAOS:

Prudence, my girls, is what we need:
yes, moderate, cautious, chaste prudence.
That's why and how your father got you here
and now that we're on dry land
I'm already planning ahead.
This is my advice:
take these words of mine
write them down in your heart
never forget . . .
(He looks toward the city.)
Wait, over there, I think I see a cloud of dust!
And when you see dust
even though it doesn't make any noise
you can bet an army's coming.
Now I hear something . . .
it sounds like wheels and creaking axles.
And now I see a crowd of men
with shields and spears, horses and chariots.
Maybe the rulers of this land
heard about us from their scouts
and are coming to see for themselves.
Their intentions may be peaceful . . .
but on the other hand they could be savages
coming to kill us.
Whatever, this is what I want you to do:
sit down over here
by this mound of Gods Assembled.
I'm going to tell you something:
an altar is stronger than any fortified tower,
it's the only kind of defense that can't be broken into
and that's an important consideration for young women.
Hurry now, get into proper position:
hold these sticks with the wool on top.
That's sure to please Zeus:
his fondness for virgins is well known.

Act pious,
remember to hold the sticks in your left hand,
and above all
when the strangers come
convince them by what you say
that you're just poor helpless girls,
virgins who have fled here to stay unbloodied.
Don't say anything that sounds bold or promiscuous,
no lifting of eyebrows, nothing like that.
Speak when you're spoken to
but don't wait too long before answering:
we don't want any trouble here.
Agree with everything:
you need help badly and it doesn't look good
when women act high and mighty.

DANAIDS:

1   Don't worry, father,
    we're as concerned for our virtue as you are.

2   We'll be true to your words
    as though they came from Zeus himself.

DANAOS:
    May his shining eye shine on us!

DANAID:
    Success is up to him.

DANAOS:
    Now do what I told you
    and say a prayer to Zeus.

DANAID:
    Can't we stay here by your side?

DANAOS:
    You need the gods' help too:

24

now pray to them.

(As he points out different statues, the girls rattle off prayers.)

DANAID:

Zeus, save us,
don't let them rape us!

DANAOS:

Here's a statue of Apollo, the son of Zeus.

DANAID:

Sungod save us,
don't let men get us!

DANAOS:

He was chaste and they exiled him from heaven.

DANAID:

Then he knows what we're going through.
Who else?

DANAOS:

Here's a statue of someone holding a trident.

DANAID:

That's the god who brought us here:
Poseidon save us,
keep away rape!

DANAOS:

This statue seems to be a Greek version of our Thoth.

DANAID:

Hermes, herald good news to the free:
keep us pure!

DANAOS:

Pray to all the gods who share this altar.
Sit in its holy shelter

as if you were a flock of doves
afraid of the hawk, their kin but their enemy.
If it's a sin for one bird to eat another
since no bird wants to be eaten,
then it's a sin for men to try to marry
reluctant daughters of an unwilling father.
If your cousins manage to carry you off
they'll pay for it in Hades
where they say another Zeus invents
final pains for the dead.
Now be careful, do exactly what I told you
if you want to win this fight.

(King Pelasgos enters from the city with advisors and soldiers.)

PELASGOS:

Who are these females?
You're certainly not Greek
with those barbarian headbands and strange outlandish dresses:
no woman of ours would dress like that.
Yet you dare to march right into our land
without heralds, allies, guides. Fearless.
From the branches lying before the gods' statues
I assume you're in trouble
and that you know something about our laws.
After that I'd only be guessing:
so you'd better give me an explanation.

DANAIDS:

1   You're right, we're not wearing Greek clothes.
    But who are you?

2   If you're an ordinary person
    why do you have a staff?

3   Are you guarding this shrine?

4   Are you one of the city's rulers?

26

PELASGOS:

You can say whatever you want in front of me.
My father was Palaikhthon, born of earth:
I am Pelasgos, king of this place.
I gave my name to the Pelasgians, they're my people.
I rule the land the river Strymon waters
from sea to setting sun
up to the Perrhaibians
and the other side of Pindos
next to the Paionians
and the mountains of Dodona.
My country's named after Apis,
Apollo's son, a doctor
who came from Naupaktos long ago to free this land
from a plague of deadly snakes
that crawled from the marshland of age-old murder.
For cutting out this deadly growth
the surgeon took no fee:
instead he asked to give this land his name.
Now you know my story: what's yours?
Remember, we don't like long speeches around here.

DANAID:

It's short and sweet.
We're Argives, a cow from here was our mother:
we can prove it.

PELASGOS:

How's that?
Daughters usually have some of their father in them:
your looks tell me you're Libyan or Cyprian,
Egyptian maybe . . . you could be some of those
Indian nomads who ride camels
(I never saw any, but I've heard).
In fact, if you had bows and arrows
I'd swear you were Amazons, you know,
women who hate men and tear at their meat.

27

Better tell me more.

PELASGOS:

DANAID:
They say Io was Hera's priestess in Argos.

PELASGOS:
That's no secret.

DANAID:
Did you know Zeus loved Io?

PELASGOS:
You mean Zeus had the virgin priestess?

DANAID:
Let's just say he wrestled her
and didn't bother telling Hera.

PELASGOS:
What did Hera do when she found out?

DANAID:
Turned Io into a cow.

PELASGOS:
Did that stop Zeus?

DANAID:
He's supposed to have grown horns
and changed to a cow-crazy bull.

PELASGOS:
And Hera?

DANAIDS:
1   Told Argos, child of earth,
    eyes over his whole body,
    to watch cow Io.

2   But Hermes killed him,

28

3   so Hera sent a terrible stinging bug
    Egyptians call the prick-fly.

PELASGOS:
   This prick-fly got Io on the run?

DANAID:
   All the way to Canopos and Memphis
   but there the hand of Zeus
   touched her and gave her a child.

PELASGOS:
   I suppose the child was a calf?

DANAID:
   The divine Epaphos/Apis
   named for the touch that saved Io.

PELASGOS:
   What happened next?

DANAID:
   Epaphos married Libya,
   rich soil to plant his seed in
   and they had a son:
   Baal, my father's father.

PELASGOS:
   And your father's name?

DANAIDS:
1   We're daughters of Danaos:
    his brother Aigyptos had the same number of sons.

2   Now you know our connection with Argos:
    it's your duty to help us.

PELASGOS:
   I admit you have an ancient claim to be Argive

but I still don't understand
why you're here and need our help.

DANAID:
King Pelasgos, people have as many troubles
as the sky has birds.
Who could have guessed that someday
we'd come to Argos, our forgotten home,
running away from a marriage we don't want?

PELASGOS:
Is that why you cut those branches so fast
and ran to the gods' altar?

DANAID:
We won't be slaves for Aigyptos' sons!

PELASGOS:
Is there a legal reason?
Or do you just hate them?

DANAID:
Does a slave love her master?

PELASGOS:
The strong ride the weak:
that's social order, girls.

DANAID:
So it's that easy for them
to dispose of us.

PELASGOS:
What do you want me to do?

DANAID:
Don't let them have us!

PELASGOS:
You could be asking me to start a war.

DANAID:

Justice is on our side,
she helps them who help us.

PELASGOS:

Only if she'd been on your side from the start.

DANAID:

The city's gods insist you protect us.

PELASGOS:

Your branches throw a shadow on their statues
that chills me.

DANAIDS:

1   Zeus will protect us from those who leave us helpless.

2   King Pelasgos,
    Palaikhthon's son,
    listen!
    You're the herdsman;
    we are calves wolves have chased
    to the cliff's edge.

3   Help us!

4   You're the only one we trust.

PELASGOS:

I don't see any calves,
just a crowd of gods
weighed down by your begging branches
nodding agreement.
But if helping you means war
I don't want it,
the city doesn't need it.

DANAIDS:

1   Themis, daughter of Zeus
    who arranges everything,

now give us shelter.

2 Pelasgos, you may be old and wise
but listen to girls younger than you:
gods don't like offerings from a man
who turns from those needing help.

PELASGOS:
That's not for me to say.
The whole city must decide
to help you or not:
if they choose badly
the blame falls on them all.
As for me, I can't promise you a thing
until I discuss it with them.

DANAIDS:
1 Why?
You're the one who counts!

2 You're the city and the people,
you answer to no one,
the public altar is yours!

3 There's only one throne
one vote, one staff
in all the land:
yours!

PELASGOS:
If I help you, I start a war with Egypt.
If I don't help, the gods get angry.
I have a choice: to act or not.
But how can I be sure
of coming out on top?

DANAIDS:
1 Maybe this will help:

kings are Zeus' subjects.
He's watching you
just as he watches the rights
of those who want help.

2   He sees
who turns away kin,
he makes those
who can't hear their cries of pain
wish they'd listened.

PELASGOS:
If your cousins have a lawful right
to you and your bodies,
if they can make good their claim
to be your next of kin,
what am I to do?
You must find a defense in Egyptian law
to prove they have no hold on you.

DANAIDS:
1   We'll never be under men:
as long as there are stars
to show us how
we'll try to escape
marriages we hate.

2   Justice is a goddess,
a stronger law:
all must obey her—
even kings.

PELASGOS:
I'm not who decides:
a king I may be
but there's nothing I can do
unless the people agree.

If things go wrong
I don't want anyone saying
"he was too quick to save those foreign girls:
he wrecked the city."

DANAIDS:

1   We tell you again—
Zeus is watching,

2   he's kin to us and the Egyptians,
he'll weigh us both
in an accurate balance,
wronging the wicked,
blessing the righteous.

3   Do what's right:
you'll feel better
in the end.

PELASGOS:

I need a way out right now:
I feel like a drunken diver
who can't open his eyes underwater.
I must figure out some way
to save the city and myself.
I can't risk your cousins bleeding my city dry
but if I let them tear you from sanctuary
another unwanted guest would take your place:
the god of vengeance
hating, never forgetting,
tracking me down alive or dead.
Now you see why
we need a saving plan.

DANAIDS:

1   The only way to save yourself
is to save us:

don't hand us over
to men we're trying to escape,
men who hate the gods.

2   It's not your city's blood
it's virgins' blood they want.
Almighty Pelasgos, you should know
why they hunt us down
and what the gods demand.

3   What will you do
when they enter this holy place,
drag us off by our headbands,
rope us like horses,
man-handle our flesh?

4   What you do now
sets the price
your house must pay:
if you're afraid to fight for us
your children will die in war.

5   Zeus is just and strong:
think about that.

PELASGOS:
I've thought and thought til
my mind's run aground.
But one thing's as watertight
as a boat in drydock: war
against the Egyptians or the gods.
I lose no matter what.
If this were an argument
or just a case of stolen property
there'd be no problem.
You give someone who's been robbed
a little more than he lost,

he'll thank Zeus, God of Property.
A misunderstanding based on words
even if it really jabs the heart
other words can always heal.
But this is blood, kindred blood:
yours, ours, theirs;
all I can think of is to
pile up sacrifices to gods and oracles
and pray that'll help.
Above all, I don't want war with Egypt:
when it comes to trouble
I'd rather be ignorant than know,
and hope for the best
although I'm afraid.

DANAID:
Wait, you haven't heard
the end of our maiden speech.

PELASGOS:
I'm still listening.

DANAID:
Our belts will keep us safe.

PELASGOS:
You mean those things all women wear?

DANAID:
Yes, they'll do something fine and useful.

PELASGOS:
What are you talking about?

DANAID:
If you don't give us a promise we can trust . . .

PELASGOS:
. . . belts will save you?

DANAID:

    . . . these statues will wear new decorations.

PELASGOS:

    Quit talking in riddles.
    Get to the point!

DANAID:

    We'll hang ourselves from the statues.

PELASGOS:

    You'd put that knife to my throat?!

DANAID:

    So you see what we mean
    now that we've given you eyes.

PELASGOS:

    I see a troubled tide coming at me,
    I see myself sinking
    in a sea of disaster,
    no harbor in sight.
    If I refuse your demand
    you'll kill yourselves in this holy place,
    a pollution the gods won't wash away.
    If I stand before the walls
    to kill your cousins
    or be killed by them
    what a bitter price we'd pay:
    men's blood splashing the ground
    for women's sake.
    But Zeus' anger outranks everything else:
    I can see now what must be.
    You, old man,
    father of these girls,
    pick up their branches,
    put them on some other altars
    of our local gods

to prove what's happened.
The people watch me closely:
I don't want anyone accusing me.
When they see the branches they'll realize
what kind of men prey on helpless girls.
People always feel sorry for the underdog:
they'll hate the Egyptians
and help your daughters.

DANAOS:

King Pelasgos
I wish I could tell you
how much this means to us,
how fortunate to find someone
who cherishes purity
and is ready to help strangers.
Now if you could do just one more thing:
I'll need guides and an armed escort
to help me safely through the city
to the altars and temples
of your various gods.
It's a fact that Egyptians
don't look like Argives,
so everybody can tell I'm not a native.
Things are looking up for us now:
that's all the more reason to be extra-careful.
People have been known to kill innocent strangers
just because they didn't know who they were.

PELASGOS:

I'll take care of that.
You there, do what the stranger says.
Take him to the public altars and temples.
If anyone asks what you're doing
just say you're bringing
a sailor to the gods' hearth.

(One of Pelasgos' attendants leaves with Danaos toward city.)

DANAIDS:

1   There he goes
now that you've told him exactly what to do.

2   When you take charge
I feel new hope:
tell us, too,
what we should do.

PELASGOS:

    Leave the branches here;
they're enough to let people know
what you've been through.
(The Danaids obey him.)
And now, please
if you'll move away from those statues . . .

DANAID:

    But how will ground the gods don't protect
protect us?

PELASGOS:

    We won't let those vultures snatch you away.

DANAID:

    Aigyptos' sons are worse than that—
worse than poison snakes.

PELASGOS:

    Watch what you're saying.

DANAID:

    How can we
when we feel like this?

PELASGOS:

    Thats the trouble with women:

their feelings run away with them.

DANAID:
Then say something,
do something,
make us feel better.

PELASGOS:
Your father will be back soon:
I'll let him tell you
what you need to hear.
In the meantime
I'll call a public meeting
and make sure the people take your side,
I'll coach your father
in all the right things to say.
You just stay here
and beg the gods of Argos
to meet your every desire.
Leave everything to me:
all I need is a speech
that will bend the people
and the kind of luck
that gets things done.

(Pelasgos and his attendants leave for Argos. When the Danaids realize they're alone, they fall to their knees.)

DANAIDS:
1   King of kings,
    happiest of happy gods,
    most perfect and almighty Zeus,
    we are yours,
    do what we want.

2   Show you despise men
    who try to take your place:
    keep them away.

3   Drown their black ship coming for us
    across the blood-faced sea.

4   Look at us:
    remember the woman
    you loved long ago,
    think back to the time
    you touched Io.

5   Now it's time to renew that story:
    we are yours,
    we lived here once before.

    (The Danaids rise and gradually become more animated, excited, rhythmic.)

6   Following the ancient foot-steps
    of our mother Io:
    we stand in the springtime meadow
    where she exchanged her body
    for a cow's,
    lifted her head,
    flowers dropping from her lips,
    to stare wild in fear
    at the prick-fly
    trying to get his sting
    into her flesh.

7   She ran
    one place to another
    from Europe to Asia
    across Bosporos,
    Earth's wet slit,

8   past the grazing flocks of Phrygia
    and the Mysian city of Teuthras,
    down Lydian valleys
    and up through the mountains

of Cilicia and Pamphylia,

9   on past streams
that never dry up,
through the rich wheat-field
of Syria's
Mistress of Love,
Aphrodite.

10   At last, pierced
by the prick-fly
she came to the place
where Zeus gives everything life,

11   Egypt, meadow
fed by melting snows,
goal of Typhoon's hot breath,
and Nile's water,
rising and falling,
free from disease.

12   Like a woman in labor
or at passion's height
Io moaned and shivered,
fighting what she wanted,
the stinging pain
that owned her:
all thanks to Hera.

13   White-faced terror
struck the heart of Egypt
for something never seen before:

14   half woman,
half cow,
ending her journey,
deliriously whirling,
Io:

who turned your pain to joy?

15 Zeus,
   king of unstopping time:
   he breathed his godness into her,
   touching her with strength
   that did not hurt.

16 Each tear she shed
   washed shame and pain away.

17 She took his burden in
   to give a sinless child birth,
   who shared his father's fortune.

18 Then all earth shouted
   "This is the true son
   of Zeus, Father of Life:
   who else could heal
   the frantic madness
   jealous Hera sent?"

19 Confess the work of Zeus,
   admit Epaphos
   is father of our line.

20 Who but Zeus
   could I claim
   for father,

21 sower,

22 creator,

23 great wise builder of our race?

24 He can take care of anything,
   he brings good weather:

ALL: who but Zeus?

43

25 No one sits above him,
their power
greater than his;
he respects
no one but himself:
whatever he says
happens in a flash,
he gets what he wants.

(Danaos rushes in, excited.)

DANAOS:

You can stop worrying, girls;
the people just finished voting:
it couldn't have turned out better.

DANAIDS:

1 Father, what happened?

2 Tell us quick, don't keep us waiting!

3 What did they decide?

4 How did the vote go?

DANAOS:

How can I say it?
Their vote, their unanimous vote,
made me a young man again!
The sky was a forest of hands
all voting to help us!
We're free to live here:
no one can harm or threaten us,
not even citizens can take us away.
If anyone tries to use force,
whoever doesn't run to our help,
they'll strip of everything and send into exile.
King Pelasgos gave a magnificent speech

44

telling them all about us
full of eloquent phrases like:
"Don't let the city become a meal
for the angry appetite
of Zeus, Suppliant-Protector"
and:
"These girls are both foreigners and relatives:
if we don't do our double duty
twin pollution will imperil the city,
our sin nourish incessant suffering."
When the people heard this
they didn't even wait
for the meeting's official start
but voted immediately.
Pelasgos' skill carried the day:
he put the fear of god in them!

DANAIDS:

1   Let's thank the city
    with the kind of prayers
    their vote deserves.

2   Zeus, God of Strangers,
    has watched over us so far:
    he'll show he cares,
    he'll make our prayers come true.

3   Undying children of Zeus,
    hear these prayers
    for Argos.

4   Ares Wargod,
    bringer of fire death,
    harvesting men
    in fields of blood,
    you who love
    war's noise first,

never make your home in
this land.

5   These people voted pity
for a helpless flock,
respect for those
whom Zeus protects.

6   They could have voted for men
but didn't,
they could have betrayed women
but didn't.

7   They kept their eyes
on the angel of vengeance
who watches them,
who wins all wars,
who brings no joy,
to those who see him
squatting heavy on the roof-top,
the grim messenger Zeus sends.

8   Zeus who loves the pure
likes those kind to helpless kin:
that's why in Argos
altars will be pure
and gods like what they offer.

(While speaking of purity, the Danaids pick up the veils previously removed and replace them on their heads and shoulders.)

9   Let's pray for the young,
for us and Argos:

10 May man-plague never
spend this city,
no blood spurt from
bodies thrown to earth,
no man pick
flowers' first bloom!

11　Ares, day killer,
　　night wrestler on Aphrodite's couch,
　　keep your bloody hands from
　　all that's clean and good.

12　Now pray for the old men
　　who tend the city:

13　May fire leap up
　　from altars where they gather,
　　may the city prosper
　　because they honor Zeus

14　above all, Zeus who watches over strangers
　　and keeps fate on the right path
　　by a law old as time.

15　Artemis, cool-eyed archer,
　　see that women always give birth
　　to men who'll guard the city.

16　May men not die
　　in war's bloody jaws
　　when the Wargod's clashing armor
　　drowns music and dancing
　　in hideous dinning
　　steel and tears.

17　Let there be nothing but
　　health and pleasure
　　for the people of Argos.
　　Apollo Lightgod,
　　be kind to boys and girls.

18　Zeus, give Argos:

19　fruit from the earth
　　in every season,

20 flocks of fat cows and sheep,

21 every citizen's wish
    met with gods' help,

22 poets singing virtue
    at the altars,

23 children's pure voices
    chanting to the lyre,

24 public officials,
    the city's backbone,
    protecting the common good,
    dealing fairly with strangers,
    never deceiving,
    never inviting war.

25 Let there be unending celebration
    to honor the city's gods:
    sacrifice and laurel-leaves
    and the rituals that
    fathers hand down to their children.
    For the three Laws of Justice are:

ALL:
    honor the gods
    honor the laws
    honor thy father.

(For some time Danaos has been standing off to the left, looking anxiously at the sea below.)

DANAOS:
    Daughters, I couldn't agree more.
    So listen to your father now
    and try not to be alarmed.
    While you were praying I spotted a boat coming.

No mistaking whose it is;
I could see the sails' rigging,
the spray-shields on the side,
even the eyes painted on the prow
staring ahead—
looking for us.
I saw the crew's black bodies
against their white clothes.
Look!
You can see the rest of the fleet now.
The lead ship already has its sails down
and is coming to land.
Listen, you can hear the oars
and the drum's heavy beat.
Stay calm,
get close to the gods' statues.
I'm going back to the city
and bring soldiers and public officials:
the Egyptians may send men ahead
to state their demands and grab you
as if you were stolen property.
Don't worry, that won't happen,
but just to be on the safe side
in case I don't get back in time,
remember the gods protect you:
if they drag you away
they're really violating the gods
and eventually they'll pay.

DANAIDS:

1   Father, I'm afraid:
    those ships have wings,
    they're coming so fast,
    they'll be here any second!

2   Father, no matter where we go,
    fear is there ahead of us!

3   What's the good of running
     if we can't get away from fear?
     We might as well be dead.

DANAOS:
     You forget the people's vote?
     Their decision to help was final,
     I'm sure of that.

DANAIDS:
1   Have *you* forgotten what kind
     of men the Egyptians are?
     The threat of war won't stop them
     they're eager for any vice.

2   Their black bodies,
     black boats
     full of spears,
     they'll stick in us
     if we refuse.

DANAOS:
     Here they'll meet real men,
     muscles tough and hard
     from glaring sun.

DANAIDS:
1   Father, please don't leave us!
     A woman left alone's nothing:
     the Wargod's not in her.

2   These men deceive and kill:
     they're like crows
     dirtying pure altars.

DANAOS:
     That's all the better for us:
     the gods will hate them

as much as you do.

DANAIDS:

1   They're not afraid of gods:
    shrines and tridents
    won't stop them from
    dragging us off.

2   What do mad dogs
    care about gods?

DANAOS:

You know what they say:
"For every dog
there's a wolf that's stronger."
The men of Greece eat real food
not water-lilies.

DANAID:

We'll need more than sayings
to fight off bloodthirsty beasts.

DANAOS:

They're not here yet.
It takes a long time
for a fleet to disembark:
they have to make sure
sails, anchors, hawsers are all secure
and even then the leaders won't rush ashore
especially in a strange land.
Besides, the sun has almost disappeared:
experienced pilots like to lie low at night.
I know you're afraid:
just don't let your fear
make you forget the gods.
I'm going to the city for help:
I may be old
but I talk young.

(Danaos hurries off toward city.)

DANAIDS:

1 Land of Io,
   land we love,
   what will happen to us?
   Where can we go?
   To what dark
   secret hiding place?

2 If only we could rise
   like black smoke
   high in the clouds
   near Zeus!

3 I would die
   and change to dust
   vanishing in thin air:
   then my heart
   would be free at last.

4 What Father saw
   rips my heart
   from my breast:
   I'll die from fear!

5 I'll hang myself
   and have the Deathgod
   for lord and master
   before I let men
   touch my flesh!

6 I want to fall
   from a place so high
   the snow's
   still cloud,
   I want to climb
   the top

of a lonely peak
vultures circle
over the cliff's
sheer edge,
then throw myself down!

7   Before I let marriage
tear my heart
I'll give my body
to dogs and hawks
to feast on.

8   Death will free me:
let it come!
I'd rather die
than feel a man's
body on mine!

9   Isn't there any way
to escape marriage?
Can prayers
and songs
that beg the gods
to fight for us
set us free?

10   Father, look at us,
send your strength
against theirs:
answer those who need you,
Earth's embracer,
Zeus!

11   Will you let
Aigyptos' sons,
howling like jackals,
hunt us down,
attacking you through us?

12   Zeus, you hold
     the scales of fate
     in your hands, everything
     that men can do or suffer.

*(An Egyptian Herald bursts on scene, accompanied by soldiers; the
Danaids shrink back in fear. The following words are spoken by no
one in particular, but emerge from a general chaos of panic and threats.)*

13   . . . they're here to rape us!

14   . . . but Father said . . .

15   . . . die, pig!

16   . . . scream for help!

17   . . . scum!

18   . . . filth!

19   . . . what will we do?

20   . . . run for help!

21   . . . to the altars!

22   . . . gods help us!

23   . . . see what kind of men they are!

24   . . . strutting cocks, chasing helpless women!

25   . . . Pelasgos, where are you?

HEARLD:
     Hurry, get to the boat
     right now!
     No?
     You refuse?
     I'll tear your hair,

burn your flesh,
cut off your heads:
a lot of blood will run!
Now get to the boat
or die!

DANAIDS:

1   Why didn't you die at sea

2   with your lecherous masters

3   and your brothel-boat?

HERALD:

You want blood?
Better be quiet
and go to the boat:
do what I say!
I don't want you
to waste passion.
You have no choice,
you're nothing here.
Now move!

DANAID:

I'll never
go to Egypt
where the River
rapes the meadow,
where men's blood boils
in non-stop rutting!

HERALD:

Obey me,
get up the ladder
into the boat.
I don't care if
you want to or not,

I'll drag you by the hair
and teach you to obey!

DANAID:

Why didn't you die
without a chance
in the rushing sea
where winds heap sand
on Sarpedon's grave!

HERALD:

Scream,
howl,
shout at the gods,
there's no way you'll jump
from the Egyptian boat.
You're just making trouble
for yourself.

DANAID:

You barking crocodile!
Jealous Nile will
drain your flooded . . .

HERALD:

Enough!
For the last time
I'm ordering you:
get to the boat!
If you don't hurry,
I'll pull you by
your pretty hair!

(Herald tries to drag a Danaid off by her hair. General screaming.)

DANAIDS:

1   Father, the gods don't help!

2 The black
  dream spider
  drags me to the sea!

3 Mother Earth,
  kill the fatal snake!

4 Help us,
  King of Earth,
  Father Zeus!

HERALD:
  Gods here
  don't scare me!
  I didn't drink
  from Greek gods' tits!

DANAIDS:
1 Two-footed snake!

2 Man above,
  snake below!

3 Fanged beast!

4 Mother Earth,
  kill the snake!

5 Help,
  Father Zeus!

HERALD:
  Get to the boat
  now,
  or I'll
  tear the clothes off you!

  (Herald tries to make good his threat.)

DANAID:
   We'll die
   before you touch us!
   Help, King!

HERALD:
   Soon you'll see
   many kings:
   Aigyptos' sons!
   There'll be many men
   over you in Egypt!

(King Pelasgos enters with other officials and soldiers.)

DANAID:
   Brave men of Argos,
   help us!

HERALD:
   I want these women!
   Better not stop me!

PELASGOS:
   You'll be sorry fast
   if you touch them!

HERALD:
   Your words hate strangers!

PELASGOS:
   I'm no friend to
   those who rob the gods!

HERALD:
   I'll tell
   Aigyptos' sons.

PELASGOS:
   What do I care?

HERALD:

I must know more.
My masters will ask:
"Who steals our cousins?"
I'm a herald,
I must know everything exact.

PELASGOS:

The Wargod doesn't need witnesses,
silver can't buy him off:
all he needs to know is the number
of men who die and kick away life.
So why must you know my name?
You'll learn it soon enough,
you and your fellow-travellers!
The only way
you'll have these women
is to persuade them
to go willingly.
The people voted unanimously
never to give them up to force.
That law is nailed shut.
You won't see it on public signs
or written on papyrus pages:
you hear it from a free man's voice!

HERALD:

No more talk!
Drag them
by their hair.

(Herald again tries to drag a resisting Danaid off by her hair, and his attendants advance with like intentions. Pelasgos steps forward and forcibly restrains the Herald.)

PELASGOS:

What are you doing?

Do you think
you're in a city of women?
Fool, you're trespassing
on Pelasgos' men!
You barbarian,
you insult Greeks!
You don't even think straight!

HERALD:
What is wrong?
What's the crime?

PELASGOS:
Don't you realize
this isn't your land?

HERALD:
What I lost,
I found,
and I'll take!

PELASGOS:
Who's your patron?

HERALD:
Best of all,
Hermes/Thoth
the Searcher.

PELASGOS:
How can a god
hurt other gods?

HERALD:
I worship Nile gods.

PELASGOS:
and mock ours.
Now get out,

I don't want to look at you!

HERALD:
This starts new war:
victory and power to men!

PELASGOS:
What do you expect to find here?
Beer-drinking sots like you?

(Herald and his attendants leave angrily. The Danaids cluster around Pelasgos, who speaks to them.)

Girls, these attendants are yours.

(At Pelasgos' words, an Argive soldier stands beside each Danaid.)

Go to the city:
you'll be safe there,
high towers and thick walls
will protect you.
You can live in houses
owned by the state
or in my own palace:
there's more than enough room
for you—and others.
But if for some reason
you want to live off by yourselves
that's all right too.
As they say,
pick the flower that makes you happy.
All the citizens,
whose vote made this possible,
and I myself
will be your guardians.
What more could you want?

DANAIDS:
1   We want you to overflow

with good things
for helping us,
divine Pelasgos!

2   Please send our father here, the
    courageous clever competent Danaos:
    he'll want to tell us
    where to live,
    where we'll be happy,
    how to avoid nasty gossip,
    how everything will
    turn out for the best.

(Pelasgos starts off for Argos. As he is about to leave the stage, he gestures to Danaos to come forward. One of the Danaids speaks to her sisters.)

3   To keep our reputation clean,
        sisters, each of us
    must keep with her
    the slave girl Danaos gave her
    when he thought
    we'd have to marry.

(As the Argives leave, Danaos emerges, followed by an attendant and a soldier.)

DANAOS:
    Girls, we must pray
    and sacrifice and pour libations
    to our steadfast Argive saviors
    as if they were gods above.
    When they heard my story
    they loved you
    and hated your cousins.
    They even gave me
    attendants and bodyguards
    as a sign of special honor.

Now no assassin's spear
will catch me unaware
or unrecognized:
that would shame this land forever,
and by preventing its occurrence
I give this land a greater gift
than they give me.
Now write this down alongside
the other wise sayings I've told you:
The real Test is Time.
Everyone likes to spread
dirty stories about strangers,
it's easy to be crude.
So please don't disgrace me:
you're the kind of girls
men take a second look at.
Ripe fruit isn't easy
to guard from animals,
especially the human kind,
winged beasts and beasts with feet.
The Sex Goddess auctions off
fruit so ripe it drips,
flowers that smell of love.
Any man who walks by
and happens to get a look
at girls as luscious as you
will be an instant slave of love,
hot arrows of seduction
flying from his eyes:
now you see what I mean
by beasts with *wings* and *feet*?
I've gone to too much trouble,
I've plowed my vessel
through too many seas,
to see it all wasted now.
So don't do anything

that will disgrace me
and please our enemies.
Now where do you want to live?
The king's palace?
Or the city's rent-free houses?
That choice should be easy.
Only obey your father's orders:
honor your virtue
more than your life.

DANAIDS:

1   The future's in the lap of the gods.

2   Don't worry about our ripe fruit, Father:
if the gods don't change their mind
we'll never leave the straight and narrow!

(The Danaids turn from their father and speak to themselves and to the men standing next to them.)

3   Let's praise the gods
who rule this city
and keep it safe,
gods of the
ancient river Erasinos.

4   You men Pelasgos gave us,
we hope you like our song:

5   Honor and glory
to Pelasgos' city,
we'll chant no more
to Nile's flood.

6   Now we sing
the rivers of Argos
caressing the land
with loving streams.

7   Eager lovers
       of fertile ground
       sweetest drink
       of life to come.

8   Artemis, look
           at us with pity:
           may we never
           have to marry.

9   Aphrodite,
               keep your distance:
               those who worship
               you win death.

(The Argive men reply, showing gentle but obvious disagreement.)

ATTENDANTS:
1   We share your happiness
     but not your slanging
     the Goddess of Love.

2   Her power's great,
     equal to Hera
     and next to Zeus.

3   She has a woman's fickle moods
     but the greatest moments
     in life bring her honor.

4   Her children are her helpers:
     Longing and Seduction
     whose charms never fail.

5   Whenever two bodies melt together
     in thrusting force and gasping breath
     Aphrodite's present.

6   I fear your troubles aren't over yet.

Better stay close to me:
the wind blows bloody wars and pain to come.

7   The speed and ease of your cousins' pursuit,
    as if someone or something were helping,
    hints at more than human effort.

8   You must take whatever Destiny gives:
    you cannot know or master Zeus' will.

9   Many women before have married:
    this could be your fate as well.

DANAID:
    Great Zeus, save us
    from Egyptian marriage!

ATTENDANT:
    Yes, that would be best.

DANAID:
    And don't think *you* can have me!

ATTENDANT:
    You don't know the future.

DANAID:
    How can I see through
    the infinite mind of Zeus?

ATTENDANT:
    Then be more moderate
    in what you say.

DANAID:
    What lesson of limit
    are you trying to teach me?

ATTENDANT:
    Don't ask too much

from the gods.

1   Lord Zeus, save us
from marriage that would destroy us,
from men we hate!

2   You stopped Io's suffering,
holding her with healing hand,
touching her with gentle force:
give victory to women now!

3   It seems
there's no joy in life
without pain.

4   May we
at least have no pain
without joy!

5   May gods
hear our prayer
and reward
our just cause.

(All leave toward Argos.)

EPILOGUE

The Suppliants was the first play in a connected tetralogy constituted by three tragedies and a satyr play, performed consecutively in a single day. The other two tragedies were *The Egyptians* and *The Danaids* and the satyr play was the *Amymone.* Although only a few scattered words and phrases from the last three plays of the tetralogy survive, it is possible to arrive at an approximate idea of their plots on the basis of these extant fragments and versions of the myth in other sources. The late Greek writer Apollodoros, for example, summarizes relevant sections of the myth of the Danaids as follows:

Aigyptos had fifty sons, and Danaos had 50 daughters, both from many wives. They quarrelled concerning the kingdom. Danaos feared the sons of Aigyptos, and at the advice of Athena he built a ship and . . . .came to Argos. . . . Now the country was waterless . . . so Danaos sent his daughters to draw water. One of them, Amymone, while searching for water threw a spear at a deer and happened to hit a sleeping satyr; he was aroused and desired to have intercourse with her, but Poseidon appeared and the satyr fled. So Amymone slept with Poseidon, and he showed her the springs at Lerna.

Aigyptos' sons now came to Argos, urged Danaos to cease from his anger, and requested his daughters in marriage. Danaos mistrusted their protestations and was bitter about his exile, but he agreed to the marriage and allotted his daughters. . . .

When the marriages had been arranged, Danaos had a feast and gave daggers to his daughters; and they, except for Hypermnestra, killed their sleeping bridegrooms. Hypermnestra spared Lynceus because he had kept her a virgin; Danaos therefore locked her up and kept watch on her. The other daughters of Danaos buried their bridegrooms' heads in Lerna and had a funeral service for their bodies in front of the city. Athena and Hermes purified Danaos' daughters on Zeus' orders. Danaos later married Hypermnestra to Lynceus and gave his other daughters to winners of an athletic contest (*Bibliotheca* 2.1.4-5).

THE EGYPTIANS

In the interval between the first and second plays of the tetralogy, there may have been a battle in which the Egyptians were victorious and Pelasgos died, as a result of which Danaos became king of Argos. At any rate, the play opens with the Egyptians in position to enforce their will on their reluctant cousins. The main events of the play would be the negotiations between Danaos and the Egyptians concerning the forthcoming marriage, the marriage itself, and perhaps a scene in which Danaos gives a dagger to each of his daughters and orders them to kill their husbands on the wedding night.

THE DANAIDS

In the interval between the second and third plays, the murder of the sons of Aigyptos by the Danaids probably took place; the single exception was Hypermnestra, who spared her husband Lynceus. Since the men were decapitated while asleep, the girls presumably did not kill in order to preserve virginity but rather in retaliation for defloration. Although Apollodoros says that Hypermnestra spared Lynceus because he respected her virginity, Aeschylus probably followed the version he used in his *Prometheus*, that Hypermnestra spared Lynceus because she fell in love with him; her motive was awakened sexual desire, not gratitude for abstinence.

By directly disobeying her father, Hypermnestra acquires an individual name and life of her own, freeing herself from her nameless sisters' compulsive repetition of the past (their re-enactment of Io's fate) and pathological attachment to their father (and to Zeus and Pelasgos, his substitutes in fantasy).

There may have been a trial scene in this play, as in the last play of Aeschylus' only extant trilogy, the *Oresteia*. The Danaids who killed their husbands may have been prosecuted for mariticide, or perhaps Hypermnestra was accused of disobeying her father. The only thing we can say for sure is that somehow Hypermnestra was justified in her new love and somehow her sisters were reconciled to marriage.

The theme of personified Love must have been important as the one sizable extant fragment of *The Danaids* indicates. The power of Eros as a cosmic principle was affirmed by Aphrodite herself, either against the Danaids or on behalf of Hypermnestra:

Love makes holy Sky lay Earth
Love makes Earth want to be laid
Rain falling from Sky's coming makes Earth pregnant
She bears flocks of sheep and grain, so men may live
The forest comes to life, watered by this marriage
Of these things I am the cause

69

AMYMONE

If the satyr play followed the usual version of the myth, we can see in the story of Amymone a reflection of her sisters' attitude towards sex. The satyr may be compared to the Egyptians, lustful beasts in the eyes of the girls, and Poseidon, Amymone's rescuer and lover, is equivalent to his brother Zeus and the other paternal figures to whom the Danaids appeal for protection and, ultimately, for love.

Prometheus Bound

Aeschylus

translated by

Emily Hilburn

Introduction

Prometheus Bound is a balanced representation of a static situation: the conflict between two opposing forces, Prometheus and Zeus. With the bleak setting of Scythia and the comparative lack of action throughout, Aeschylus forces the audience's attention to that conflict.* There are no diversions from scenery, props, or superfluous action on stage. The characters are mythological essences—symbols in the purest sense. The scene is marked by no sense of time: the past is recounted and the future predicted, but the present is a vacuum. Aeschylus has stripped down the trappings of the theater to present a nowhere and an eternity. The reality of the play is brutal confrontation, rope-tight tension against a blank and silent landscape, which can be felt from the moment the giant Prometheus is dragged in until he and the chorus of sympathetic Oceanids are blasted to Tatarus by Zeus's thunderbolt.

The force of the tragedy lies in the language of the characters and in their strategically placed entrances and exits. The play opens with the most spectacular of entrances—that of Prometheus—ends with his dramatic exit, and is punctuated by the entrances and exits of other characters who come to sympathize, plead, consult, or threaten. The central character, Zeus, does not appear, but his presence is reflected by every other character. Power and Violence are manifestations of the tyranny of Zeus and the means by which he enforces it; Hephaistos, Ocean and Hermes are less dramatic manifestations—echoes of Power and Violence, reminders of the subservience that Zeus demands and to which Prometheus will not bend. Prometheus and Io are victims of Zeus, and can be considered masculine and feminine parallels. Prometheus's transgression is his active threat to Zeus's power; his punishment is forced passivity. Io, by her mere existence, is a threat to Hera's sexuality; she is driven by the gadfly to frenetic activity. Timid throughout about stating its loyalties, the chorus ultimately identifies with Prometheus. It makes the only character transition in the play by standing in defiance of Zeus at the end.

Several years have passed since I began this translation of *Prometheus Bound*; originally it was a class project, an exercise. I first produced a very literal version of the first scene, completing the assignment. I found that that wasn't enough, that it did not express in English a theme that has been with me for years. I stripped the translation down into the most primitive words I could think of, "fossilizing" the English. I then recorded the words and found that the sounds suggested to me imagery— part visual, part symbolic, part kinaesthetic—which may or may not be in the original. I reconstructed the English to fit that imagery and the sense of character, speech, and form that it demands. To treat one's own language at an almost pre-verbal level, to focus on both the smallest linguistic and etymological elements and also on the Gestalt of the whole —that is, I think, what translation is about. If some of the excitement I felt in making that discovery has emerged in my work, I am grateful to share it.

The translation is based on the text of Gilbert Murray, *Septem Quae Supersunt Tragoediae,* Oxford Classical Texts, 2nd ed., 1955. It was undertaken with the encouragement, advice, and inspiration of James Hynd, to whom in deepest respect and appreciation, this work is dedicated.

Emily Hilburn

*The authorship of *Prometheus Bound* is a matter of some controversy. For a full discussion, see C. J. Herington's *The Author of the "Prometheus Bound"* (University of Texas Press, 1970).

CHARACTERS

PROMETHEUS, son of Themis

POWER ⎫
      ⎬ servants of Zeus
VIOLENCE ⎭

HEPHAISTOS, god of fire

OCEAN

IO, daughter of Inachus

CHORUS of Ocean's daughters

(Power and Violence enter, dragging the giant Prometheus across the stage to a large rock. Hephaistos follows, limping, chains and tools in hand.)

POWER:

We have come to the end of the earth.
No nomad rests his head upon this rock,
no plowman plows this ground.
Hephaistos—now! The father's orders!
Bind this rebel to the cliffs
with fetters made in fire, cold steel bonds.
Your flower he plucked, all crafts' pure flame,
and stole it fast, gold hope for mortals.
Mortals! He'll pay the gods for that;
he must learn to love the father's power,
and stop loving men.

HEPHAISTOS:

Enough. You've dragged him here to Scythia, world's end,
your job is done.
I must carry through the father's black command,
to bind Prometheus, a brother god,
and nail him to this precipice.
My heart says no, but Zeus's power compels.
I must obey.
        Contriving child of Themis!
I too recoil from my hammer's strokes;
and yet the spikes drive deep.
They'll keep you on this barren ridge, alone.
You'll hear no human voice,
see no human form.
Poor scorched flower! The sun's blind flame
will wither your fresh skin—darken it
to burning crimson. You'll yearn
for night's star-studded cowl to blanket day,
and long to feel the sun
melt morning's flowers' frost. Icebit blossom!

76

The pain will cut you through
as water does the stone,
from day to night, night to day,
for neither night nor day can give you rest.
No one yet born can do that.
Nothing is what you get for loving men.
A god not fearing god's rage,
you gave god's right to men.
For this you sentinel a bitter rock,
upright, never sleeping, your legs straight as sticks,
the desert silence racked with screams unheeded,
not unheard. Your empty cries
will crack the heart of Zeus
no more than they will this rock.
His power is new and rough.

POWER:

Why fret, blacksmith?
Why not hate this thief, this god-galling god?
Not pity—anger! He stole your tools of trade,
and gave god's gift to men.

HEPHAISTOS:

The bonds of blood and company break hard.

POWER:

Zeus's laws—they aren't hard?
You don't fear his thunder?

HEPHAISTOS:

You are proud and pitiless.

POWER:

Why pity the doomed?
Why waste pity on god's enemy?

HEPHAISTOS:

Then pity me. I hate my craft. I hate these sootblack hands.

POWER:
Your craft? I do not damn my strength.
We serve the law's demands.

HEPHAISTOS:
Perhaps. But I would shirk this burden.

POWER:
Everything burdens except to rule the gods;
Zeus alone is free.

HEPHAISTOS:
Yes. None of this denies it.

POWER:
Quick! Throw the chains around
or Zeus's hawk-eye sees you idling!

HEPHAISTOS:
I have shackles for his wrists.

POWER:
Nail them down. Take up your hammer.
Strike! Pin him to the rock.

HEPHAISTOS:
Done. They won't come loose.

POWER:
Harder! Bind him fast. And crush your pity.
You know he contrives.

HEPHAISTOS:
One elbow's down.

POWER:
Now nail the other.
He must smart to learn from Zeus.

HEPHAISTOS:
Only *he* could justly fault my work.

POWER:
Drive your nail through his chest.

HEPHAISTOS:
Prometheus! Every stroke pierces my heart.

POWER:
Again you shrink—and shrink for him.
Save pity for yourself.

HEPHAISTOS:
There: a painful sight.

POWER:
To see him getting what he deserves?
Stop yammering. Strap his ribs.

HEPHAISTOS:
Only because I must—don't dog me on.

POWER:
By Zeus I'll hound you till the job is done.
Go below. Hoop his legs with iron.

HEPHAISTOS:
Done.

POWER:
Strike! Strike harder! Fix the fetters tight!
His eye is on you.

HEPHAISTOS:
Your words fit your face.

POWER:
You are steel forge-warm and twisted easily.
Do not reproach my hardness.

HEPHAISTOS:
Let's go. Prometheus lies bound, stonestill.

POWER:
So stand here, man-lover,
filch gifts from gods for creatures-of-a-day.
Let's see your people help you here.
The gods have named you wrong, Prometheus: 'He-Who-Thinks-
Ahead.'
Divine into eternity! Nothing can free you
from this blacksmith's trap—
or from the wrath of Zeus.

*(Power, Violence, and Hephaistos leave Prometheus strapped to the
rock.)*

PROMETHEUS:
Shining air, swift breeze,
clear streams, laughing waves,
Earth Mother! All-seeing circle of the sun!
Hear me. See what I, a god,
endure from gods.
See what wastes me,
will wear me a thousand years.
See the trap the gods' new ruler
shaped for me.
Skies hear! I wail the pain that grips me,
the pains that will.
                    Where will it end?
What? All coming
I know clear before it comes;
no new pain takes me unforeseen.
I must endure, for fate will.
Ohhhhhhhhhh—
the pain will not make me silent,
it will not let me speak.
Ohhhhhhhhhh—

what I gave mankind yokes me to my fate.
I hunted out the fount of fire,
stole it in a fennel stalk,
to show a shining path
and teach men craft.
I pay that sin's price chained
beneath the open sky.
                    Who's there?
What do I hear? What's that smell?
God, man, half-god?
Witness to my pain?
See me then, a bound, wretched god,
hated by Zeus, by all the gods;
hated for loving men.
Do I hear birds rush?
The sky above me flutters;
fear draws close with all that closes near.

(A chorus of five Oceanids dressed in flowing grey robes enters, suspended above Prometheus.)

CHORUS:

Don't be afraid. We're friends.
On light wings we come to Scythia,
our father's will scarce won.
Breezes brought us.
A steel sound clanging
darted through our cave
and struck away shyness.
We rushed here in our chariot.

PROMETHEUS:

Children of fertile Tethys,
daughters of Ocean
who circling earth
streams sleepless,
see me pinned

to chasm's cliff
suffering dismal watch.

1st OCEANID:

Yes, Prometheus.
I weep to see you wither
ironbound, outraged on this rock.
A new king rules Olympus,
Zeus, who cruelly wields new laws.

PROMETHEUS:

I wish he'd hurled me shackled
under Hades, host of the dead,
down to endless Tartarus.
There no one would laugh at my chains.
But here I suffer, played by the wind,
my torments joy to my enemies.

CHORUS:

What god is so hard-hearted
to revel in your pain?
Who suffers not your suffering,
but Zeus? Stone set
he will not bend his will, and
heaven's race lays low, not stopping
till his glutton's gut is filled,
or cunning wrests away his power.

PROMETHEUS:

Hear me. Though I am humiliated,
tortured in chains, one day Zeus will need me
to reveal a plot against his scepter.
His honeyed words won't sweeten me,
his storming threats will not
shake secrets trembling from my tongue.
No. Until he breaks these straps and apologizes,
I will not tell.

2nd OCEANID:

> You are bold, you don't give in.
> Words fly from your unfettered tongue,
> and pierce me with fear.
> I shudder for you.
> Where will you dock your sorrow?
> Iron-hearted Zeus shuns mercy.

PROMETHEUS:

> I know he's harsh.
> He holds himself above the law.
> But truth will make him soft.
> He'll approach me friend to friend,
> and I'll welcome him.

CHORUS:

> Tell, uncover all:
> Why did Zeus take you?
> Why are you tortured?

PROMETHEUS:

> Speech and silence pain me.
> I suffer both; neither stops the pain.
> When balance broke among the gods,
> splitting them against themselves,
> some wished to unseat Kronos
> and give his throne to Zeus.
> The rest wanted Kronos' son
> never to rule.
> I gave my best advice
> to the Titans, sons of Sky and Earth.
> I failed. Power made them deaf.
> They set to win with Violence.
> Many times my mother Themis, Earth—
> one god—many names—told me
> the ruled would not need force
> but craft to rule the rulers.
> They never glanced my way.

With Earth's support, I offered.
Zeus accepted.
Thanks to me Zeus buried Kronos
and his friends in Tartarus.
His profit is my pain;
his gain the tyrant's plague:
he fears his friends.
                    Why he tortures me—
listen. When he finally sat where Kronos did
he gave each god part of his realm,
assigned the powers. People got nothing.
Zeus planned to raze the race to plant another.
Of all the gods I stood against him—
alone I dared rescue man
from Zeus's fire and Hades' murk.
Now he lays me low and tortures me,
cursed to suffer, pitiful to see.
I did not give myself the love
I gave to men.
Ruthlessly chastised,
I disgrace his reign.

3rd OCEANID:
Heart of rock and will of iron
he has who stands unmoved
by your suffering.
I did not want to see;
what I see grieves me.

PROMETHEUS:
To friends I am pitiful.

CHORUS:
Did you do anything else?

PROMETHEUS:
I kept men from seeing destiny.

CHORUS:
How?

PROMETHEUS:
I blinded them with hope.

CHORUS:
A good thing.

PROMETHEUS:
More than that—I gave them fire.

CHORUS:
Time-bound creatures know fire's red tongue?

PROMETHEUS:
From it they'll learn a lot.

CHORUS:
And on these charges Zeus—

PROMETHEUS:
Torments me without rest.

CHORUS:
This has no end?

PROMETHEUS:
It ends when Zeus ends it.

4th OCEANID:
But when? Why hope? You went wrong.
To say so hurts me, tortures you.
Don't speak—think of an escape.

PROMETHEUS:
You aren't hurting—
easy for you to talk.
I know I wronged—I chose to!
In helping men I helped myself to trouble.

I never thought these jagged rocks,
this empty place, would waste me.
Stop weeping, step down,
hear what's to come.
Know my struggle, listen,
suffer with me.
Suffering wanders all over,
and greets everyone alike.

CHORUS:

Our hearts hear you, Prometheus.
We leave the air, the way of birds,
and light upon the rugged ground
to hear your tale.

(Ocean enters on a great white bird.)

OCEAN:

Prometheus! At last!
I was determined to find you.
Know I suffer with you—
blood binds me—blood and highest awe.
It's true—I cannot flatter.
How can I help? Tell me.
There's no better friend than Ocean.

PROMETHEUS:

So, you too have come to gawk?
How did you leave
the streams that name you,
your rock-arched caves, to visit Earth?
You came to hear my tale, add your tears to mine?
Look at me, Zeus's friend
who helped him to his throne,
now bound, wrenched with pain.

OCEAN:

I see. This is my advice:

know yourself. Find new ways.
A new king rules the gods.
Toss rough words into the wind
and Zeus on high may catch them.
Then this will seem child's play.
Unhappy friend, put wrath away.
Seek freedom from your bonds.
You are paying for your big mouth—
yet you still aren't humble.
You don't yield to pain. You ask for more!
Don't kick against the pricks.
I'll try for your release.
Stay quiet, don't rave.
Don't you know the cost of foolish words?

PROMETHEUS:

    Innocent, you dare share my struggle?
Give up—go home.
There's no convincing one
who will not be convinced.
Look to yourself—concern for me
ruins you.

OCEAN:

    It's clear you advise your friends
better than you do yourself.
I'm going now, don't stop me.
I'm sure Zeus favors me,
yes, sure he'll free you.

PROMETHEUS:

    Thanks a lot.
Do nothing—nothing you can do helps.
Keep still, keep clear of danger.
If I suffer— do I want all the world to suffer too?
No. My brother Atlas' fate disturbs me.
Out west he stands, propping on his shoulders

the pillars Sky and Earth,
Always with his heavy load.
I pity Sicily's earthson living in a cave—
raging hundred-headed Typhon.
He fought the gods alone,
hissing terror from his monster jaws,
flashing flame from fiery eyes
to crush the throne of Zeus.
But the thunderbolt unsleeping,
breathing flame, struck out of him
those vaunting braggart's boasts,
blasted out his strength,
and burned his heart to ash.
Now his powerless hulk sprawls
by the narrows of the sea,
pinned by Aetna's roots,
while on its highest peaks
Hephaistos forges red-hot iron.
From there one day will leap
streams of flame, devouring
Sicily's garden with savage jaws.
Typhon then shoots lava-balls,
a fiery spray, though charred
to cinders by the thunderbolt of Zeus.
    You aren't stupid, you don't need examples.
Save yourself if you can.
I'll wear this ordeal
till Zeus abates his anger.

OCEAN:
    Don't you know
    words can heal an angry heart?

PROMETHEUS:
    If used to soothe in season,
    not force a swelling down.

88

OCEAN:

Do you see risk for me,
risking care for you?

PROMETHEUS:

Only heavy work and a light mind.

OCEAN:

I'll be simple then;
a wise man often profits seeming foolish.

PROMETHEUS:

But *I'll* be deemed the fool.

OCEAN:

Your words send me home.

PROMETHEUS:

Then go. Don't let pity cast you into hate.

OCEAN:

With the king young on his throne?

PROMETHEUS:

Watch out—don't make him mad.

OCEAN:

Your fate teaches me.

PROMETHEUS:

Hurry up. Save yourself.

OCEAN:

No need to shout. I'm going—
my four-legged bird already fans the air.
He wants his stall.

(Ocean departs)

5th OCEANID:
I weep for your misery,
Prometheus. Tears
flood my cheeks,
streaming sorrow.
Zeus who cruelly reigns
with private rules
disdains the gods of old.

CHORUS:
Now all Earth chants a dirge
for your time-told brilliance,
the glory of your blood.
The Asians wail in pity for your pain;
the dwellers of Colchis,
girls, unafraid to fight,
and the Scythians who live on
Lake Maiotis' shore—earth's last place;
warring Arab's flowering youth
camped near the Caucasus,
army of terror, raging with spears that rip flesh.

1st OCEANID:
I have seen only one other Titan
bent in steel humiliation:
strong Atlas, who groans beneath the weight
of heaven's lid.

CHORUS:
The tide roars mourning as it breaks.
The hollow depths lament your pain.
Black Hades rumbles pity.
Clear swift rivers weep.

PROMETHEUS:
Neither pride nor stubbornness
makes me silent. Anger eats my heart.
Who but I doled out privileges

to these upstart gods?
You know that. Now hear about men's misery.
They were stupid till I gave them thought.
Let me list for you—not blaming them—
the gifts I gave.
    They had eyes but didn't see,
ears but did not hear. As in a dream,
they confused senses. They knew no skills—
couldn't build with brick or wood.
Like ants they drudged in sunless caves,
not knowing winter, flowering spring,
or fruitful summer. Their lives were chance.
Then I taught them how the stars move.
    I made numbers, first of sciences,
syllables, then words, memory of all,
the Muses' mother.
I yoked to cross-bars beasts
instead of men, relieving them from labor.
To the chariot I hitched horses,
delight of wealth and pride.
I designed the sailor's ship to cross the sea.
    All this I contrived for men. But for myself,
I don't know how to spring this trap.

CHORUS:
    Misery has worn your mind away.
    Like a doctor fallen ill,
    you cannot cure yourself.

PROMETHEUS:
    Hear the rest. Marvel at the tools
    I found for men.
    If people were sick before,
    they had no food, drug,
    no drink to heal them.
    Their only cure was death—
    until I showed them potions,
    herbs, to drive disease away.

I marked the ways of prophecy,
which dreams will be reality,
unriddled chancing sounds and wayside meetings.
I carefully compared the flights of birds—
which bode good, which evil—
their ways of life, their feuds and friendships,
the smoothness of their guts, what color gall
gives gods the greatest pleasure,
the liver's mottled balance.
I burned loin-meat and thighbones
thickly wrapped in fat,
letting humans join secret rites.
I read fiery omens, obscured before.
    The inner earth concealed from men
iron, bronze, silver, gold.
I bared them first—*that* no one else can claim.
In short, know this:
Prometheus gave mankind all arts.

CHORUS:
Do not then, helping people,
be careless of yourself.
You'll soon be free, I hope,
and prevail no less than Zeus.

PROMETHEUS:
Fate has yet to make your hope
come true. She won't, until infinities of pain
sap me. Then I will be free.
Necessity is stronger than craft.

CHORUS:
Who's in charge?

PROMETHEUS:
Three Fates and unforgetting Furies.

CHORUS:
Even Zeus submits?

PROMETHEUS:
He can't escape.

CHORUS:
What's for him except to rule forever?

PROMETHEUS:
Don't ask—you mustn't know.

CHORUS:
You veil a mystery.

PROMETHEUS:
Speak of something else; it's not
the time to tell but conceal.
Only by keeping my secret
will I loose these chains.

1st OCEANID:
May Zeus who gives all gifts
never set his face against my will.
May I never slow in offering oxen
to the gods beside my father's stream,
my tongue never offend.
Hold this unfading prayer, heart.

2nd OCEANID:
Sweet to live
in buoyant hope,
sweet to swell the heart
with golden joy.
I quake to see these thousand tortures
wasting you.
You have no awe for Zeus,
but in defiance worship men.

93

3rd OCEANID:

See how thankless all your help?
What helps you, anywhere?
Creatures-of-a-day? Don't you see
the murky dream that shackles them?
Their purpose never hinders Zeus's harmony.

4th OCEANID:

From you I learned
this somber song, Prometheus.
How strange this tune
beside the melody I wove around
your bridal bath and bed,
to woo Hermione, my sister,
to be your wife.

(Enter Io, dress torn, screaming, pursued by gadfly.)

IO:

What land? People? Who's this,
bound on rock, open to the seasons?
What crime deserves this death?
Where am I?
Ohhhhhhhhhh—
The gadfly, Argus' ghost,
stings again. Ahhhh!
Keep him away!
The herdsman of a thousand eyes
stalks me, his crafty glare
unglazed by death.
Out of his grave he goads me
to wander hungry by the shore.
The wax-pipe drones a lullaby—
where will I go?
Zeus, why me?
You drive my heart to frenzy!
Away! Ohhhhhhhhhh—
Better burn me, bury me,

throw me to a nest of water snakes—
eat me alive!
Take me to heart, King.
I'm tired of roaming—I can't stop.
Listen! Hear the girl you crowned with horns!

PROMETHEUS:
How can I ignore the girl the gadfly maddens,
Inachus' child, who softened Zeus's heart
with love, exhuasted runs from Hera's hate?

IO:
You know my father's name?
Who are you?
Tell me, you who rightly called me
maddened girl, and
named the wasp god sent
that crazes me.
Ohhhhhhhhhh—
The pain! Hera!
Who feels what I do?
Ohhhhh—
What else? What remedy
Cures my disease?
Tell me—speak.
Show me misery.

PROMETHEUS:
I'll tell you plain—
no riddles—
friend to friend.
You're looking at Prometheus, who gave men fire.

IO:
You lit a brilliant light—
why do you suffer now?

PROMETHEUS:
I just told that story.

IO:

Why not repeat it?

PROMETHEUS:

What do you want? I can't tell all.

IO:

Who bound you here?

PROMETHEUS:

Zeus's will, Hephaistos' hand.

IO:

Why?

PROMETHEUS:

I've said enough.

IO:

Then show me when and where
I stop wandering.

PROMETHEUS:

Better you don't know.

IO:

Don't hide my misery.

PROMETHEUS:

I can't.

IO:

Then why not tell?

PROMETHEUS:

Truth hurts.

IO:

Don't love me more than I, myself.

PROMETHEUS:
   All right, I'll tell.

CHORUS:
   Wait! Include us in the pleasure.
   First we'll ask about her sickness,
   let her tell that story.
   Then you foretell her future.

PROMETHEUS:
   Io, this favor is your duty
   to your aunts, Ocean's daughters.
   It's worth the time to weep
   when you can win a tear.

IO:
   How can I refuse? All you want,
   you'll know. How I weep
   recalling heaven's storm,
   my body's shameful marring
   and who did it!
      Phantoms haunted my bed at night,
   beckoning soft, 'Why still a virgin?
   The highest marriage is yours.
   Zeus, pierced with passion's arrow,
   longs to lie with you in love. Don't spurn him.
   Go to Lerna's grassy meadow
   where your father's oxen graze,
   give Zeus rest from yearning.'
   Each night these dreams enfolded me;
   at last I told Father.
   To Pythos, to Dodona, he sent messengers
   to learn what act, what word would
   please the gods. They brought oracles,
   obscure and darkly worded. Then Inachus
   heard a clear response,

charging him to banish me from home
and fatherland, to roam at random to Earth's limits,
or with his race be blasted off the planet.
He drove me out, barred me from his house
against his will and mine, forced by Zeus.
I changed—see these horns he gave me?
The gadfly stung—
I ran to Cerchnea's sweet stream and Lerna's spring.
Argus, sharp in anger, followed,
watching every step, all eyes,
till sudden death came on him.
I'm driven land to land, lashed
by the whip of god.
    Predict my future—
can't you? Don't lie—don't pity me.
To me deception's the sickest shame.

5th OCEANID:
    I never dreamt
of hearing such strange words,
such crushing cruelty,
bitterness,
it stings my soul.
Fate! Fate!
Io's anguish shakes me.

PROMETHEUS:
    You weep too soon;
there's more.

CHORUS:
    Tell us. To the ill it's sweet
to know the pain that's coming.

PROMETHEUS:
    You've heard her past—
know her future, too:

98

the revenge Hera makes her bear.
You, child of Inachus,
cast my words into your heart—
know your end.
    Turn to the east. Cross the plains
until you see Scythia's nomads, armed with bows,
living in tents on wagons. Keep away.
Follow the rocky shore through.
To the left live the Chalybes, ironworkers.
Watch out—they're savage.
You reach the river Hybristes, the Violent,
rightly named. Don't cross—
you can't—walk on to Caucasus' crest,
where from its brows the river pours its fury.
Over that peak climb south, to meet an Amazon army,
manhaters. They'll found
Themiscyra on the Thermodon,
where Salmydessus juts its rugged jaw,
hostile to sailors, witch to ships.
You reach Cimmeria's isthmus. Be bold—
pass through Maiotis.
People will always praise this crossing—
they'll name it for you: Bosporos—the Cow-Strait.
Then leave Europe for Asia.
    Does Zeus seem completely violent?
On the girl he desired he now casts endless
wandering. What a lover, poor girl.
And this is only the beginning.

IO:
    Ohhhhhhhhh—

PROMETHEUS:
    Do you want the rest?

CHORUS:
    There's more?

PROMETHEUS:
A wintry sea of ruin.

IO:
Ohhhhhhhhhh—
why live? Why not
break myself on these rocks,
dash myself to death?
Better end all in a flash than
suffer on!

PROMETHEUS:
You wouldn't like *my* situation.
No death frees *me*.
My misery doesn't end
till Zeus falls from rule.

IO:
Zeus lose his tyranny?

PROMETHEUS:
That pleases you.

IO:
Why not? He gave me all this.

PROMETHEUS:
It's to be.

IO:
Who strips him of his scepter?

PROMETHEUS:
His own empty purposes.

IO:
How?

PROMETHEUS:
He'll make a bad marriage.

IO:
His wife will drive him from the throne?

PROMETHEUS:
No, his child—stronger than its father.

IO:
There's no escape?

PROMETHEUS:
None, unless I'm freed.

IO:
Who breaks Zeus's law to do that?

PROMETHEUS:
One of yours.

IO:
What? My child free you?

PROMETHEUS:
Yes—the third-born after ten generations.

IO:
I don't understand.

PROMETHEUS:
So don't ask.
IO:
Don't break a promise.

PROMETHEUS:
I'll tell you one of two tales.

IO:
Which ones? Name them, let me choose.

PROMETHEUS:
Either hear your story,
or mine.

CHORUS:

Tell us one, her the other.
Both want words.
Tell her her journey to the end,
us, who'll free you.

PROMETHEUS:

First I'll show you your journey,
Io. Write it on your heart.
    After you cross the Bosporos,
walk toward the flaming East,
over the sea to Cisthene's Gorgon plain
where Phorcys' daughters live:
three old swannish spinsters.
They have one eye, one tooth;
on them no sun shines by day,
no moon at night. Nearby are three winged
sisters, Gorgons who hate people, snakes in their hair.
Look at them—you die.
You'll see the griffins, Zeus's watchdogs,
and the one-eyed Arimaspian horsemen,
riding near Pluto's golden stream.
Stay away. You'll reach
a distant land, where black people
live by the waters of the sun.
There's the river Aethiop—follow it
until it falls, where from the Biblos mountains
Nile lets down his sacred stream.
He'll lead you to the delta,
where you and your descendants
make your home. Is this clear?
Ask questions, know it all. I have more
spare time than I need.

CHORUS:

If you've left out some part
of her trip, go on.

If you've finished, keep your word.
Who'll free you?

PROMETHEUS:

Io's heard her journey.
So she'll know my words are true,
I'll tell her recent wanderings,
not from the beginning
but beginning with the end.
When you reached the Molossian plain,
and Dodona with its high circling ridge,
where Thesprotian Zeus keeps a seat of prophecy,
his talking oaks—a marvel past belief—
called you Zeus's famous bride-to-be—
right? Then the fly stung—
you flew along the shore to Rhea's gulf,
bounding there to here.
People will call that Io's bay
to remind everyone you passed.
These details prove I see more than I tell.
    I'll go on with the story now.
At Nile's silty mouth stands Canopus,
where Zeus's hand will stroke you—restore your senses.
You bear a dark-skinned child, whose name, Epaphus—
'From-a-Touch'—tells how he was fathered.
He'll harvest fruit from every land
broad Nile waters. Five generations later,
fifty girls return to Argus,
fleeing marriage with their cousins.
These boys, hearts afire with love,
like falcons tailing doves will lust
for wives not to be wed:
god denies the brides they want.
Greece will welcome them,
where night's black veil hides
these women's blows

103

that murder pride, lust, and life.
Each woman bathes her knife in man's blood—
may my enemies know such love!
But sex will charm one girl to save her love,
to blunt her purpose, choosing cowardice
over butchery. She'll live in Argus
and mother a race of kings.
Her daughter's daughter
will bear Herakles, an archer
who will free me from my fetters.
Themis told me: it will be.
Ask no more—you'll get nothing.

IO:

Madness—fire—my mind!
Ohhhhhhhhhh—
My soul!
The gadfly's arrow burns!
Ohhhhhhhhhh!
Heart, break against my ribs!
My eyes
are popping!
Blow icy gust—blast me away!
Ohhhhhhhhhh!
Why speak?
What are words against a tidal wave?

(Io leaves, tearing at her clothes, screaming, etc.)

CHORUS:

He was wise,
who said marriage
to one's own is best.
Not with her pampered by gold,
swollen with pedigree,
should he whose hands labor
want to wed.

Never, Fate,
never see me
share Zeus's bed.
Never may my lover be a god,
for Io's sorry love,
drained by Hera's hate,
shakes all desire from me.
A fair match is free
from fear. Gods,
never cast a trapping
love on me. This is war
that is no war, a bitter
well of sorrow.
I would not know my fate—
how could I escape the love of Zeus?

PROMETHEUS:
Even Zeus will be brought low
by a love that hurls him from power
to nothingness. What Kronos,
driven from his throne, divined,
will be.
No god but I can save him
from his fall. I know all.
Let him strut, plume, trust
the crash of power, brandishing
his thunderbolt. Nothing
saves him from falling.
Even now he readies for a rival
whose flash, whose crash,
will split Poseidon's trident.
Zeus cracks on this reef;
he learns what splits
ruler from ruled.

CHORUS:
Your threats are only your desire.

PROMETHEUS:
They're what will be—and my desire.

CHORUS:
Zeus mastered?

PROMETHEUS:
By pain bitterer than mine.

CHORUS:
You aren't afraid to taunt him?

PROMETHEUS:
Me, afraid? I can't die.

CHORUS:
He could make more pain.

PROMETHEUS:
Let him— I'm ready.

CHORUS:
Wisdom submits to necessity.

PROMETHEUS:
Then worship him, please, fawn on him.
What do I care for Zeus?
Let him have his way, his little day:
it can't last.

(Hermes enters.)

Who's this? Zeus's errand-boy,
a lackey of the new regime?
Well? What's new?

HERMES:
To you I speak, crafty, bitter god,
who wronged us with your love of men,

to you, fire-thief. The father
means to know what marriage overthrows him.
Speak! None of your tricks!
Don't make me come twice, Prometheus.
Your bragging doesn't soften Zeus.

PROMETHEUS:
Your job to serve the gods
has made you arrogant.
You're young—like your power—
don't you think you'll come down?
I've seen two kings fall already,
and soon a third.
You think I cower, I fear your gods?
Far from it.
Get back to Zeus—stop wasting time here.

HERMES:
Your pride put you in these chains.

PROMETHEUS:
But I'd never trade them
for your servitude.

HERMES:
Better to be trusted with this rock
than the messages of father Zeus?

PROMETHEUS:
Your words match your insolence.

HERMES:
Seems you like your bonds.

PROMETHEUS:
These? I'd like to see my enemies
revelling like me. You, too!

HERMES:
I'm to blame for your bad luck?

PROMETHEUS:
I hate all the gods who repay
my help like this.

HERMES:
You're mad.

PROMETHEUS:
If hating enemies is madness, yes.

HERMES:
You'd be hateful free and ruling.

PROMETHEUS:
Ohhhhhh— *(cries out in sudden pain)*

HERMES:
Ohhhhhh? A word Zeus doesn't know.

PROMETHEUS:
Time teaches all.

HERMES:
It hasn't taught you wisdom.

PROMETHEUS:
Or why would I speak to you?

HERMES:
You're not telling me what the father needs.

PROMETHEUS:
I'm in his debt? I owe him favors?

HERMES:
You tease me like a child.

PROMETHEUS:

You're not a child—or worse?—
expecting to learn anything here?
He can't torture or trick
me into telling before my chains break.
Shoot all the curls of fire he wants,
upheave earth with blizzards, crashing thunder,
this won't wrench the answer from me:
whose hand will crush him.

HERMES:

Choose your words wisely.

PROMETHEUS:

I am resolved.

HERMES:

Submit, fool, submit
to reason in the face of pain.

PROMETHEUS:

Speak to the waves!
Never, fearing Zeus, will I
ape woman's hands and
face the sky
to beg my captor to release me.
I'm far, far from that.

HERMES:

I've said enough—
nothing softens you.
Unbroken, you champ the bit
and jerk against the rein.
You're violent because you can't think straight.
What's a stubborn fool? Nothing.
Think again—the hurricane,
the muddy waves of agony that break on you

unless you hear me.
First Zeus cracks this rock
with lightning, flame and thunder,
then sinks you, still clasped in stone.
But you'll see light again:
the eagle, Zeus's hound with blooky beak
will rip you in rags, an uninvited guest
to dine upon your black, bloody liver.
Your pain has no end, unless
some god descends to sunless
Hades to take it on himself.
I'm not bragging: it's all true.
God cannot lie: his every word is truth.
Reflect—don't put pride over good advice.

CHORUS:

Hermes makes sense.
He wants you to leave your
stony will and reason.
Obey. Don't, knowing better,
stay in the wrong.

PROMETHEUS:

I already knew of these threats
announced so loudly.
For one enemy to hate another
is no disgrace. Let the fire burn,
angry winds blast, thunder shock.
Let cyclones uproot Earth,
roaring waves devour the stars.
Let him take me up,
hurl me to Tartarus.
Let Fate's muddy whirlpool
suck me down.
    Do what he can—
he can't make me die.

HERMES:
A madman's words!
This prayer proves it!
Where does his madness stop?
You, who share his agony,
get out—or thunder's crash
crazes you.

CHORUS:
Say that again—beg us
in a different tone.
We're no cowards—
we'll stay with him through
any pain. We've learned
to hate traitors;
nothing is sicker.

HERMES:
Remember my warning—
be content with what you get.
Don't say Zeus hurt you unfairly.
Blame yourselves instead.
By your own will you'll be caught
in misery's tight net—
tangled in your own stupidity.

PROMETHEUS:
His threat is real: the earth quakes.
Thunder bellows deep—
fire's spiral flashes.
Ashy whirlwinds swirl,
the winds blow mad.
Air and sea convulse as one.
Zeus's chaos is here!
O Holy Mother,
air rolling round the common light,
you see the wrongs I suffer!

111

(In a fiery holocaust, Prometheus and the Chorus sink beneath the stage.)

EPILOGUE

PROMETHEUS BOUND

Some important fragments of the sequel to *Prometheus Bound* have survived. The play must have begun with the entrance of the Titans, who recount to Prometheus (still chained to the rock, but in daylight, not Tartarus) their recent release from Tartarus, a reconciliatory measure of Zeus, whose power has now been tempered with mercy. As at the beginning of the first play, Prometheus is silent. His silence, however, is probably a result of pain rather than obstinance.

Prometheus's opening speech survives in a Latin translation by Cicero. He beseeches the Titans to look at his bonds, and describes the eagle's frequent visits. Zeus has given him the worst; his defiant strength is sapped, and he longs for death. So we see the beginnings of a compromise in Prometheus's position as well as in Zeus's. The Titans, like Ocean and the chorus in *Prometheus Bound*, urge Prometheus to show wisdom and submit to Zeus. He probably rejects their advice to tell Zeus the secret he demands.

The next visitor to the rock may be Themis, Prometheus's mother and Goddess of Earth, to whom he appealed at the beginning and end of *Prometheus Bound*. She, too, urges him to submit, and he finally listens. Perhaps he consents to allow his mother to divulge to Zeus his secret— that if Zeus marries Thetis, she will bear him a son who will overthrow him. Themis would then exit to go begin her mediation between Zeus and her son.

Herakles might then appear. He kills the eagle, discovers who Prometheus is, and perhaps becomes reluctant to help his father's enemy any further. Prometheus might change his mind by recounting the story of his ancestor, Io, and promising to predict Herakles' wanderings as he did Io's, if Herakles will release him. Herakles agrees to the arrangement, and, after hearing the story of his future wanderings, breaks Prometheus's chains.

It may be that Hermes reappears with the news that Themis's mediation between Prometheus and Zeus has been a success. He might remind Prometheus that Zeus demands that another god be found to take his sufferings upon himself. Here Herakles intervenes, explaining that he has accidentally wounded Cheiron, the Centaur, who wants to die but can't. Cheiron is accepted by all as a substitute for Prometheus. Herakles departs to fulfill Prometheus's predictions.

PROMETHEUS THE FIRE-BEARER

Prometheus now supplicates himself before Zeus to be re-admitted to Olympus. It may be that some higher god or goddess intervenes with Zeus on his behalf. Perhaps Athena, who has an ancient connection with Prometheus as the collaborator with him in the creation of mankind, uses her influence with Zeus for a complete reconciliation. The play probably also portrays Herakles' wanderings, and might picture his attempt at initiation in the Eleusian mysteries. The object of the third play is, at any rate, reconciliation between all the conflicting forces of the trilogy—Prometheus and Zeus, Zeus and Hera, Zeus and Herakles, Herakles and Hera. It all works nicely. Zeus punished Prometheus for his salvation of mankind. When time taught them both wisdom, Prometheus saved Zeus from downfall and was himself saved by Zeus's son. Herakles continues Prometheus's work in advancing the progress of human beings. The Olympian conflict is finally resolved by Athena, goddess of wisdom, who is also patroness of the city, the peak of human civilization. The close of the trilogy may be a celebration or festival honoring Prometheus, Herakles, and Athena, who together have reconciled the forces of intelligence and power and promoted the destiny of mankind.

Philoctetes

Sophocles

translated by

Armand Schwerner

Introduction

How to have them say what they must?

you have to con Philoctetes, use the language
....
....
if he sees me and has his bow with him I'm dead,
and so are you, because of me
....
.... *you shrink*
from the music of deceit
....
............................*if* you *fail,* we *fail*
Troy will elude us, the Greeks will grieve,
we must have this man's bow

(this version; all quotes by Odysseus
to Philoctetes, from ll. 55-86)

—the translator looks again at his adventures in the latitudes of speech-modes. Reasonably colloquial, intermittently hieratic. As in any transmission, to enter into the work, the body, and re-make. . . . What can help? Historical perspective, some understanding of class structure, Eliade on the sacred, Kitto, Bowra. . . . And what remains is almost everything. These powerful aristocratic men, power-lust and righteousness, and nevertheless the subtly pervasive harmonics of moira, ananke. And pain, a lot of pain. When an unbearable hurt comes, the words,

117

the rhetoric, go: παπαî, απαππαπαî, παπαππαπαππαπαππαπαî Near the extreme point on the continuum; from that wrenched cry to the lyricism and compassionate clarity of the Chorus:

᾿῾Υπν᾽ ὀδύνας ἀδαής, ῾῾Υπνε δ᾽ ἀλγέων,
ε᾽υαες Ημῖν ᾽ἐλθοις,
ε᾽υαίων, ὦναξ
ὄμμασι δ᾽ ἀντισχοις
τάνδ᾽ αιγλαν, ἁ τέτατει τανῦν
ἰθι ᾽ἰθι μοι παιών.

The translator, *carrier-over*, owes the play-language and himself an immersion in the extensive field of those possibilities. Faithfulness to the tone. If in doubt, cut. But why still *another* translation of the play? The Harvard Loeb edition (1913) gives:

Sleep immune of cares,
    Sleep that knows not cumber,
Breathe thy softest airs,
    Prince of painless slumber!
O'er his eyes alway
Let thy dream-light play;
Healer come, we pray.

ababccc, not too reasonably, the text giving abcbda. 7 lines for 6. Diction the old trap. What's the compulsion for this kind of *ordering*? Thomas Francklin (1938) gives:

Sleep, thou patron of mankind,
Great physician of the mind,
Who dost nor pain nor sorrow know,
Sweetest balm of every woe,
Mildest sovereign, hear us now;
Hear thy wretched suppliant's vow;
His eyes in gentle slumbers close,
And continue his repose;
Hear thy wretched suppliant's vow,
Great physician, hear us now.

118

aabbccddee; 4-stress couplets, arbitrarily; metronomic, almost; 10 lines
for 6; the deadly language of 'poetry' in a sterile version of 18th century
modes. When in doubt, add? enforce symmetry? David Greene, 1957:

Sleep that knows not pain nor suffering
Kindly upon us, Lord,
Kindly, kindly come.
Spread your enveloping radiance,
As now, over his eyes.
Come, come, Lord Healer.

6 lines for 6; more skillfully restrained and apposite; a significant lyrical
movement; a workable decision about the rhymes; but still the continuing afflictions of syntactical inversion and archaic diction, the traditional
'nobility' mode—*knows not . . . nor, kindly come,* etc. Here the lines
read:

lord Sleep, breathe
a quiet music for him
lord of peace not pain
flow in your calm over his eyes, come
lord healer come

Is this 'better'? In any case it does represent the effort to work in pretty
straight conversational syntax, to minimize interruptive punctuation in
the interest of flow, to commonly de-emphasize phrasal and clausal webs.
   Can this tragedy work on the stage today and tomorrow, in the context
of good plays working through the complex presence of our American?
I wanted very much to produce a translation whose language has a play-
able vivacity—a version essentially faithful to the original, but subject to
my sense of pace and rhythm in the language we speak. For instance I
felt the need to cut through what I experienced as the prolixity of sticho-
mythia, the full-sentence formalities of line-for-line conversations. I
hope I succeeded in rendering the force and sharpness of many colloquies
without calling on the rhetoric or implicit world-view of naturalistic
theater. The various dramatic embodiments of subtle and shifting
psychological states—which talk to us with such extraordinary *presence*—
evoke constant recognition. The play does establish temporal disjunction

with the sudden appearance of its god-from-the-machine, Herakles. But that event, easily felt as intrusive and inorganic, works a power. It's in the conjunction of two orders: Philoctetes' and Neoptolemus' moral and psychological growth in self-awareness, and the matrix of that Necessity to which they finally submit.

Armand Schwerner

CHARACTERS

ODYSSEUS

CHORUS, sailor companions of Odysseus and Neoptolemus

NEOPTOLEMUS, Achilles' son, prince of Scyros

PHILOCTETES, Poeas' son

HERAKLES

A SPY

SCENE

The play takes place in a lonely place on Lemnos Island.

ODYSSEUS:
  finally, Lemnos island, see how dreary
  this place, no people, no houses, nothing and no one
  except Philoctetes, Poeas' son.
                    Neoptolemus
  you're the son of our shining father Achilles,
  let me make it absolutely clear I left Philoctetes here
  on the prince's orders: it was unbearable,
  his rotting foot and its pus, his screams and moans
  unnerving everyone, souring our rites and our sacrifices

  well, no point going on about it. there's no time
  if he finds me here I'll never be able to take him back
  I need your help, take a look around, we're looking
  for a cave with a double entrance. it'll have one alcove
  the sun warms in winter, in the other
  cool breezes dissipate the heat
  over to the left a little you'll see a fountain
  where he drinks, if he's alive. if you see anything
  signal, then we'll talk further

NEOPTOLEMUS:
  I think I see it. a cave

ODYSSEUS:
  where? up or down?

NEOPTOLEMUS:
  up there. but there's no sign of a path

ODYSSEUS:
  maybe he's lying down. have a look

NEOPTOLEMUS:
  nobody

ODYSSEUS:
  no food? how about utensils? anything?

NEOPTOLEMUS:
  just a bed of leaves

ODYSSEUS:
  and?

NEOPTOLEMUS:
  a wooden bowl. pretty crude. some kindling

ODYSSEUS:
  his whole treasure . . .

NEOPTOLEMUS:
  here are some rags, drying, grayish-yellow with pus

ODYSSEUS:
  this must be his place. he's probably nearby
  with that bad leg, out to find food I suppose
  or medicinal herbs. set a watch on him
  he's one man I'd rather not be surprised by
  he'd rather take me than any Greek alive

NEOPTOLEMUS:
  I'll arrange for the guard. now
  go on. you have more to say

ODYSSEUS:
  son of Achilles today you must prove
  who you are, and not just with your body
  I'm setting you a task, strange to you; but you must
  do it. you came to serve

NEOPTOLEMUS:
  what do I do?

ODYSSEUS:

you have to con Philoctetes. use the language.
when he asks you about yourself, tell him
'Achilles' son.' no need to lie about that. but
tell him more, that you're sailing home in anger,
having left the fleet in anger
the Greek chiefs lied to you and betrayed you.
to take Troy they had to have you, seduced you
into leaving home and when you joined them
they ripped you away
from Achilles' weapons, your father's
weapons, that you had a right to, and gave them
to Odysseus, gave those arms to Odysseus.
when you say my name curse me, spit on Odysseus
that's no pain for me: if *you* fail, *we* fail
Troy will elude us, the Greeks will grieve,
we must have this man's bow

I'll explain why you can meet him and why I can't
you're here freely, not bound by a pledge or an oath
nor did you belong to the first fleet
but I *am* bound, and I *was* present. that's it.
if he sees me and has his bow with him I'm dead,
and so are you, because of me

can you deliver that unconquered bow? I know
the dishonesty sickens you, you shrink
from the music of deceit. but winning is sweet,
today is for courage, tomorrow for honesty; be mine
for one hour of lies; as to the rest, your probity,
the endless future will bear witness

NEOPTOLEMUS:

son of Laertes, what I hate to hear, what rasps
my ears, I hate to do. that's how I am. I loathe the smell
of deceit and they tell me my father did too. I *am* ready
to deliver Philoctetes. by force. I won't by fraud.
he can't withstand us, crippled as he is. prince,

123

since I am sent to help you
I'm worried about seeming passive, but
I'd rather fail with honor than sink
into victory

ODYSSEUS:
son of great Achilles, when I was young
I bound my tongue and winged my hand, like you
but our common pain has taught me
the tongue's ultimate power

NEOPTOLEMUS:
you want me to lie

ODYSSEUS:
to snare Philoctetes

NEOPTOLEMUS:
and not persuade him? deceive him?

ODYSSEUS:
persuasion's as useless as force

NEOPTOLEMUS:
why are his weapons so incredible?

ODYSSEUS:
they never miss. death comes immediately

NEOPTOLEMUS:
but if a brave man . . .

ODYSSEUS:
no. only stratagems will work. I told you that

NEOPTOLEMUS:
lies don't shame you?

ODYSSEUS:
not if success depends on them

NEOPTOLEMUS:
an adult is responsible for his face . . .
how can he confront the world if . . . ?

ODYSSEUS:
if you have qualms you lose

NEOPTOLEMUS:
how do I profit if we do get him to Troy?

ODYSSEUS:
without the bow we can't sack Troy

NEOPTOLEMUS:
you said *I* would take the town

ODYSSEUS:
you and the bow; the bow not without you

NEOPTOLEMUS:
in that case the quarry's worth going after

ODYSSEUS:
if you make it you win twice

NEOPTOLEMUS:
make that clear and I'll try

ODYSSEUS:
they'll call you brave; but they'll also say: 'a wise man'

NEOPTOLEMUS:
I'll throw out my shame and do it

ODYSSEUS:
you remember my instructions?

NEOPTOLEMUS:
enough; I said I'd do it; I'll do it

ODYSSEUS:

stay here then; wait till he comes
I don't want to be seen so I'll go
and bring the guard back to the ship with me.
if you stay away for long, he'll come back
disguised as a sailor. you won't know him
so be alert. listen carefully, his cryptic words
will cloak his message. it's up to you now
and back to the ship for me.

HERMES:

God of cunning
be with us
Athene, mistress of victory, Goddess
of the City, who have never failed me
support us now

(exit Odysseus.)

CHORUS:

sir, we're strangers in this strange place, how
will we talk and what should we hide
how should we act with the man we're looking for
let us know: you have a special power of perception
handed you from Zeus; you hold the scepter
and the skill is yours from your father's father's fathers.
young lord, what can we do

NEOPTOLEMUS:

if you want to find his hiding place go on—
when you see the wanderer come back, leave
his cave and come back too. I may need you

CHORUS:

we will do what we've done and will go on doing,
care for you
now we should know
where he lives and rests, we must be on guard

and watch for an attack. where does he walk?
is he at home?

NEOPTOLEMUS:

there's the double door of his cave
and there's the inner rock he uses for a bed

CHORUS:

where is the poor man?

NEOPTOLEMUS:

probably out looking for food
his wound never heals, and goes on hurting
so he limps around, stumbling
on game, his arrows between him and famine

CHORUS:

poor man, forgotten by every man, how we pity him
plagued by his disease and the absence of love
how can he stand the endless aloneness?
a man shudders his way to death and the path is pain
in spite of his lineage he's bereft
and endures his hunger and incurable wound
with only wild and spotted beast for company
except for the blabbing of far away echo
that returns his bitter cries to him

NEOPTOLEMUS:

his pain's no accident, sent
I think by pitiless Chryse,
there's a design to what distresses him:
a wise god knew about the war before the war began,
knows now the harsh
minute of Troy's death, and fixes the song
of Philoctetes' marvelous bow
to the one hour where his absolute arrows
will realize for Troy the promise of its end

CHORUS:
   shh

NEOPTOLEMUS:
   why?

CHORUS:
   listen. a man, limping? is it here?
   here? it's getting nearer now, clear
   sound of groping feet and now still far
   but nearing, distinctly, a voice of pain.
   get ready prince

NEOPTOLEMUS:
   for what?

CHORUS:
   new trouble. he's closer. he's no shepherd
   and that sound's no syrinx melody.
   just listen to the harsh cries born maybe
   from his stumbles on the wounding road. or is he still, eyes
   clearly fixed on the cold port,
   his trial one with the inhospitable sea.

PHILOCTETES:
   you, strangers,
   who are you, your stock, from where,
   ending up here on this island
   of depression and refusals? your clothes, the way
   you look, you must be Greeks, you make my eyes
   happy, talk to me, let me hear you talk.
   if I look strange to you let it be
   I have no friends; I'm alone; I'm stranded here,
   pity me. if you're here as friends I beg you
   talk to me as I do to you

NEOPTOLEMUS:
   your first question: we're Greeks, you're right

128

PHILOCTETES:
wonderful how wonderful to hear Greek again
what quest brought you? the wind
that ordered your sails was a happy wind
tell me everything, I want to know my friend

NEOPTOLEMUS:
I'm from Scyros, where the waves lap the coast
and I'm going home. my name is Neoptolemus
my father's Achilles. you know everything now

PHILOCTETES:
son of a dear father
son of a very dear land
foster-son of old Lycomedes, what
do you need here? what port did you sail from?

NEOPTOLEMUS:
I sailed straight from Ilium

PHILOCTETES:
Ilium? is it . . . could you . . . were you on board
when our fleet first sailed for Troy?

NEOPTOLEMUS:
what do you mean? were you there?

PHILOCTETES:
o my son you don't know who you're talking to?

NEOPTOLEMUS:
should I know a complete stranger?

PHILOCTETES:
not even my name? you don't know
even my name? they never told you
the growing rot in my body?

NEOPTOLEMUS:
I don't know anything about all this

PHILOCTETES:
o the gods forsake me, not one word
of my misery has reached home
but the jackals who marooned me laugh, keep
quiet, my wound keeps hurting
and gets worse every day.
o my boy, Achilles' son, you never heard
about that man, me, Philoctetes, son of Poeas,
inheritor of Heracles' bow, me, thrown
out by the Atridae and the Cephallenian prince,
me, wasted, a tramp, struck by plague, chosen
for death through the hollow envenoming tooth
of a man-killer snake.
that's how they left me, plagued.
exhausted from tossing sleeplessness, I'd fallen
into sleep under a beachrock and they laughed
at my state, as they left for the ships
they donated some used rags, a beggar's alms
and table left-overs. may the gods
lay them this low one day soon.
picture, my son: I wake,
all men gone, what a waking, tears
and distraught cries when I see the ships that had borne me
sailed from my life, no man left to share
the absences or care for me and my hurt.
I looked everywhere my son and found pain, nothing
else as the days and months grew years. I cared
for myself under this sad roof. when hunger came
I shot doves and crawled to retrieve what my taut
bowstring and my arrow had delivered, and all the time
my wasted foot kept dragging heavily on the ground.
if I needed water, if I had to have firewood
when winter frosted the ground, I'd get them. no fire
except for hard rock flint on flint, the hidden spark
that keeps me alive. the bare roof and the fire's all I need.
except for the healing of my hurt.

130

now my son, about this island:
no sailor *wants* to sail here, no anchorage, no
market for goods and profit, no place to sleep and eat.
prudent men stay away. the rare accidental visitors
give me pity, food or clothes
but when I talk of home they leave alone.
so it's ten years now for me, lingering on,
hungry, dying piece by piece.
only the worm that gnaws me flourishes.
my son I owe this misery to the Atridae and Odysseus.
may the gods lay them this low one day soon.

CHORUS:
o son of Poeas as much as those visitors I pity you

NEOPTOLEMUS:
I'm witness to the truth of your story
I've lived with the evil of the Atridae and of Odysseus

PHILOCTETES:
they hurt *you*? a wrong that maddened you?

NEOPTOLEMUS:
o I wish I could act on my resentment,
then both Mycenae and Sparta would learn
that Scyros has also given great sons birth

PHILOCTETES:
well said my son, but I must understand
about your anger: why, what charge, why you're here

NEOPTOLEMUS:
that's not easy for me, I'll try to explain
what I suffered at their hands.
when Fate determined Achilles' death . . .

PHILOCTETES:
what? enough. but . . . he's dead?

131

NEOPTOLEMUS:

    dead. killed by Phoebus, not by a man, pierced
    by an arrow from the bow of the god

PHILOCTETES:

    high lineage in killer and victim, what
    to do first, open to your griefs or weep for him?

NEOPTOLEMUS:

    you have enough pain dear Philoctetes
    without crying for me

PHILOCTETES:

    that's true. so tell me again, from the start
    how they hurt *you*

NEOPTOLEMUS:

    Odysseus and my father's fosterfather Phoenix
    sent for me in a bright ship, told me,
    true or not, my dead father's power
    had descended to me, only *my* hand
    would topple Troy. I yielded and sailed.
    how I lusted to see my father in his death
    my father I'd never seen alive, and I *was* flattered:
    without me Troy was lost to us.
    on the second day swift by sail and oar
    we'd reached Sigeum. I hate that name.
    those men all honored me! "you're Achilles come back to us."
    there lay my father dead and me, poor fool, I mourned him
    a while and accepted the Atridae almost as family,
    claimed my father's arms, and they, inconceivable, they said:
    "child of Achilles, whatever was your father's yours
    but not his arms, assigned to Laertes' son."
    I cried out, I got up furious and I spoke bitterly
    to Odysseus: "you. how dare you give these arms
    to any man but me? they're mine by right,
    I've given *you* no right." then Odysseus said:

"yes boy I have the right, I rescued
the body and arms of your father Achilles." that
maddened me, I burned with abuse and insult, none
adequate for that gross embezzler, who said, stung but so calm:
"you weren't with us, you managed to stay away.
try this response to your boasting and your arrogance:
you'll never reach Scyros with these arms."
in the sleet of attacks like those I left
and now I'm sailing home, the victim of Odysseus the Burglar.
and yet he's less the blame than rulers,
each soldier is subject to authority
all crimes spring from the seed of poor teachings.
that's my story. whoever hates the Atridae
will find me his friend, as I hope he'll find the gods.

CHORUS:

o mother Earth
mother of Zeus
ultimate provider, the golden
Pactolus river courses
between its golden shores
through your body. you were riding
your team of lions and I called to you
when the Atridae dishonored themselves
that day, diverted from Neoptolemus
the arms of his father shining Achilles
to hand over to Odysseus, Laertes' son

PHILOCTETES:

you good men bring me a token of shared pain
I can just see Odysseus' hand and tongue
at their conspiratorial work, anything as long as false.
no surprise there. but did Ajax see and bear all this?

NEOPTOLEMUS:

my friend, Ajax was dead. otherwise
my rights would have been respected

133

PHILOCTETES:
   o is he dead too?

NEOPTOLEMUS:
   yes. he's left the light

PHILOCTETES:
   yes. *he* has. but not those who should never have seen it

NEOPTOLEMUS:
   those prevail, and the Argives call them 'mighty.'

PHILOCTETES:
   and my old good friend Nestor, is he
   alive? his wisdom often checked their intemperateness

NEOPTOLEMUS:
   he's not what he was since he lost
   his most loved son Antilochus

PHILOCTETES:
   o the two men I could spare the least.
   your account inflicts a double loss
   o what hope when two men like that die and Odysseus
   survives, Odysseus—why not *him*? why?

NEOPTOLEMUS:
   a crafty gamesman, but you know
   they're the ones who commonly lose

PHILOCTETES:
   tell me, where was Patroclus, once
   your father's dearest friend?

NEOPTOLEMUS:
   dead like the rest. it's true: war
   spares the villain and dooms the decent man

PHILOCTETES:
my life tells me that too: and about another,
worthless, shrewd and glib . . .

NEOPTOLEMUS:
Odysseus?

PHILOCTETES:
no. Thersites, who babbled when silence
mattered. does he live?

NEOPTOLEMUS:
I didn't see him, but heard he lives

PHILOCTETES:
I thought so. evil never dies. are the gods
perverse? I think they turn back hopelessly bad men
from the mouth of hell but trample the righteous.
of if the gods are unjust, how to find them just?

NEOPTOLEMUS:
I will avoid the men who irrigate villainy
I will see the Atridae and Troy only from a great distance
I will sail to my native rocks in Scyros island, they
will do for me. love and farewell, Philoctetes,
may the gods hear your heart's cry and heal you
we go now and ready the ship for the moment
when the gods grant us a favorable wind

PHILOCTETES:
you leave so soon, my son?

NEOPTOLEMUS:
it's time, to go and watch the tide from the beach

PHILOCTETES:
o in your father's and mother's name, by all

the household gods, my son, don't leave me here alone,
I beg you, abandoned to the pains you've seen
and worse ones you've been told about. think of me
as a stowaway. I know it's burdensome.
please take on the burden. the high spirit weighs shame and honor
it would dirty your honor to leave me here. fame
and glory are yours if you bear me alive to Oeta.
please. it's just a day's bother. take heart. stow me
wherever you like, the hold, the bow, the stern, whatever,
wherever I'm least likely to offend.
by Zeus the god of suppliants please take me. look I'm falling
at your feet, me the cripple. don't condemn me
to this empty place. take me safe to your home
or take me to Euboea, from there I can cross to Oeta
to the Trachnian passes, to the broad Spercheius river
to see my father once more. these heavy years
filled with nightmares of his possible death. . . . every time
visitors came I sent word to him, would he
fetch me home in his own ship. he's dead I suppose
or the bearers of my message dismissed me
from their cares and hurried home. but you now
my messenger *and* my savior, please, pity me.
you understand how fortune and misfortune stand
on slippery ground. so the prospering man at ease
should look for the rocks ahead.
the unexpected shipwreck waits.

CHORUS:
  prince,
  pity
  this agony of grief.
  may the gods keep any friend of mine
  from such an end.
  pity.
  I know the pungent bitterness
  of your hate for the Atridae. turn their rotten plot

to this poor man's profit.
take him home.
bear him through the waves on our ship,
away from the Avengers

NEOPTOLEMUS:
you must hold to your compassion.
if it's only a passing mood, the closeness of his wound
may shake and wither it

CHORUS:
I'll be true

NEOPTOLEMUS:
I couldn't bear the shame
of not helping a stranger in pain
I couldn't lag behind
the light of your insistence. so
we'll sail. let him board. I cannot think
our ship will reject him. may the gods
bring us home safe and soon

PHILOCTETES:
the day now glows. I'm happy
how can I prove my heart's thanks to you
my dearest friend, and to you kind sailors
my son we leave but before we leave go in
and recognize this homeless home, enter into
my heavy life and the obstinacy of my hanging on.
I think no other man could have lasted
but I learned from the needs that were my Fate.

(Neoptolemus and Philoctetes start to enter the cave)

CHORUS:
wait. two men are coming, one a sailor
one a stranger. let's see what they want first.

(two sailors enter, one disguised as a Merchant Captain)

137

SAILOR:
son of Achilles, I'm docked next to you by accident
I asked this shipmate of yours, on guard with two others,
where you were. I command a ship that's sailing home
from Ilium to Peparethus, rich in wines.
I found the crew on liberty was yours
and decided as a man should to tell you
what you probably don't suspect:
the Argives' plans against you, I mean their plots.

NEOPTOLEMUS:
I won't forget your concern. say more clearly
what the Greeks will do to me

SAILOR:
old Phoenix and the sons of Thesus
are after you in a warship

NEOPTOLEMUS:
to bring me back, or to force me back?

SAILOR:
I don't know; that's all I heard

NEOPTOLEMUS:
is it to please the Atridae that Phoenix and his cohorts. . . .?

SAILOR:
I can't say; they're coming

NEOPTOLEMUS:
and why didn't Odysseus come himself—afraid?

SAILOR:
he and Tydeus' son were searching for someone else

NEOPTOLEMUS:
who? for whom would Odysseus sail on his own?

138

SAILOR:
he . . . wait; who's this next to you? whisper.

NEOPTOLEMUS:
this is world-famous Philoctetes

SAILOR:
no more talking. go. get away from here immediately.

PHILOCTETES:
boy, what's he saying, and why in whispers
as if I were a thing

NEOPTOLEMUS:
I don't know yet. but he'll tell us all. out loud.

SAILOR:
give secrets away, child of Achilles? I'm poor
and owe the commanders some regard. they've paid me well

NEOPTOLEMUS:
they're my enemies. Philoctetes here because he hates them
is now my dearest friend. if you come
"as a man should," to help, you must say what you know

SAILOR:
You don't realize what you're asking

NEOPTOLEMUS:
I do

SAILOR:
the consequences . . .

NEOPTOLEMUS:
are mine

SAILOR:
well, Odysseus and Tydeus' son are headed here

to take this man, by persuasion or force.
they've sworn an oath to do it. bold Odysseus proclaimed
his purpose in public, his reputation's now at stake

NEOPTOLEMUS:

why now? all these years. they'd left this man
and forgotten him. is it compassion? is it the fear
of retribution, the anger of the gods?

SAILOR:

I'll tell you some things you don't know
I'll tell you about a prophet of high lineage,
Helenus son of Priam, seized by foxy Odysseus
in a night's prowl. who else but rotten Odysseus
would tie him up and show him off to the Argives?
Helenus said, "you'll never take Troy
unless you get Philoctetes from Lemnos to help you."
Odysseus took on the job. *he* would bring the man
willing or not. "If I fail," he said, "anyone here
can have my head." that's it. beware, you and your friend.

PHILOCTETES

that sneak and burglar really swore to take me?
back to those Greeks? that's as likely as death
loosing me because some one has said a prayer.

SAILOR:

I can't say. back to my ship now. so goodbye.
the gods be with you both and order all things well

PHILOCTETES:

I can't believe it boy, that Odysseus
would seduce me to his ship, exhibit me to those Greeks.
monstrous. I'd rather deal with the snake
that crippled me. nothing's too low
for Odysseus. he'll come. hurry my boy, let's put
the ocean between him and us. now's the time
to work, when we rest we'll rest peacefully.

140

NEOPTOLEMUS:
the wind's in our teeth. when it drops

PHILOCTETES:
all winds favor the man who's running from evil

NEOPTOLEMUS:
not this wind, even for him

PHILOCTETES:
for pirates looking to rob and pillage
any wind will do

NEOPTOLEMUS:
all right. we'll sail. take what you want from the cave

PHILOCTETES:
I haven't got much, but need a little

NEOPTOLEMUS:
my ship has what you'll need

PHILOCTETES:
not that wonderful herb that quiets my pain

NEOPTOLEMUS:
bring it with you. what else?

PHILOCTETES:
I may by chance have dropped some arrows
anyone could pick up. let me go look

NEOPTOLEMUS:
what you're holding, is that the famous bow?

PHILOCTETES:
it is

NEOPTOLEMUS:
let me get closer to it. may I handle it

worship it like a god

that and whatever else I can do to please you

NEOPTOLEMUS:
it's true my longing masters me.
if it seems improper I'll withdraw

PHILOCTETES:
thank you for that. but you have the right
to this privilege. you alone
give me daylight
and Oeta
and my old father
and my friends. I was the lowest of the low
and you uplifted me above the heads
of my tormentors. the bow is yours
to handle and return. think of it: your service
makes you the only man to have earned *that*.
the bow came to *me* for kindling
the funeral pyre of Herakles

NEOPTOLEMUS:
I've found a friend, and hope I am one.
some men recognize good done to them
and give of themselves in turn, they know
a friend outweighs, outshines, mocks an infinity of gold.
go on inside now

PHILOCTETES:
I will. please come too. my wound needs you.

(they go into the cave)

CHORUS:
not from out of my own life but from the tradition
a story which turns out to be true: of a youth

142

who dared to approach Zeus' bed.
Kronos' great son
bound him for endless torture
to the endless round of the wheel,
aside from him
what life known or heard of is sadder
than Philoctetes'? innocent man
dragging to his end
he robbed or wronged to man
how can I understand him? I see
the waves of the years of his anguish
break and break on the grey cold stone
he is his own neighbor, he groans
to his neighbor, limping through the heavy
for Herakles, Zeus' son, and received the bow you're holding.
no friend to mirror his misery to him, to offer
healing attentiveness, to calm the rage
and quell the pain
with herbs from the good soil.
no choice: between spasms his infant's crawling's
all he can manage on his hunt for his drugs.

alone among the sons of men he's cast out of earth's
gifts, the sowing and the reaping.
enough if now and then his arrow downs
any living thing. poor man
in those ten black years
what did he find to drink
not wine but stagnant water

he's found a good friend now.
the music of his life deepens
through his suffering; he will rediscover a green
continuity
goodbye to the black months.
homing in with our ship
to his Spercheios' banks, his old

countryside, the naiads' woods, he will roam
where the hero of the brazen shield
climbed in fire to the sky over Oeta.

NEOPTOLEMUS:
go on in if you feel like it. why
so quiet all of a sudden?

PHILOCTETES:
oh no

NEOPTOLEMUS:
what?

PHILOCTETES:
nothing, boy. go on

NEOPTOLEMUS:
you feel the pain again?

PHILOCTETES:
no. just a tiny . . . . I think it's going away— o god

NEOPTOLEMUS:
what is it—groaning like that, calling on god

PHILOCTETES:
to help me, to rescue me, oh . . . .

NEOPTOLEMUS:
please, what's wrong? won't you tell me? you won't
talk to me? I'm not blind or deaf. what is it?

PHILOCTETES:
my son, I'm lost. it's over. I can't
hide it from you any more. lost. it shoots through me
shoots through me, can't, o it hurts so much, utterly
wasted o my son eating me up my son ogod/ogod
ogod/ogod, ogod/ogod/ogod/ogod/ogod/ogod/ogod/ogod

144

a sword my son if you have a sword at hand cut
my foot off. whatever else, my life, forget it, quick
quick my son quickly

NEOPTOLEMUS:
what is it all of a sudden? you're crying

PHILOCTETES:
you know

NEOPTOLEMUS:
what is it?

PHILOCTETES:
you know

NEOPTOLEMUS:
no. what's the matter?

PHILOCTETES:
don't you know? ogod/ogod/ogod

NEOPTOLEMUS:
o Philoctetes you're in such pain again

PHILOCTETES:
beyond words. o pity me

NEOPTOLEMUS:
what shall I do?

PHILOCTETES:
don't be afraid of me. stay with me. my pain
lets me be then comes back home after its holiday

NEOPTOLEMUS:
poor man, all this misery, lean on me, let me help you

PHILOCTETES:
no please don't touch me. take my bow. you wanted to hold it

145

take it, care for it until my shaking stops and sleep comes
that's medicine, follows the drowsiness after the spasm.
so let me sleep then and if they come
keep it. it can't be theirs
it can't be theirs, however you hold on to it, force
foxiness, do it or you're twice a murderer
death for you and for me your suppliant

NEOPTOLEMUS:

it's yours and mine alone I swear it, I swear
I'll do what's needed. let me have the bow
and good luck attend it

PHILOCTETES:

take it my son, but first propitiate
the Jealous God. this bow: for its first owner
a plague, and for me; don't let it be for you

NEOPTOLEMUS:

may the gods look on us kindly, whatever way
we're destined to go may the trip prosper

PHILOCTETES:

o my son. your prayers may be useless, look
at my wound, the flow of this black blood's a sign
of worse to come. o how I hate this foot, now
pain, later increase of pain. it prowls and stalks,
I know it will spring on me. o now that you know
please stay with me stay with me
if only I could rivet this spasm forever in Odysseus' chest . . .
and those two generals—Menelaus, Agamemnon—may the worm
reign in their guts as long as it has in mine
and you Death I call on you every day Death you
don't answer me. my boy noble boy take me burn me
in those fires. consume me. I did such a service
for Heracles, Zeus' son, and received the bow you're holding.
answer me. why don't you talk to me?

146

NEOPTOLEMUS:
I was thinking about your endless pain, my heart
so heavy

PHILOCTETES:
understand, this pain leaves as it comes, fast,
but don't leave me here by myself

NEOPTOLEMUS:
courage. we'll stay

PHILOCTETES:
you will?

NEOPTOLEMUS:
I promise

PHILOCTETES:
it wouldn't be right to swear you to that

NEOPTOLEMUS:
my honor's at stake: I couldn't leave you

PHILOCTETES:
give me your hand on it

NEOPTOLEMUS:
here. my pledge

PHILOCTETES:
over there then, I'll go. . . .

NEOPTOLEMUS:
where?

PHILOCTETES:
up

NEOPTOLEMUS:
are you delirious again? why

147

are you staring up at the sky?

PHILOCTETES:
let me go let me go

NEOPTOLEMUS:
let you go where?

PHILOCTETES:
I tell you let me go

NEOPTOLEMUS:
no

PHILOCTETES:
don't touch me or I'll die

NEOPTOLEMUS:
I'm letting you go. you're calmer now

PHILOCTETES:
o mother Earth take me in my last sickness
I'm dying now and can't even stand on you

NEOPTOLEMUS:
I think he'll be asleep soon, his head's falling
back, sweat trickles over his body, a black
and bloody mess breaks out of his foot. friends,
let's leave him in peace till he falls asleep

CHORUS:
lord Sleep, breathe
a quiet music for him
lord of peace not pain
flow in your calm over his eyes, come
lord healer come

boy consider where you are and how
you must go. consider

and be clear. why wait? this time
right now is the ready fruit

NEOPTOLEMUS:

we could sail on alone, we could
steal the bow, we could not succeed
without him. the God said so. this man
crowns our victory. otherwise we're shameful frauds

CHORUS:

boy leave the burden of such thoughts
with the God and whisper
your answer in my ear
the sick man sleeps lightly, he can hear
in his febrility, his closed eyes see

boy if your plan still holds
work it out privately now. do I need
to repeat it? there's no doubt his endless torments
stretch vastly ahead.
it's a fair wind boy, and there he lies
gladly asleep in the sun, deaf and blind,
his feet and his hands like those of Earth's buried guests
absolutely still.
may this whole scene be your teacher
and let me say shortest way round is best

NEOPTOLEMUS:

quiet, and be alert. his eyes
are opening, his head's moving

PHILOCTETES:

how wonderful, waking up to brightness with you
near me, concerned about me
I never hoped for that, never dared.
the Atridae, those courageous captains
had no heart to accept my cries

and my wound. I afflicted their eyes, I insulted their ears, my hurt
was foul in their nostrils but you have a noble nature my son
and made light of all that.
a space of peace seems to have come.
absence of pain.
so help me up, my boy, up onto my feet,
soon, the attack spent, we'll sail

NEOPTOLEMUS:

how glad I am to see you, so happy
and amazed you're well and free of pain
to look at you before was almost
to look at death
can you get up now? or should these men lift you?
they won't mind in the least since you and I
have come to an understanding

PHILOCTETES:

thank you my son, but would you do it?
if they carry me I may sicken them.
my wound. the smell of my wound.
not yet for that closeness. soon they'll be my shipmates
and I think that voyage will ask of them
all that they have to give

NEOPTOLEMUS:

very well. get up now. hold on to me

PHILOCTETES:

don't be afraid. I'm used to this

NEOPTOLEMUS:

o my God what do I do now?

PHILOCTETES:

what's wrong? your words are drifting strangely

150

NEOPTOLEMUS:
I don't know what to say. I'm at a loss

PHILOCTETES:
but why? don't say that my son

NEOPTOLEMUS:
it's true. I have no choice

PHILOCTETES:
are you disgusted at my wound?
is that stopping you now from taking me?

NEOPTOLEMUS:
everything's disgusting when a man denies
his essential self, his acts violating his understanding

PHILOCTETES:
look, you're helping me. nothing in all of this
can sully your lineage

NEOPTOLEMUS:
time will uncover my treachery; that tortures me

PHILOCTETES:
not in what you're doing now; but your words. . . .

NEOPTOLEMUS:
o Zeus what shall I do? to be shown up twice—
hide what I shouldn't and persist in the lie. . . .

PHILOCTETES:
unless I'm wrong this man will betray me
and will leave me stranded here

NEOPTOLEMUS:
leave you? no not that. far worse: bring you
with us. that's what tortures me

151

PHILOCTETES:
strange words. their meaning's hidden from me

NEOPTOLEMUS:
well, here it is, straight out. you're sailing
for Troy, to the Atridae, to all those Greeks

PHILOCTETES:
o no

NEOPTOLEMUS:
can you listen to me quietly?

PHILOCTETES:
"listen to me" he says, and what now for me?

NEOPTOLEMUS:
well, first to rescue you from this terror,
then waste Troy—with your help

PHILOCTETES:
would you do that, really do that?

NEOPTOLEMUS:
there's no choice. try to accept it

PHILOCTETES:
you, how rotten you are, so hard to believe this betrayal,
give me the bow I want the bow, give me back my bow now

NEOPTOLEMUS:
impossible. I owe my chiefs allegiance
and share their sense of necessity

PHILOCTETES:
and can you look me in the face, fire,
monster, you've really done me in haven't you?
champ, champion o how I hate you, master
of treachery. and me the suppliant, me

you rob of my bow, my life.
o give it back, I beg of you my son
if you feel for me at all give it back
don't take my life away.
o he turns away, says nothing, meaning
he'll never part with it.

I'm crying out to you rivers, headlands, lairs
of wild beasts, sharp cliffs, only you—
lasting witnesses of my pain—will listen to me
listen to the torment brought to me
by Achilles' son:
he swore to bring me home; it's Troy I go to.
our hands sealed a contract and he borrowed the bow,
now it's his, the sacred bow of Zeus' son Herakles
and he'll flaunt it in front of the Argives,
and me as well, as if he'd taken a strong man
and doesn't understand he's killing the dead
a shadow, a diaphanous ghost.
he could never take a healthy Philoctetes
and even as I am, a cripple, he still needed guile.
I'm trapped now. o what can I do?
please give my bow back to me
be your true self again. will you?
no answer. lost.
cave with a double entrance, I'm back
to you once more, but without arms and so
without food. I'll wither and die here. the quarry
of bird and beast I pursued will now pursue me,
those who served as food will feed on the hunter,
blood for blood. this man's innocent posture
earns me my death.

I curse your life—no I'll wait
until I know if you'll go the other way
if not may my curse wither you

CHORUS:
what shall we do? it's up to you prince
do we sail, or do what he asks?

NEOPTOLEMUS:
I feel a strange pity. from the very start
I've been moved with pity for this man

PHILOCTETES:
please be merciful. do you want to be known
as the shrewd liar who betrayed me?

NEOPTOLEMUS:
what shall I do? I wish I'd never left Scyros,
to experience this awful circumstance

PHILOCTETES:
you're not a bad man, but learned your foul part
from evil people. leave that for those
naturally corrupt. sail, but first return my bow.

NEOPTOLEMUS:
well men. what shall we do?

(Odysseus appears suddenly)
ODYSSEUS:
are you crazy? give me that bow

PHILOCTETES:
who's that? is that Odysseus' voice?

ODYSSEUS:
as you see. Odysseus. me.

PHILOCTETES:
now I'm really sold out. it was Odysseus
who captured me and stole my bow

ODYSSEUS:
yes. I. I did it.

PHILOCTETES:

son. give me back my bow.

ODYSSEUS:

that he won't, even if he wants to. in fact
either you come along with it or we'll drag you with us

PHILOCTETES:

you corrupt, arrogant . . . . these people
of yours will take me by force?

ODYSSEUS:

yes if you don't come freely

PHILOCTETES:

o Lemnos you with your volcanic fires
lit through Hephaestus' fall will you
allow this man to rip me away from you?

ODYSSEUS:

it's Zeus, Zeus who rules here, Zeus
who gives the orders; I do his will

PHILOCTETES:

how disgusting—to invoke the Gods
and put lies in their mouths

ODYSSEUS:

it's the truth. you must come
you must travel the appointed road

PHILOCTETES:

I will not

ODYSSEUS:

I say yes. you must

PHILOCTETES:

I must have been born to pain.
did my father give birth to a slave?

ODYSSEUS:
  no, to one among equals of high lineage
  with whom you will destroy Troy

PHILOCTETES:
  never. anything but that as long as this sharp
  precipice thrusts its harshness under me

ODYSSEUS:
  what would you do?

PHILOCTETES:
  throw myself down and shatter
  my head in the rocks underneath

ODYSSEUS:
  hold him, both his arms, tight

PHILOCTETES:
  o my hands how weak you are, imprisoned
  by that man, all because my bow's gone.
  you've done it again haven't you con man,
  fungus heartrot, using this stranger, just a boy
  to get at me. he grieves right now
  for his rashness and the wrong done to me.
  in fact he's too good for you and stands
  appropriately alongside me. but you like a shadow
  voice you were always
  giving the boy his cues
  and he studied at your vicious school
  against his own characteristic grain
  and now you sickening cheat you intend to wrap me
  in rope and carry me from this island where
  you first left me homeless and alone, living dead.
  my curse on your life. I've spent
  so many years cursing you. but the Gods
  embitter my life, and you dance on

156

as my endless misery defines my life.
you laugh at me, you and Atreus' two sons
who mock me as well; you tried
to escape induction by playing mad
but they put your son in front of your plough
and they had you, forced you to sail with them.
though I volunteered my seven ships and me
I was marooned, they say by you and you by them.
so I'm dead to you, why seize the corpse?
the gods despise you.
I still limp, my wound still stinks, I'll still sour
your rites and sacrifices. my curse on your life
for what you've done to me. if the gods are just
you will be cursed. I know they're just
because they touched your hearts to think of me
and come here. o my own country
and you watchful gods avenge me, however
long it takes, if you pity me as I deserve.
if I could see them shattered I'd be almost free of pain

CHORUS:

he's full of spite, and hard. suffering
hasn't gentled him

ODYSSEUS:

I haven't time to say more than this;
I'm a man who fits the occasion.
when it requires even-handedness, justice, that's
what I furnish. I always want to win
except in your case. I give in freely.
you sailors let him go. he can stay.
we don't need you Philoctetes, we have
your bow, we have two great bowmen, Teucer,
and myself, who can shoot with your skill.
who needs you? you can keep
your Lemnos. we go. your prize

157

may earn for me the honor you'd have had

PHILOCTETES:
what can I do? and you strutting
for the Greeks in my arms. . . .

ODYSSEUS:
enough talk. I'm leaving

PHILOCTETES:
son of Achilles, are you going too,
not a word from you?

ODYSSEUS:
let's go Neoptolemus, and don't look at him
you'll spoil everything

PHILOCTETES:
and you men, you'll leave me by myself now?
no pity in you?

CHORUS:
this young man, our captain, governs
what we say. he's our ¹aw

NEOPTOLEMUS:
I know Odysseus will call me weak
but if Philoctetes wants you men to stay with him
until we finish our prayers and our preparations
do so. maybe he'll relent. so we go.
when we call you come on the double

(Odysseus and Neoptolemus leave)

PHILOCTETES:
cave in the rock I'm married to you forever
hot and freezing by turns you'll witness my death
tell me sad home haunted by my suffering
how will I go on?

158

I free all the birds, their flight now
endless, wherever they land they've won
immunity from me and my bow

CHORUS:

it's you, you've fashioned your own doom
don't blame the gods for your stubbornness.
faced with the good you chose otherwise

PHILOCTETES:

o endless endless unhappiness
totally wasted by unhappiness
barely lingering, hanging on
without a single friend
to accompany me to my end.
my arrows' work on Lemnos done forever
the hunting season of my life is dead.
I suspected nothing and the liar seduced me
I'd love to see him fixed in my agony

CHORUS:

fate fate not the works of our hands
threw you down. don't curse us, we cared
for you and we care for you now

PHILOCTETES:

Odysseus sits on the sand by the grey sea
and laughs at Philoctetes
he plays with my bow, it was my life.

o my bow how I loved you
mine the only hands that bent you
if you could feel, what power of grief.
they've forced us apart, you from me Herakles' friend.
a bad man is stringing you, you serve a master
of deceit—shareholder in that company of men
who have hurt me.

159

CHORUS:
a man should stand his righteous ground
but moderate his venom's toxin.
as for Odysseus, he represents the communal will,
which he obeys, which speaks through him.

PHILOCTETES:
you birds once my bright-eyed prey
in these hills, keep flying near the hunter's home.
untouchable you own the air
my hands hang, the bow's gone and with it your caution
your weakened enemy's flesh will turn
into your food. come do your will
as I diminish into death, the only
voyage left in the absence of anything to eat

CHORUS:
can you still open yourself to a friend? if so listen.
it's you who feed your pain and grief
you can choose your freedom

PHILOCTETES:
of all the men who've come to Lemnos
you've touched my heart, but also rekindled
the old grief. why afflict the afflicted?

CHORUS:
what do you mean?

PHILOCTETES:
I mean you want to take me to hateful Troy

CHORUS:
for your sake too

PHILOCTETES:
then go. now

CHORUS:
good. good. we will. men, to the ship and our oars

PHILOCTETES:
please please in God's name stay

CHORUS:
calm yourself

PHILOCTETES:
please. stay.

CHORUS:
why?

PHILOCTETES:
o dark darkest spirit, it's over for me
damn foot what will I do with it?
friends please come back

CHORUS:
what do you want? you say
'go.' you say 'come back.'

PHILOCTETES:
don't be angry. man in pain
undergoes the rash cries of his own discord

CHORUS:
unhappy man, come sail with us

PHILOCTETES:
never never. if the God of the Lightning
fixed me with his lance of fire
I'd still say 'never.'
let Ilium die and all those in the siege
whose hardened hearts were pleased
to throw me out and let me rot.

may I make just one request?

CHORUS:
what?

PHILOCTETES:
let me have a sword, an axe, whatever

CHORUS:
why? to do what?

PHILOCTETES:
to shred my body, to rid it of its limbs
blood blood suffuses my thoughts

CHORUS:
but why?

PHILOCTETES:
I want to find my father

CHORUS:
where?

PHILOCTETES:
down in death's house.
he's gone from earth. o how much
I long for my city where I was born,
the sacred stream encircling my house. I left
to help the Greeks who have destroyed me

CHORUS:
I should have gone to the ship by now
but I saw Odysseus coming near
with Neoptolemus

ODYSSEUS:
why are you going back so fast?

NEOPTOLEMUS:
  to undo what I've committed

ODYSSEUS:
  what does that mean?

NEOPTOLEMUS:
  I shouldn't have obeyed the Greeks and you

ODYSSEUS:
  what did you do that was so terrible?

NEOPTOLEMUS:
  I lied. I betrayed a man

ODYSSEUS:
  who? I hope you're not verging on something rash

NEOPTOLEMUS:
  no nothing rash. I've got to see the son of Poeas

ODYSSEUS:
  why? your words are upsetting me

NEOPTOLEMUS:
  I'm going to return the bow

ODYSSEUS:
  o Zeus— give it back, you can't mean that

NEOPTOLEMUS:
  I'm ashamed of how I got it

ODYSSEUS:
  you can't be serious

NEOPTOLEMUS:
  I am, unless you think seriousness is a joke

163

ODYSSEUS:
Achilles' son, exactly what are you saying?

NEOPTOLEMUS:
do I have to repeat myself?

ODYSSEUS:
I wish I hadn't heard you in the first place

NEOPTOLEMUS:
I have nothing else to say

ODYSSEUS:
there's someone who'll stop you

NEOPTOLEMUS:
who?

ODYSSEUS:
the whole Greek army, me among them

NEOPTOLEMUS:
you're a shrewd man Odysseus
but your words are foolish

ODYSSEUS:
and you're foolish not only in words
but in your acts as well

NEOPTOLEMUS:
better just than clever

ODYSSEUS:
is that justice—to give back
what I helped you get?

NEOPTOLEMUS:
I lied. I'm ashamed of that
I want to make amends

ODYSSEUS:
and the Greeks. you're not afraid of their response?

NEOPTOLEMUS:
I'm more afraid of being unjust

ODYSSEUS:
your justice will face our power

NEOPTOLEMUS:
you can't make me do what I won't

ODYSSEUS:
then we'll fight you, not the Trojans

NEOPTOLEMUS:
whatever comes comes

ODYSSEUS:
you see my hand near my sword?

NEOPTOLEMUS:
be ready for me to do as much, quickly

ODYSSEUS:
I'm going, and I will tell the army
they'll punish you

NEOPTOLEMUS:
very cautious of you. such discretion
may keep you alive indefinitely

(exit Odysseus)

Philoctetes, son of Poeas, come out of your cave

PHILOCTETES:
what's this noise at my door?
what do you want with me?

(Philoctetes appears at the cave's mouth)
I don't like what I see. some new terror
to top the old ones?

NEOPTOLEMUS:
wait a minute. I have news

PHILOCTETES:
I'm afraid. last time you came
I believed you and suffered for it

NEOPTOLEMUS:
can a man be sorry?

PHILOCTETES:
you sounded sweet as this in your treachery
when you stole my bow

NEOPTOLEMUS:
I'm not lying to you. I want to know
if you're completely sure about staying

PHILOCTETES:
you can stop right now

NEOPTOLEMUS:
you have no doubts?

PHOLOCTETES:
absolutely none

NEOPTOLEMUS:
if I could have convinced you to come
I would. but there's no point. so I'll stop.

PHILOCTETES:
you might as well stop talking. did you really think
we could ever be friends again? you lied, stole

my life and came preaching. rotten son
of a great father. damn you all, the Atridae,
Odysseus and you

NEOPTOLEMUS:
you can stop cursing now. here's your bow

PHILOCTETES:
what? another trick?

NEOPTOLEMUS:
no. I swear by Olympian Zeus

PHILOCTETES:
if these words are true they're wonderful

NEOPTOLEMUS:
believe me. stretch out your hand. here's your bow

(Odysseus appears)

ODYSSEUS:
stop. as the Gods witness, and in the name
of the Atridae and all the Greeks

PHILOCTETES:
whose voice my son; was that Odysseus?

ODYSSEUS:
yes it is, here to carry you to Troy
I don't care what Neoptolemus thinks

PHILOCTETES:
if this arrow flies straight
you'll regret your words

NEOPTOLEMUS:
stop, in the Gods' name don't shoot

PHILOCTETES:
by the Gods dear boy let my hands go

NEOPTOLEMUS:
I won't

PHILOCTETES:
why did you stop me
from killing the man I hate?

NEOPTOLEMUS:
would you be proud of that? would I?

PHILOCTETES:
one thing's clear. the generals, the Greeks'
lying heralds, talk big, and run fast

NEOPTOLEMUS:
whatever. the bow's yours again. you have
no further quarrel with me

PHILOCTETES:
none my boy. you've shown what you're made of,
sprung not from Sisyphus but Achilles, noblest
in life as now in death

NEOPTOLEMUS:
what you say about my father and me
makes me happy. but now, a request.
a man must bear the fate the Gods dictate
but some, like you, are attached to their wounds.
who can pity or accept such self-destruction?
you listen to no-one, a friend who loves you,
who tries to talk to you, becomes your enemy.
nevertheless as Zeus is my witness I'll say
what I have to. inscribe
these words in your mind forever:
your wound results from the anger of the God

that you blundered onto Chryse's roofless
sacred place and stirred the serpent guardian.
there's no relief for you in the endless rerun
of the sun's courses
until you come to Troy freely.
there our healing Asclepiadae will ready you
to stand with your bow and me, to conquer Troy.
I'll tell you how I know this: it's from
our Trojan prisoner, the prophet Helenus.
he also said that Troy must crack
this summer, his life on it.
now that you know come, please,
willingly. look at your future—healed, hailed
as pre-eminent in war and prince
who closed the agonized chapter of Troy

PHILOCTETES:
o how I hate this life that reins me in
from the darkness, I long
to gallop into the grave, and my friend,
what will I do, my dear friend who tells me go back,
back to those I can barely look at, who'll have to say
welcome to me, and will have to forgive me—
what my eyes have already seen has almost closed them
and soon they must see me eating and sleeping
with Atreus' sons, my murderers,
with Odysseus, the well-head of my misery. . . .

I could forget the long flow of my pain
but what about tomorrow? don't I know by now
about all those infected minds waiting
to drown me in their pus? and what about you, you
should talk me into staying here, and stay away from Troy.
they've defrauded you, stolen your father's arms
and you want to help them fight, and send me too?
no. you promised to take me home. do it.

you go to Scyros and let those vipers rot
from each others' fluid poisons. your father and I
will thank you. if you help the killer you become him

NEOPTOLEMUS:
what you say makes sense. still
I wish you'd believe the God's promises
and mine. I'm your friend. trust me. sail with me.

PHILOCTETES:
are you crazy—me on the Trojan plains,
with the foul sons of Atreus, with this damned foot

NEOPTOLEMUS:
no. to men who'll heal your agonizing wound

PHILOCTETES:
a very cryptic statement. you mean...

NEOPTOLEMUS:
I mean full flowering for you and me

PHILOCTETES:
can you tell me that and not shake in shame
at the judgments of the Gods?

NEOPTOLEMUS:
should a man who gives to his friend be ashamed?

PHILOCTETES:
gifts for me, or for Atreus' sons?

NEOPTOLEMUS:
for you my friend

PHILOCTETES:
o yes a real friend, who'll hand me over

NEOPTOLEMUS:
don't let your misery turn you sour

PHILOCTETES:
I can tell your advice would destroy me

NEOPTOLEMUS:
you're the stubborn destroyer. not me.

PHILOCTETES:
did the Atridae maroon me? did they?

NEOPTOLEMUS:
they did. but now they'll save you

PHILOCTETES:
not if I can help it. not Troy.

NEOPTOLEMUS:
what can I do, I can't convince you
I should stop talking and leave you here
marooned, absolutely hopeless

PHILOCTETES:
my way's my way. but we joined hands
in an understanding: take me home my son
no more mention of Troy. I can't take any more

NEOPTOLEMUS:
all right. let's go

PHILOCTETES:
thank you for that. let's go then

NEOPTOLEMUS:
can you walk well enough?

PHILOCTETES:
I'll try as hard as I can

NEOPTOLEMUS:
but the rage of the Greeks will follow me

PHILOCTETES:
  ignore it

NEOPTOLEMUS:
  and if they penetrate my boundaries?

PHILOCTETES:
  I'll be there

NEOPTOLEMUS:
  what good will that do?

PHILOCTETES:
  the good of the bow

NEOPTOLEMUS:
  and you'll....

PHILOCTETES:
  I'll make them run

NEOPTOLEMUS:
  kiss the earth. it's goodbye. let's go

(Heracles appears on the rocks behind the cave)

HERAKLES:
  stay son of Poeas
  until you've heard me
  Herakles stands in front of you
  the voice of Herakles sounds in your ears
  I've come from Olympus because of you
  through me great Zeus
  turns you back from your way
  listen

  first my story, of intense endurance and pain,
  of a final arrival, to final recognition
  beyond death. your life

like mine will come through pain
to such heightenings.
go to Troy with this man
to be healed, to be first for your power
and with my bow to topple Paris
seed of all the suffering.
you will waste Troy, your peers
will honor you, you will bear the spoils
to your father Poeas and your country Oeta.
and remember as tribute to my bow
some part of those spoils on my pyre

and you son of Achilles, you cannot take
city alone, nor he without you.
you shall guard each other
like two lions on the hunt.
I will send the healer Asclepius to Troy
to return your health, my arms
will crack Troy twice.
but remember—when you burn the city
honor the Gods, for Zeus the highest virtue.
the sacred survives the graves.

PHILOCTETES:
   I've longed so long for your voice
   your form returns after such losses
   I will not disobey you

NEOPTOLEMUS:
   neither will I

HERACLES:
   then get ready. the time is right
   and the breeze able

PHILOCTETES:
   so it's goodbye to you companion cave,

nymphs of river and shore, beach-hollows
echoing ocean's deep music.
sometimes the South wind brought me
the water's spray and wet my hair, myself
back by my cave's far wall, and I thought
mount Hermeaum answered my cries in kind.
goodbye Lycian well I'm leaving you. I'd thought
Lemnos perpetual,
o my island listen to me, sea-
surrounded host, your guest is going, wish him well
to his new harbor, appointed
by the powers of Fate and the great
Voice whose will orders our event

CHORUS:
    let us pray to the sea nymphs
    for bountiful winds and safe return
    and then we can go

The Cyclops

Euripides

translated by

George Economou

Introduction

When I was three or four, I climbed into bed with my father and asked for a story. He told me about Odysseus and the Cyclops. It was the first story I had ever heard, and it remains so for me to this day—the first story of all stories. To read the episode in Homer, I must admit, is a weak experience compared to my recollection of our mutual intensity. I will always hear him telling it in my mind's ear.

My father had not read *The Odyssey*, but he KNEW the story—from whom or what source doesn't matter—and gave it his own personal emphases, like any good oral poet. Odysseus, a whispering tough guy, blinded the one-eyed giant with courage, a bit of glee, and the thrill of righteous treachery we feel when we do in some one who has gotten us into his power. But the fallen Cyclops was the more affective of the two: though a brute to the Ithacans, he showed great concern for his flocks and especially his lead-sheep (with Odysseus clutching its belly). The dominant quality was not one of irony: that at this moment that the Cyclops speaks to his old friend—who comes last now instead of first— Odysseus is making his escape from the cave. It was rather a quality of sad ambivalence, of the recognition that even the meanest of us can be and need to be soft and tender to somebody. I remember admiring Odysseus but feeling strongly for the blind Cyclops, whose remote sheepherder's world had been disturbed by these strangers.

Some years later I sensed a similar ambivalence in Euripides' satyr play. The hero has guts and ingenuity *but* is a vain and boastful man who can come up with a good speech—or deadly trick—for any occasion. His

177

moral imperatives are to be "civilized" and opportunistic. Odysseus can contemplate betraying his own kind while the heavy, Polyphemus, can think of being generous with his. Though allegedly a good part of it is alien to men, the Cyclops' world is not at all so to him. It is natural for him to bully and devour other creatures, especially the men who come so rarely into his sphere. When they do, their leader plays the game the Cyclops' way—violently—for survival's sake, though he seems to shift to the imperatives of Etna with relative ease. Without trying to build a case for it here, I think Euripides is showing us that Odysseus and Polyphemus are not so different or opposite as their dramatic antagonism appears to state. It is this theme which Silenus and the satyrs so brilliantly support in their intermediate role of "mananimals." It is a picture of the complexity of human nature from several angles—all of them showing that it is far from perfect, a kind of anti-pastoral. To this Euripidean end, Silenus, Polyphemus, and Odysseus are most exemplary.

The touch of W. C. Fields in the voice and manners of Silenus—I hope it can be heard—is intentional. Odysseus, as we've seen, is not quite Homer's man and is often affected by the sound of his own voice. Polyphemus might be dressed as a lumberjack or mountain man, American style, just to reinforce visually the language bridge over the gap of centuries.

The play should be staged with lots of music and dancing. These suggestions, along with a few stage directions in the text, are all I offer to those who might want to produce this play in this version. Having worked in the theater, I know that a director, actors, and everyone else involved begin where the text leaves off, with private and artistic motives for collectively shaping the whole as they will. Such were my own motives in selecting this play and recreating its language.

(Text: Loeb Classical Library Edition.)

George Economou

178

CHARACTERS

SILENUS

ODYSSEUS

POLYPHEMUS (called Cyclops)

CHORUS OF SATYRS

LEADER OF THE CHORUS

ODYSSEUS' MEN

Sheep, goats, lambs and kids

The Scene: high on the slopes of Etna, gapes the mouth of Polyphemus' cave-home. Silenus, old and weary, but still game, comes out of the cave and speaks:

SILENUS:

Bacchus! What a pain I still get in my—
because of you just like when I was young and tough.
First Hera turned you into a maniac
and you skipped out on your mountain-girl nurses;
then in that war with the Giants
like a good right-hand man I stood by you
and stretched out one of the big lugs with a bull's-eye
in the shield—but wait, am I dreaming?
No godamnit! I showed the spoils to Bacchus.
But now I have to stick out bigger troubles.
Good old Hera made Etruscan pirates
haul you off on a long trip
and hearing about that I set sail
with my boys to search for you. I stood tall
on the poop holding the tiller to steer us,
while the boys pulled hard, churning up
the green water to a foam, searching for you, chief.
Now just as we approached Malea
a sudden east wind blew us
right up onto this lousy rock, Etna,
land of the sea-god's one-eyed spawn,
home of the cave-living-man-killing Cyclopes.
One of them—Polyphemus the name—caught us
and simply declared us his slaves.
So long Bacchic song and dance
hello herding sheep and goats for an unholy one-eyed brute.
Up on the steep hillsides, my boys,
just young fellas themselves, watch his tender flocks,
while I'm stuck with trough-filling,
sweeping up the place, and rustling up
Old Evil Eye's messy grub.

Now my orders call for me
to clean up the cave with this rake
to welcome home Boss Cyclops
and his herd to a spotless grotto.
But here come my boys, punching the mutton home.
What's up? Isn't that the patter of dancing feet—
just like old times when gathered for Bacchus'
doings you swished your way
   with singing strings to Althaea's place?

CHORUS *(entering with flock)*:

STROPHE *(to a ram)*:
   Hey, Mister Blue-Blood
   on both parents' sides
   why spring for the rocks?
   Don't you have a gentle breeze
   grassy pastures
   water swirling from the stream
   into troughs beside the cave?
   Don't your babies *mbehhhhh* for you?

   Shoot! where you going,
   to sip dew on the hill?
   Move it or I'll fling a pebble!
   Go-go horny fella
   listen to your keeper
   who's kept by farmer Cyclops!

ANTISTROPHE *(to a ewe)*:
   Relax those swollen titties,
   come suckle the babies
   you left in the kid-pens!
   Dozing by day they *mbehhhhh*
   they need you now.
   Stop that grassy nibbling,
   come home to your yard
   in your own piece of the Rock!

[Shoot! where you going,
to sip dew on the hill?
Move it or I'll fling a pebble!
Go-go wooly mama
listen to your keeper
who's kept by farmer Cyclops!]

EPODE:

Here's no Bacchus, here's no dancing
wild-women with pine-cone wands in hand,
and no rumbling drums
or bright drops of wine
beside the gushing water,
and no dancing mountain-girls.
Hey hey calling hey
chasing swiftly
after Aphrodite
with bare-assed wild-girls.
O master mine where are you roaming
shaking your auburn locks?
I, your rightful servant,
slave for Big One Eye,
an itinerant worker
with nothing but a lousy goatskin
and wholly lacking your love.

SILENUS:

Quiet my boys, get the flock
out of here and under the rocks.

LEADER:

Keep moving. So what's the big hurry, pop?

SILENUS:

There's a Greek ship on the beach,
crew and captain marching this way.
They've got bottles and empty buckets

round their necks—looking for food
and water for their barrel. Poor sons-a-guns,
I wonder who they are? They can't know
Polyphemus is in charge here, the way they come
right up to the mangobbler's door
expecting a welcome—but bound to get his jawbone.
Quiet now so we can find out
where they're from and what they're up to.

(Enter Odysseus and crew)

ODYSSEUS:
Say, brothers, show us some running water
to stop our thirst? And maybe some food
for hungry sailors? Make a deal? But whaaa?
Looks like we've come to Bacchus' city.
Satyrs all around this cave.
Better say hello to the old man first. Hello!

SILENUS:
Well, now howdy, stranger. Who you and where from?

ODYSSEUS:
Je suis Odysseus—King of little Ithaca.

SILENUS:
No shit! The well-known conman and illegitimate of Sisyphus?

ODYSSEUS:
That's right. And cut the crap.

SILENUS:
So what are you doing in Sicily?

ODYSSEUS:
On our way home from the Trojan War.

SILENUS:
Yeah? Charted a direct course home, didn't you.

ODYSSEUS:
A storm drove us here.

SILENUS:
Well, surprise! Same thing happened to me.

ODYSSEUS:
Really? Bad weather forced you here?

SILENUS:
Chasing the pirates who kidnapped Bacchus. I stood tall on th . . . .

ODYSSEUS *(interrupting him)*:
What kind of place is this? Who lives here?

SILENUS:
This is Etna, top o'Sicily.

ODYSSEUS:
So where are the walls and towers?

SILENUS:
This ain't a burg! No people here, fella.

ODYSSEUS:
Well who or what is? Wild animals?

SILENUS:
Cyclopes. Live in caves, not houses.

ODYSSEUS:
Who do they take their orders from? Or is this a "republic"?

SILENUS:
Wandering shepherds, they, and not to nobody they listen for nothing.

ODYSSEUS:
That so? What do they live on? Do they farm?

SILENUS:
Milk, cheese, and lotsa meat.

ODYSSEUS:
How about wine? Any vineyards?

SILENUS:
Not a grape! Not a song or a dance in the place!

ODYSSEUS:
Well, are they at least friendly to strangers?

SILENUS:
Sure, they just eat them up.

ODYSSEUS:
Wait a minute. Are you trying to tell me something?

SILENUS:
Everyman that's come here has wound up on the table.

ODYSSEUS:
Where's this Cyclops now? Not home I hope?

SILENUS:
No. He's off on Etna with his hounds.

ODYSSEUS:
Will you help us—to get away from here?

SILENUS:
What do you want, Odysseus? You know I'd do anything for you.

ODYSSEUS:
Sell us some bread. We've got nothing to eat.

SILENUS:
Like I said, there's only meat.

ODYSSEUS:
That'll do.

SILENUS:
There's fig-cheese, too, and a lake of milk.

ODYSSEUS:

Let's see it. This is no mail-order.

SILENUS:

Then show me your cash.

ODYSSEUS:

No money. But I do have . . . Dionysus' juice.

SILENUS:

Wine? Beautiful! Ohhh, it's been so long.

ODYSSEUS:

Maron, your god's own son, gave it to me.

SILENUS:

The baby boy I reared in these arms?

ODYSSEUS:

Bacchus' own baby boy—that's the plain truth.

SILENUS:

It isn't down in the ship—the wine—you have it with you?

ODYSSEUS:

Right in this skin. Look here, old guy.

SILENUS

Why that's hardly a mouthful.

ODYSSEUS:

This holds twice as much as it seems to give.

SILENUS:

A veritable fountain! I like, I like.

ODYSSEUS:

How about a little sample—straight?

SILENUS:

Good enough! I'll seal our contract with my lips.

186

ODYSSEUS:
Then use the cup that hangs from the flask.

SILENUS:
Pour. A little drink to stir up old memories.

ODYSSEUS:
Say when.

SILENUS:
O my god! What a bouquet!

ODYSSEUS:
Do you see it?

SILENUS:
See it? I smell it!

OSYSSEUS:
Drink up and then give your testimonial.

SILENUS *(drinks and does a couple of Zorba steps)*:
Oooh, Ahh, Bacchus—this calls for a little dance.

ODYSSEUS:
How'd that go down the old throat?

SILENUS:
All the way down to my tippy toes.

ODYSSEUS:
We'll throw some change into the bargain, too.

SILENUS:
Just keep the wine flowing and pee on the money.

ODYSSEUS:
OK, then show us some cheese and mutton.

SILENUS:
Sure thing. I don't give a damn about the big bad boss.

187

I'm so freaked out over this here wine
I'd trade off all of Big-Eye's flocks for it,
Drive 'em right off these rocks into the sea.
When you're drunk your troubles just disappear.
Say, don't trust a man who doesn't drink.
Why it makes this little man stand up big and tight
so you grab a boobie and get ready to explore
the bush country, then do a little frug
and forget your blues. Why shouldn't I worship
drink like this and let Cyclops bug off,
the dummy with an eye in the middle of his brow?

(Silenus goes into the cave.)

LEADER:
Hey, Odysseus, can we ask you something?

ODYSSEUS:
For friends, no favor's too big.

LEADER:
When you got Troy, did you get Helen, too?

ODYSSEUS:
We creamed the whole house of Priam.

LEADER:
So when you caught that woman,
did you all line up
and give her a good fucking?
That little bitch, along comes a man
decked out in fancy pants and a gold belt
around his middle and she gets all shook up
and leaves Menelaus, the scrappiest
little guy around. It'd be a good thing
if there were no more women in this world—except for me.

SILENUS *(returning)*:
Here's some baby lambs for you,

188

the pick of the flock for Captain Odysseus,
and plenty of dairy dishes too.
Take them and get away from here right now.
So you can give me that sacred grape juice.
Christamighty! Here comes Cyclops! What to do?

ODYSSEUS:

We've had it old man. Where can we go?

SILENUS:

In the cave, you can hide in there.

ODYSSEUS:

Are you kidding—walk right into a trap?

SILENUS:

No—lots of hiding places in those rocks.

(He enters the cave)

ODYSSEUS:

Never! Great Troy itself would cry out
if we fled from one man. Many times I stood up
to a swarm of Trojans with nothing but my shield.
If we die, let it be death with honor,
if we live, let it be with fabulous glory.

CYCLOPS *(entering):*

Hey hey hey hey! Taking a break?
Bacchus games? No Bacchus in these back woods!
No fruity finger cymbals or drum drumming here!
How are my little kids doing in the cave?
Are they sucking mama's tits and
snuggled close, are my wicker-crates
full of fresh cheese, huh? huh?
So? What d'yuh say? Maybe my stick
will draw some tears! Look up here, not down.

LEADER:
See, we're looking up to Zeus himself,
I can see the stars and Orion.

CYCLOPS:
Have you grub-worms got my brunch ready?

LEADER:
All set. Ready for your waiting throat.

CYCLOPS:
And are my milk-jugs full up?

LEADER:
Drink all you want, a whole barrel.

CYCLOPS *(picking up one of the jugs Silenus had brought)*:
What's this? Sheep's-milk? Cow's? Half 'n half?

LEADER:
Anything you want. But please don't swallow me.

CYCLOPS:
No way. It would kill me
to have you cutting your capers in my gut.
Hey! Who's this bunch at my front door?
Have pirates and thieves invaded us?
And look—lambs from my own cave
all tied up with cords,
tubs of cheese all over the place, the old man
coming out with his bald head all banged up!

SILENUS *(entering)*:
Ohhhh. They beat me up. I think I'm running a fever.

CYCLOPS:
Who? Who's clobbered you, old man?

SILENUS:

Those greasers, Cyclops, I tried to stop them from robbing you.

CYCLOPS:

Didn't they know I'm a god descended from gods?

SILENUS:

I told them, but they went right on taking.
Even though I said no they ate up the cheeses
and stole the sheep. Then they said they'd loop
a huge dog collar around your middle
and squeeze the dog shit out of your only eye,
and they said they'd horsewhip your ass
and tie you up nice and neat,
toss you aboard a ship and sell you off
as a rock-lifter or a living mill.

CYCLOPS:

No kidding? Well then get moving,
sharpen my meat cleavers, take a bunch of faggots
and light my fire. I'll butcher them right away
and feed my face with their meat
hot off the charcoal, which is
faster than making a stew.
I'm tired of mountain vittles!
Had to eat too many lions and stags
and it's been a long time since I had a man.

SILENUS:

Yessir, a change from the routine
can be sweet. It's been a long time
since we've had company at the cave.

ODYSSEUS:

Cyclops, listen to what we strangers have to say.
We needed food, so we came from our ship

to your cave to bargain for it.
This guy sold us your lambs
for a drink of wine the minute he tasted it—
of his own free will, no force was used.
There's not an honest word in what he says
now that he's caught selling your goods on the sly.

SILENUS:
Who me? May you rot in hell!

ODYSSEUS:
If I lie.

SILENUS:
Cyclops, by your father Poseidon,
by Triton and Nereus, by by
by Calypso and all her sisters,
by the holy waves and all the fishies in the sea,
I swear, my beautiful, my baby Cyclops,
my cute lil' master, I did not sell
any of your stuff to the strangers. If I did
may misfortune overtake my boys whom I love so much.

LEADER:
Screwyou, Silenus-my-boys. I saw you myself
making a deal with them. *(to Cyclops)* And if I lie,
may my old man die! Don't be unfair to the strangers.

CYCLOPS:
Liar. I'd sooner believe him
than the father of our country—he's right I say.
Now I want to question you. Where you from, strangers?
What's your nation? What's your hometown?

ODYSSEUS:
Ithaca. After we wasted
the town of Troy, sea winds drove us
ashore here, in your territory.

CYCLOPS:
And so slutty Helen's kidnapping
made you go after poor Troy-town?

ODYSSEUS:
That's right. We saw our duty through all the way.

CYCLOPS:
Shame on you—to raise a whole campaign
for the sake of one lousy woman!

ODYSSEUS:
God's doing. Mere men didn't cause it.
But as free men we're asking you,
great son of the sea-god, don't kill
strangers who came to your cave as friends,
and don't defile your jaws by eating us.
We're the ones, sir, who have saved
your father's shrines all over Greece.
Taenarus' holy harbor is safe, and
his sanctuary on high Malea, so is
Athena's Sunium, that motherlode of silver,
and the refuge on Geraestus—in fact
we just wouldn't surrender Greece to Trojan wrongs.
And you're part of this—here where you live
on Etna, the smokestacked rock, here is Greece.
Human decency—would you please pay attention—
calls for receiving poor shipwrecked sailors
and giving them hospitality and clothing,
not for sticking them on ox-roasting spits
like so much shishkebab to stuff in your mouth and belly.
Priam's country has left Greece desolate enough,
soaked up the blood of thousands dropped by spears,
unmanned women's beds and made white-haired
grandparents childless. If you put the survivors
to the fire just so you can have your vicious meal,
what justice is there? Believe me, Cyclops,

drop this mad hunger, be good
and forget this sacrilege. "Many a man
has paid the price for ill-got gains."

SILENUS:

Wow! Hey take my advice, if you gobble up
all his meat, especially his savory tongue,
you'll become a sharp, verbal Cyclops.

CYCLOPS:

You monkey, wealth is the smart man's god.
The rest is bullshit and sweet talk.
My father's seacoast shrines can
kiss off. Did you think I cared about 'em?
And I don't tremble at Zeus' thunder, boy,
in fact, I'm not sure he's tougher than me.
Anyhow, I don't care, and I'll tell you why.
When he sits up there and pours the rain down,
I settle down in my comfy cave,
munch on some veal or venison and
chugalug a whole barrel of milk on my back,
spilling it all over my tummy. Then I fart up
a bigger storm than Zeus could ever make.
When the north-wind blows in a blizzard,
I wrap myself up in furs
and light the fire—so let it snow.
Whether it wants to or not, the earth has to
come up with the grass that fattens my flocks.
And I make no sacrifices—except to the
greatest god of all, my own gut.
Plenty to eat, plenty to drink, everyday,
that's Zeus for men who know what's what,
to have no worries at all. As for those
who set up laws to cramp my human life-style,
let 'em suck wind! I'll just go right on
indulging my heart's desire—by eating you.

O I'll be hospitable enough—to stay on the safe side—
and give you fire, father's water, and a kettle,
which will do very nicely by your little bodies.
So step inside and stand round the altar
of this cave's god, and wish him "Hearty appetite!"

(He drives Odysseus' crew into the cave)

ODYSSEUS:

Damnit! Did I survive the troubles at Troy
and at sea just to wind up here,
held by a foul will and hard heart?
Pallas Athena, child of Zeus and my own goddess,
now, help me now. Worse than dangers at Troy,
I've come to the very brink of disaster.
And you, glowing in your starry throne,
Zeus-for-strangers, look here, 'cause if you don't,
you're no Zeus at all, but a Zero!
(enters cave)

CHORUS:

Open up wide, One Eye,
your lip-rimmed hole. Come get it
boiled, roasted, charcoal broiled,
to nibble and chomp, prime cuts of company,
as you relax on a fleecy skin.

But don't ask me along.
You can stow that cargo yourself.
I'd just as soon stay clear of you,
stay clear of the godless
offerings Cyclops of Etna makes
out of converting strangers
into the fixings for his supper.

Ruthless, reckless, he
who butchers his suppliant houseguests

195

on his very hearth,
bears down on them,
the boiled flesh stuck between his terrible teeth,
human meat hot off the fire.

ODYSSEUS *(returning from cave):*
My God! How can I describe what I saw in that cave—
incredible horrors, more like a story than reality?

LEADER:
What happened, Odysseus? Did that godamn
beast kill some of your shipmates?

ODYSSEUS:
He weighed them in his hands by two's
until he found the fattest pair.

LEADER:
Poor man! How did your ordeal turn out?

ODYSSEUS:
Well, after we went into the cave,
first he lit a fire, then threw logs
from a tall oak on the huge hearth—
at least three wagon loads.
Next he spread his bedding
all of pine-needles beside the fire.
Then he milked his ewes
and poured the milk into a hundred gallon tub.
Beside it he set an ivy box
about four feet wide and six deep.
And he set his brass pot to boil on the fire;
also there were thorny spits sharpened by ax
and then fired in the flames,
and blood-bowls big as Etna.
After he'd laid everything out, this,
this demonic cook grabbed two of my men

and making like a drummer killed them:
he knocked one's head against the hollow kettle,
the other he held by the heels
and smashed against a sharp rock,
braining him; then he sliced their flesh
with a sharp knife and put it on the fire,
throwing what was left of them into the pot to boil.
With tears running down my cheeks,
I approached the Cyclops to wait on him.
The others, scared to death, cringed
like birds in the rocky nooks and crannies.
Then as he lay back, bloated on the flesh
of my friends, and exploded a belch,
a great idea came to me! I filled a cup
with Maron's wine and offered him a drink.
"Cyclops," I said, "you son-of-the-sea-god,
meet the glorious wine that flows
from Greece's vineyards, Dionysus' pride!"
Stuffed with his horrible meal,
he took it and knocked it down,
then raised his grateful hands: "My friend,
you've helped me top off a great meal with a great drink."
When I saw how much it pleased him,
I poured another, knowing he'd get
stoned on that wine and that I'd get my revenge.
He started to sing; I just kept pouring out
drink after drink until the stuff warmed his guts.
So the whole cave resounds with his singing
and my crew's moans—some harmony. I sneaked out
to save myself and you, if you're with me.
So tell me now whether or not you want
to escape from this savage and live
in Bacchus' halls with his river-girls.
Your old father inside approves this,
but he's too weak to help; he's made a big investment in the wine,
it's as if he's glued to the cup—

going nowhere. But you're young,
so help save yourselves with me and return
to your old friend Dionysus, who's so unlike this Cyclops.

LEADER:
Friend, if we could only see the day
when we'd finally escape the brute!
(holding his cock)
For a long time this old nozzle has been
forsaken, with no goodies to snarf up.

ODYSSEUS:
Then listen to my plan for your liberation
and revenge on this inhuman criminal.

LEADER:
Tell me. I'd rather hear about his destruction
than listen to the best music out of Asia.

ODYSSEUS:
He's so drunk he wants to go out
and party it up with his relatives.

LEADER:
I get it. You want to trap him in a lonely wood
and kill him—or push him off a cliff.

ODYSSEUS:
O no. I was thinking of something more clever.

LEADER:
Well, what? For years I've heard how smart you are.

ODYSSEUS:
I'll talk him out of this party, I'll say
he shouldn't have to share such good wine,
that he should keep it for his private pleasure.
Then as soon as he passes out, well—

there's an olive tree in the cave,
I'm going to sharpen it with my sword
and set it in the fire, and then when it
catches I'll whip it out all hot and shove it
right in Cyclops' eye and dissolve it.
Just like a ship builder fitting timbers
twirls his drill with a leather strap,
I'll screw that torch right into his eye
and push until his eyeball scorches.

LEADER:

Out of sight!
I'm crazy about your plan!

ODYSSEUS:

Then I'll put you, your old man,
and my friends aboard my ship,
and with this double crew we'll speed away.

LEADER:

Since everybody's supposed to participate in rituals,
I'd like to lay a hand on the pole
that blinds him. I want to share this job.

ODYSSEUS:

Sure. The log's heavy. Everybody pulls his weight.

LEADER:

I'd lift the weight of a hundred wagons
so that Cyclops would come to an evil end—
we'll smoke out that eye like it was a wasp's nest!

ODYSSEUS:

Quiet now. You know the plan.
When I call, obey—I'm the boss. *(pauses)*
I just won't abandon my men inside
and escape by myself, as I might.
I made an easy exit through a tunnel.

But it wouldn't be right to leave those
I came here with, and save myself, would it?
(returns to cave)

O who'll be first and who'll be next
working along the long firebrand
to shove it up the Cyclops' eyelid
and put out the light, put out the light?

(Singing inside the cave is heard. Then Cyclops comes out with Odysseus and Silenus.)

Shhhh shhhh. Here he comes, Mister Drunk,
singing an awful song
off-key, out of tune, utterly unmusical,
here he comes stumbling out of the cave.
Now let's teach that unteachable
a good drinking song.
It won't be long before he's blind.

A happy man cries "cheers"
when the grape fountain flows
and he stretches out for fun,
arms opened for a friend,
like a curvy blonde
on his bed for company
with sweet, shining curly-
locks, who whispers, "I want you to want me . . . "

CYCLOPS:

Man o man o man, am I full of wine!
I just love a good feed.
I'm a merchant ship
loaded right up to the deck.
This fine meal makes me
feel like a picnic

with my Cyclopes brothers.
Hey you! My friend, hand me the wine-skin.

CHORUS:

With a gleam in his handsome eye,
Mister Hey Good-looking steps out of the house.
"Somebody loves him, we wonder who?"
And the bridal torch is burning
for a touch, as the soft bride
waits in the cool of the cave.
Soon we'll crown him
with the reddest garland!

ODYSSEUS:

Listen, Cyclops, I've put in a lot of time
with this drink of Bacchus I've given you.

CYCLOPS:

So who's this Bacchus? A recognized god?

ODYSSEUS:

No greater when it comes to giving men pleasure.

CYCLOPS *(belching)*:

Well, he makes for a pleasant belch.

ODYSSEUS:

Right, he's the kind of god that wouldn't hurt anybody.

CYCLOPS:

What kind of god likes living in a flask?

ODYSSEUS:

No matter where you put him, he's happy.

CYCLOPS:

A god just shouldn't wear a wine-skin.

ODYSSEUS:

So what if you like him? Or don't like the skin? Big deal.

CYCLOPS:
I hate the skin. But I love that wine.

ODYSSEUS:
So stay here and have a ball.

CYCLOPS:
Shouldn't I give some to my brothers?

ODYSSEUS:
Naw, keep it for yourself, like a big-shot.

CYCLOPS:
But it's more responsible to share.

ODYSSEUS:
Well, that kind of party often ends up in a brawl.

CYCLOPS:
I may be drunk, but nobody'd lay a hand on me.

ODYSSEUS:
Nobody? My good man, when you're drunk, stay home.

CYCLOPS:
I think it's stupid not to party after drinking.

ODYSSEUS:
A smart man stays home when he's polluted.

CYCLOPS:
What do we do, Silenus? Stay home?

SILENUS:
Stay. Why bring more drinkers into this?

CYCLOPS:
This grass is soft and thick.

SILENUS:
It feels good to drink in the warm sunshine.

Lie down on your side like the king you are.

(He puts the wine behind Cyclops' back)

CYCLOPS:
Hey, why'd you put the wine-bowl behind me?

SILENUS:
Somebody could spill it.

CYCLOPS:
You're just trying
to swipe a drink. Put it in the middle.
Now, fella, tell me the name you go by.

ODYSSEUS:
Nobody. You have a reward for me?

CYCLOPS:
Sure. You'll be the last one of your crew I eat.

SILENUS:
O Cyclops, that's a really neat present. *(drinks)*

CYCLOPS:
What do you think you're doing? Stealing another drink?

SILENUS:
O no, the wine kissed me because it adores my eyes.

CYCLOPS:
Watch it. You're in love with the wine, but it's not mutual.

SILENUS:
O yes, it says it's crazy about my good looks.

CYCLOPS:
Pour! Up to the top! Keep pouring!

SILENUS:
Is it mixed right? Let me check it out. *(drinks again)*

CYCLOPS:
Goddamn! Give it!

SILENUS:
No-no, not till I
crown you with this wreath—and have a little drink.

CYCLOPS:
You cheating bar-rag!

SILENUS:
For heaven's sake, no!
Now the wine is sweet, so wipe yourself before you drink.

CYCLOPS *(wiping himself)*:
OK. My mouth and beard are clean.

SILENUS:
Now set your elbow so—easy does it—and drink
just as you see me—and now you don't. *(drinks)*

CYCLOPS:
Hey, what's going on?

SILENUS:
Happy days!

CYCLOPS:
You take it, buddy, and pour for me.

ODYSSEUS:
That wine and my hand are well-acquainted.

CYCLOPS:
Just fill'er up.

ODYSSEUS:
I am. Take easy.

CYCLOPS:
Hard not to talk when you're drinking.

ODYSSEUS:
All right, here, and down the hatch.
Never say die till you've finished it off.

CYCLOPS:
Buddy, the vine must be the smartest tree around!

ODYSSEUS:
When you've had a big meal and you feel like more than one,
just drown that thirst and you'll sleep great,
but leave just one drop and Bacchus'll dry you up.

CYCLOPS:
Wheeeeeeeee-O!
I can hardly keep my head above water. Pure pleasure!
The earth's flying and seems to blend
with the sky. I can see Zeus
on his throne and the perfect wonder of the gods.

(The satyrs dance sexily around him)

No kissy-kissy you—the Graces come on with me—
(grabs Silenus)
but I'll take Ganymede here and make it
with him beautifully; by these goats—Graces—
I've always preferred boys to girls.

SILENUS:
What? I play Ganymede to your Zeus?

CYCLOPS:
Yeah, you're that Trojan boy and I snatch you up.

SILENUS:
My boys, I'm finished! You know what he'll do to me!?

CYCLOPS:
Object to your lover because he's tight? Real tight!

SILENUS:
O shit! This is the worst drink of all!

(Cyclops carries Silenus into the cave)

ODYSSEUS:
Let's get to work, good sons of Dionysus,
our man's inside. Soon he'll fall asleep
and shamelessly barf up chunks of meat.
The stake, I see, has started to smoke inside.
This is what we've been waiting for, to burn
out Cyclops' eye. Show what you're made of.

LEADER:
Wills of rock, nerves of steel.
Hurry in now before our father is
uhh—violated. We're all ready for our orders.

ODYSSEUS:
Hephaestus, fire-king of Etna, burn to a crisp
your evil neighbor's eye and be rid of him for good,
and you, Sleep, child of black Night,
jump with all you've got onto this abomination.
Don't let it come about that after their glorious
test at Troy, Odysseus and company die
at the hands of one who doesn't give a damn for god or man.
Or else we'll have to accept Chance as the goddess
who stands above all the gods.

(Enters cave)

CHORUS:
Let grim pincers
nab him by the throat
who eats guests. Soon fire
will corrode his large eyeball.

Right now a charcoal torch
hides in the ashes, big as a tree.
And you, wine, do your work.
Tear out the eye of crazy
Cyclops, make him rue the day he drank you.
As for me, the sight of ivy-loving
Bacchus is my heart's desire,
and to leave this desolation.
Will I ever make that trip?

ODYSSEUS *(returning)*:
Shutup, for god's sake, you animals,
shut your traps! Don't you breathe,
or clear your throats, or even wink,
so that devil doesn't wake up
before we gouge his eye out.

LEADER:
Mum's the word. Lockjaw, too.

ODYSSEUS:
Let's go! Grab the stake with both hands
when you get inside. The point is red-hot.

LEADER:
Then you line us up, first to last,
on the fiery pole, to scorch Cyclops'
eye out, as we all want equal shares in this.

FIRST SATYR:
Where we stand here by the entrance
is too far away to reach his eye.

SECOND SATYR:
O we've just come up lame.

THIRD SATYR:
Same here, just sprained our ankles
standing on this spot—don't ask me how.

ODYSSEUS:

Sprained your ankles standing still?

FOURTH SATYR:

Me, too,
I've got something in my eye.

ODYSSEUS:

You chicken-shits, you're no help!

LEADER:

So I care about my back
and don't want my teeth
knocked out, so that makes me chicken?
But I do know a very fine Orphic spell
that will make the pole fly all by itself
right into his skull and burn the one-eyed son-of-a-bitch!

ODYSSEUS:

I've known all along what type you are,
and now I know even better. I'll use my own men,
in fact, I have to. Even if you're too weak to help,
you can still be our cheering squad
and inspire my men with some hearty rooting.

(Enters cave)

CHORUS:

Hold tight! Hold tight! Go right for the head!
Smoke him out, smoke him out, smoke out Cyclops!
Go! Go!
In-Out-Back and Forth, do it!
Burn his eye
beastly fiend
stick it in and burn him—
the big sheep-man of Etna!
Now twist and turn and watch yourselves
he's up against the wall.

208

CYCLOPS *(from within)*:
Aeiiiiiiii! My eye's turned into a burning coal!

LEADER:
Pure music! Sing it for us, Cyclops!

CYCLOPS:
Ohhhahhh! They've ruined me, I'm through!
But don't think you'll escape out of the cave
to celebrate, you tiny turds. I'll stand
here in the entrance and block the way.

(He comes and stands in the cave's mouth)

LEADER:
What are you screaming about?

CYCLOPS:
I'm dying.

LEADER:
You do look pretty awful.

CYCLOPS:
I *feel* awful!

LEADER:
Did you pass out into the fire?

CYCLOPS:
Nobody wiped me out.

LEADER:
Well then, you're OK?

CYCLOPS:
No! Nobody put my eye out.

LEADER:
Then you're not blind.

CYCLOPS:
Blind as you—

LEADER:
Please explain how nobody could possibly blind you.

CYCLOPS:
You're making fun of me! Where's Nobody?

LEADER:
He's nowhere!

CYCLOPS:
The stranger, jerk! who's killed me,
the scum who broke me down with booze.

LEADER:
O wine is treacherous, very tough to wrestle with.

CYCLOPS:
For god's sake, is he still inside or did he get away?

LEADER:
They're quietly taking cover
under a rock—over there.

CYCLOPS *(moving away from entrance to cave)*:
Which side?

LEADER:
On your right.

(Greeks begin to file out of cave)

CYCLOPS:
Where?

LEADER:
Right up against that rock.
Got 'em?

CYCLOPS *(bumping into rock)*
Ah! There's no end to my troubles. I just
busted my head.

LEADER:
And did they get away?

CYCLOPS:
Over here? You said they were over here?

LEADER:
No, the other way, I said.

CYCLOPS:
Which way?

LEADER:
Turn this way, to your left.

(The Greeks are all out)

CYCLOPS:
You're mocking me, rubbing salt into the wound.

LEADER:
Not at all. There's Nobody right under your nose.

CYCLOPS *(lunges)*:
Fucking bastard! Where are you?

ODYSSEUS:
Out of your reach,
and watching out for Odysseus' safety.

CYCLOPS:
Who'd you say? Have you changed your name?

ODYSSEUS:
Odysseus, the exact name my father gave me.
Thought you'd get away with your fiendish meal?

It would have been wrong to have burned down
Troy and not avenged the murder of my men.

CYCLOPS:

O no! So the old prophecy comes true.
It said you'd blind me on your way home
from ruined Troy. But is also said
you'd pay for what you did to me:
for years and years you'll be adrift at sea.

ODYSSEUS:

You're making me cry. I've done the very thing
you're talking about! Now I'm going to the beach
and set sail through Sicily's sea for home.

(Exits with his men)

CYCLOPS:

O no you won't. I'm going to tear a boulder
off this cliff and crush you and your miserable men under it!
I'll climb this mountain even though I'm blind,
I'll make my way up through a secret tunnel.

(Gropes his way to cave)

LEADER:

And we'll sign up with Odysseus.
From now on we work only for Bacchus.

(Satyrs help Silenus move off stage with them)

The Bacchai

Euripides

translated by

Charles Doria

Introduction

Somehow I've never been able to answer the question—and I'm not sure I want to anymore—that Ezra Pound said Mussolini put to him once: "Perché vuol mettere le Sue idee in ordine?" ("Why do you want to put your ideas in order?"). I don't think Pound ever answered it either except by demonstrating that ideas create their own order, and not the other way around. Or: without ideas there would be no order. In fact I wonder if the whole business of setting priorities or sequences doesn't somehow in itself violate the nature of our primary experiences and of our experiencing these experiences; if order doesn't go counter to whatever fragmented notions are left in me concerning the nature and operation of event itself which, as I see it, is neither random nor controlled either from within or without, but simply another occurence—sometimes a surprise—that takes place within known parameters of whatever sort we care to define. So this introduction to *The Bacchai* will come out in bits and pieces, a little at a time. Let the chips fall where they Heisenbergianly may.

There are two plots in *The Bacchai*, Epiphany and Vengeance: each reflects Dionysos' dual nature and double ancestry: half-human, half-divine. Dionysos wants people everywhere, not just the Greeks, to recognize him as a god. His 'coming out party,' as far as the Greeks are concerned, he decides will take place in Thebes, their oldest and in some ways holiest city. But this is also where his human family lives: a grandfather who drove his mother, pregnant by Zeus, out of the palace for reasons of scandal, plus three aunts who encouraged their father to do this to their sister by planting blasphemous rumors that denied Dionysos' father was Zeus, not to mention a cousin of about the same age who may or may not have benefited by Semele's death and Dionysos' forced removal to Asia, since he grew up to become king of Thebes and rule it in a most unDionysiac manner.

As a result—or possibly in deference to some higher order or plan of Zeus's (briefly alluded to towards the end of the play)—Dionysos assumes human form as a young priest of his own faith and proceeds to work out a perfectly poetic, if somewhat cruel and arbitrary, scheme of vengeance against his family. In this way he demonstrates (Epiphany) that he is a son of Zeus, while through his followers and the ways in which he punishes his family, he provides a picture of all the various phases and facets his cult and divinity can manifest.

In that sense the movement of *The Bacchai* is a lot like that of a good drunk, a weekend bender even. First there's all this partying and fun-making and good times up in the mountains and down in the city. Even the young prude, King Pentheus, gives in long enough to enjoy himself in his voyeuristic capacity as guardian of the public morals and key-hole peeper into his mother's bedroom and the girls' locker room's showers. But then comes the morning after: so many headaches that turn into heartaches for some. Cadmus and Agave wake up to themselves and their bleak future after Dionysos compels them to sober up from the euphoria he first aroused in them. For Pentheus, the fun is short-lived and his remorse almost thrust upon him as part of the desperate plea he makes to his mother and the other Theban women to spare his life.

This would probably be all right if no one in the play except the audience listened to the choruses of the Asian Bacchai. At first they sing ecstatically about the wonders of nature and the miraculous Dionysos whose godhead they enjoy one step below sainthood and one or two degrees short of spiritual whoredom. But by the end—and this is no sudden transition—they are singing about the wondrous fulfillment of a revenge administered by their god to people too stupid to be aware of or feel guilty for the crimes they committed against the embryonic god and his

216

mother and who are as well too weak to fight back. No matter how many soldiers Pentheus commands, Dionysos still has god on his side.

For Dionysos is a jealous god, resenting and needing the love his human family denied him. He punishes, either to the limits of his strength or to the letter of the latitude allotted him by Zeus or Destiny, all those who should have loved him and his mother, who should have acknowledged him as one of their flesh and blood and recognized Zeus's paternity and continuous involvement with his son which leads him eventually to nominate Dionysos to join the Twelve Olympians, his Divine Family.

The divine in Dionysos appeases his all-too-human need for vengeance. That's his strange character which makes it hard for some to see him as god—this catering or tailoring of his thoughts and acts to respond to mortal, rather than immortal, fears or hopes. But as I see it, for better or worse, Dionysos is an involved god and humanity forms his principal involvement. He is not a cold, aloof divinity on the standard Olympian model or a perfect exemplar of justice tempered with mercy on the Christian ideal who punishes and rewards for all eternity according to a rule book of his own composition. Dionysos seems to want to play according to our rules—it's only that his capacity for harming or helping, since he is also a god, has been enormously increased. Play fair with him is how I think it goes, and he'll play fair in return—even though the rules, in this case those governing family relations, appear more our doing than his. So there is very little elevation or 'majesty' in Dionysos; at times he doesn't even seem very bright: in short a figure eminently suitable for hero-worship—which is precisely what the Chorus and Teiresias do with him both in their own way. But definitely no god for Massachusetts.

On the other hand there is nothing vague or 'mystical' about him: he is a very exact and exacting god. This explains, I think, his strange passivity in the play; he seems to function as an emcee. Whatever anyone, particularly Pentheus, wants, Dionysos is right there to grant it and provide every possible assistance. Another instance of the vanity of human wishes? Well, perhaps.

217

All these possibilites lead me to think that Dionysos, despite his many pronunciamentos to the contrary, basically sees no difference between people and gods. He treats every one alike. He's a very democratic god. That's a very good thing for those who come in innocence with no outstanding guilts on their conscience to be initiated by him into his religion and be lifted temporarily and joyfully from care and woe through the sacrament of his wine. But what happens to those who, like the members of his own family, come to him with sullied hands and unacknowledged crimes against the god laid up in their hearts? That's where the real center of this tragedy lies. For Dionysos apparently is capable of devising reward and punishment within the unfolding of his myth and mystery that gladden the innocent with innocent happiness and depress and destroy the guilty by forcing them into the remembrance of past unnatural crime, by compelling them while under his magic spell (or the influence of booze) to commit still further crimes against nature—e.g. the cannibal feast Agave and her sisters make of Pentheus.

But there are other issues at stake here besides revenge. Dionysos offers everyone the gift of wine which Teiresias compares to Earth's gift of wheat, 'the staff of life,' and which the Herdsman ranks with Aphrodite's gift of sex—that is to say—reproduction, the passing on and preserving of that supreme gift, life, from one generation to the next. It is the validation of wine and the wine-cult as an active and worthwhile element in the human community that Dionysos is after. And so it comes to pass that all in the play sooner or later submit to wine or some form of Dionysiac intoxication and, freed of shame and guilt, proceed to act out their private selves and private dreams, hopes and wishes in public, with all the world their stage. *In vino veritas,* after all.

This more or less forms the plan of *The Bacchai* as I see it, and which I've tried to bring out as much as I could in the translation that follows. I've also attempted one other thing: to capture the generous, apparent spontaneity of the play, remembering that since everyone in it is Euripides, nothing has been left out.

When a class of mine staged *The Bacchai* some years ago, they performed it as an improvisation—that is, they learned the outlines of the play but concentrated their main efforts at building in themselves some common notions concerning the personality and role each character in it has. So without actually memorizing lines, they staged the play as an impromptu or spoken charade. Every time they did it, it was a wholly new thing yet still recognizably *The Bacchai*. They also double-cast Dionysos as a short blonde girl and a tall dark boy and kept them both onstage at the same time. While one spoke the other mimed. This worked especially well in the two interview scenes with Pentheus where a seduction of sorts is going on, only it involves the soul, not the body. This double-casting also served another purpose, besides making for good theater: it threw into sharp relief the schizoid but complementary breaks in Dionysos' own make-up that make it possible for him to be one and many things all at the same time.

This translation is dedicated to Lucy Williams, who never quits, and to Charlie Potts, who taught me how to spell.

Charles Doria

CHARACTERS

DIONYSOS

CHORUS OF ASIAN BACCHAI

TEIRESIAS

CADMUS

PENTHEUS

GUARD

HERDSMAN

MESSENGER

AGAVE

CHORUS LEADER

Guards, slaves, attendants, Thebans, etc.

THE SCENE

On the right are the palace of Cadmus and his family and the walls and towers of Thebes. In the center of the stage but recessed is the grave shrine of Semele which is covered with ivy and smokes constantly. On the left is the road that leads to Mount Cithairon and the hill country around Thebes. It is late winter but the beginning of spring, a Mediterranean January, in *alcheringa*/dream time.

(Enter Dionysos disguised as a girlish-looking teen-age boy with long blonde hair. He is dressed like a bacchant in a long, flowing robe, a fawn skin draped over his shoulders, and an ivy wreath in his hair. In his right hand he carries a thyrse—a long rod or staff wrapped in ivy and tipped with a pine cone. He acts and talks as if he is on a continual alcoholic high.)

DIONYSOS:
Hi, everybody! I'm Dionysos,
the son of Zeus and Semele.
This is my native Thebes,
where, if they'd of let me stay,
I'd a been prince an
maybe eventually king.
But instead—whoopie!
I'm a god—in fack
the god of wine, of joy, of endless ecstasy.
It was right here
that Zeus with a fire bolt
slashed me from my mother's womb,
then stitched me to his thigh,
so that my father became my mother.
From him I leapt into the world, a god.
I've come back home,
but the Thebans, such dim wits,
don't know who I am:
course that could be cuz
I've made myself look

just like a normal tourist,
standing around gawking
at Dirce's spring and the Ismenus river.
Right over there's my mother's grave—
where she married the lightning.
Ever since my father's immortal flame
still flickers, still smoulders there,
while the shattered embers of my mother's house
bear eternal witness to what
Hera's jealous hate can do.

But Cadmus, my grandfather, did something nice:
see—he turned her tomb into a shrine
and made it sacred to her name.
Nacherly I made a few improvements:
all that lattice work of grape and clustered vine's
my doing—to shield her grave from public view.

I've traveled a long ways to get here,
I've left a good many places behind.
I've been where rivers flow in gold:
Lydia and Phrygia—where my odyssey began,
whose mountains I scaled
to reach the Persian plains
where the sun beats down without mercy.
I made my way across Bactria's empty distance
and the mind-numbing wastes of Media
until I came to rich Arabia.
Traveling along the Asian coast,
I passed towering cities
where Greek and non-Greek alike live in peace.
Everywhere I went I taught my Mysteries,
I showed people how to move their feet in dance for me.
I established my rites and my religion,
so that everyone on earth could see for themselves
I am who I am: god.
Now it's Thebes' turn.

So watch out, all you nice, stuffy people—
my show's headed your way.

This city, the oldest in Greece,
screams, cries, echoes with my women's trebling melodies.
Listen—can you hear the joyous shout they raise?

(Shouts and cries of women can be heard from inside Thebes.)

Here for the first time
I clothed Greek women's flesh
in dappled fawn hide
and armed them with the thyrse,
a spear tipped with a pine cone,
around which my other plant,
the ivy, winds.

Now for the reason
I picked Thebes:
I returned to throw the lie
back at those champion liars,
Agave, Ino, and Autonoe,
my mother's sisters—
who therefore had least cause
to slander her.
But did that stop them? Nooo . . . !
They went around telling everybody
my mother'd slept with some man
who knocked her up, and that Semele,
to make her swollen belly
appear holy and respectable,
tried to persuade people
it was Zeus who'd done it to her.
Oh, how they snickered and giggled!
They'd stick their itsy-bitsy hands
half over their mouth

and whisper pizpizpiz! blasphemous lies
behind my mother's back:
until they finally convinced Cadmus
he'd simply have to kick that no-good bitch
right outta da palace—
'to protect her good name,' they said,
'as well as ours. And that's that, humph!'
Then when Zeus entered her with a thunderbolt
and blew her to shreds,
ya know what my dear, sweet, kind, lovable aunts claimed:
that this was Zeus's way of punishing her
because she'd named him as the father
of me—her child.

Now you can see why I drove
the women of Thebes mad with joy
and chased them from their homes into the hills
where they run around in giddying circles,
where, sick of mind, they are forced
to wear my bacchants' fawn skin and have
chaplets of live, writhing snakes in their hair.
Yes indeedy—that's what I did
to every female in Thebes—but only them:
the men aren't affected—yet.
But young and old, high-born and low,
all the women are up there in mountains,
this time of the year,
as Bacchai, celebrating my divinity—
and guess who's leading them? right:
it's those three liars,
those Regal Dames of Cadmus' House.
Yes—it's them who're putting the girls
through their paces, big as life
out there under the white pines,
under rocks that give no roof,

they're dancing, they're singing my Name.

Like it or not,
it's high time Thebes got acquainted
with my Mysteries.
Something else they'd better attend to:
I want Semele's name cleared.
I'll show her to them as mother of god
and reveal myself the son she gave Zeus.

King Cadmus has resigned
and turned over his throne and royal power
to his grandson, my cousin Pentheus,
who fights against the god in me,
who deprives me of my diet of sacrifice and prayer.
I'll prove to him and every Theban
I'm exactly what I say I am: god.
Once I've established myself here
and everything's going the way it should,
I'll be on my way,
revealing my supernal majesty
to other people throughout the world.

If the Thebans try to complicate matters
by trying to chase my Bacchai from the hills,
hunting them down like animals,
I'll just wear another of my many hats:
I'll turn general
and lead my maenad army
against this city and smash it to dust.
Now you know why
I've temporarily put my divinity in mothballs
and go about wearing the mask of man.

(Dionysos turns to address the Chorus.)

Come, ladies, pleasure me:

I've led you from Asia
where Mount Tmolus lifts her crest high above Lydia.
Come, you who have shared my journey:
come pounding Phrygian drum, Rhea's drum, and now my drum.
Beat a compelling tattoo
before the gates of Pentheus' palace
to let the Thebans know who you are,
while I go back to Cithairon's freshly greening forests
where the Theban Bacchai wait for me
to wind them through their dervish dance.

(Dionysos leaves for the mountains while the Chorus of Asian Bacchai
enters, carrying thyrses, drums and tambourines, to dance in front of
the palace.)

CHORUS:

From Asia—
from Tmolus Mountain's sides—
we bring the rites of Bacchus Bromius Thunder Shouting Lord.
We come to serve,
we come to work for him,
to find from him sweet reward,
sweetly following,
sweetly screaming:
'Bacchus Evoi! it's you we want, we love!'

Anyone else,
doesn't matter where you are—
on the streets,
the plazas—
get out of our way.
Hold your tongue. Shut up.
No bad luck word leave your mouth,
fouling the air.
Gang way.
Stand aside.

And silence!
We sing the old, old Bacchus Song:
'Happy is she who learns the Secrets of god,
Happy the girl who makes her life holy a slave to this god,
Happy she whose breath the god owns, becoming one with her:
with every woman whose body fleshes the body of god.
Happy those dancers, bright, clear forms
that dance on hill ridges the dances of god—
Happy to honor the paths Cybele, Great Mountain Mother, makes,
Happy to raise the thyrse, the god wand, in their hands,
Happy, yes! those girls who weave themselves crowns of ivy of god,
they are Happy,
Happy Dionysos is their god.'

Move, Bacchai! Keep it moving:
bring our god triumphantly home.
Carry god, son of god.
Follow him home.
Lead him down from Phrygia's hills.
Parade him proudly through the streets of Greece.

Does it matter
his mother gave him bitter birth,
the baby whipped from her by lightning bolt,
drawn away by flame Zeus sires?
Shriveled in that fire
Semele died,
split before her time,
though she labored with godchild.
Blown by light she fell:
by light the child was born.
The child Zeus saved
faster than eye can see:
saved and thrust into his secret womb,
hooped in bands of gold.

For his son he made his thigh a womb,
he sewed him there
to hide him from Hera's eye.

Looming Fates spun their threads:
soon the child's was knit.
Son of Zeus, bull-horned boy,
FatherMother Zeus bore,
who found it joy
crowning his son with ivy
weaving snakes in and through his hair:
so that it falls to us in holiness
to wear the maenad's crown,
this living, pulsing garland of snakes.

Thebes!
you bore his mother:
now bear our crown.
Let briony give you green,
berries stain you red.

Thebes!
wear oak and pine.
Dance the dance that commands.
Wrap shoulder and arm in spotted leathers fawns provide.
Hem skirts with curled, tufted wool.
Careful with the thyrse!
It is strong and violent.

And dance!
Roarer Bromius
takes to the mountains
where his women tribes are waiting:
whom he owns,
whom they profess,
for whom they've left loom and shuttle behind.

Holy acts Cretans know:
caves Kouretes Armored Lads danced in front of,
that cave where Zeus was born,
where Korybants leapt,
circling the thudding drum,
on their heads helmets done triple-fold:
they are,
they were
the first
whose flashing feet beat out our sacred measure
the taut-hided drum unerringly taught
while flutes screeched.

This holy drum they gave Mother Rhea.
Fool Satyrs stole it.
Now the drum is ours.
Now it instructs our feet to dance.
Every second year it makes
your name a holiday: Dionysos—

Who makes sweet mountain music,
Who falls to earth,
Whose women run after him in packs,
Who wears dappled fawn skin leather,
Who hunts wild goat and flays it alive,
Who loves to eat its meat raw,
Who races along Phrygian ridge lines,
Who runs over Lydian mountains,
Who is named Bromius Ranter Roarer our Leader:

   Eván! Evói!

Earth's teats pour forth milk.
They give wine,
brimming over with honey from the bee.
Our god, the Torch, burns,
making frankincense in air.

Flickering fires waver through air.
He races. He dances.
He scorches with flame those who lag behind.
He harries, he hurries them on.
He screams.
His long blond hair flows with the wind.
He shouts:
his Bacchai shout:

>   *Eván! Evói!*

Go, Bacchai: go go go!
Go and doncha stop for nothing.
Chase our god, Tmolus' Golden Glory.
Sing. Chant.
Pound drum.
Shout *evoi!* for the Lord *evoi* names.
Wail tunes in Phrygian mode
while the godling pipe plays honeyed tones.
Sing the holy songs
of those who race
up mountains up mountains
up like colts clicking hooves beside their mares grazing grass,
Bacchai, leap! Leap!
And leaping,
leave yourself behind.

*(The Chorus moves away from the palace. Teiresias the Prophet enters
from Thebes. He is dressed like a bacchant. Since he's blind, the thyrse
he carries he uses as a cane to tap his way forward.)*

TEIRESIAS *(addressing one of the palace guards):*
You there—
go call Cadmus, Agenor's son,
that old hero
who left his native Sidon
to come here and found this city,

fortifying it with seven towers
to guard its walls.
Tell him Teiresias is waiting for him:
he'll know why.

(One of the guards goes into the palace.)

As one old man to another,
we made an agreement,
Cadmus and I,
to make thyrses,
wear the bacchant's fawn skin
and crown our heads with sprigs of ivy.

(Enter Cadmus from the palace. He is dressed just like Teiresias as a bacchant.)

CADMUS:
Hello—hello, my oldest, dearest friend!
I could hear you while I was inside.
I knew immediately it had to be you,
for I heard a wise man speaking wisely.
I'm all set, ready to go. Like you
I'm wearing what the new god,
my grandson, Dionysos, wants.

He has revealed his divinity to mankind,
so now it's our pleasant duty
to worship him and augment his godhead
insofar as it in our power lies.
Where shall we go?
Where foot it neatly frolicking,
our hair white with years?
Teach me, Teiresias:
let old guide the old,
for you are one who knows.
I'll never tire day or night,

pounding earth with my thyrse,
to free our eldage from care,
drawing on the god's sweet joy
to renew our days
and make us young again.

TEIRESIAS:
Your heart and mine now beat as one.

CADMUS:
Come to the mountain. Ride this chariot with me.

TEIRESIAS:
No, we must walk. Riding dishonors the god.

CADMUS:
Then I'll show you the way
if we have to walk at
our age.

TEIRESIAS:
Don't worry, we won't get tired.
The god wants us there with him.

CADMUS:
Are we the only men of Thebes
who go to join the dance?

TEIRESIAS:
Yes, since we're the only ones who know.
The rest are fools.

CADMUS:
Well, what are we waiting for?
Give me your hand. Let's go.

TEIRESIAS:
And, see: I'll take yours

(They join hands.)

CADMUS:
I will curse no god.
Though I was born to die,
yet I will not blaspheme.

TEIRESIAS:

Framing arguments about the divine—
such a useless waste of time.
What our fathers believed,
and their fathers before them,
constitutes our whole faith.
No silly chains of logic shall bind our minds,
even though our wisdom comes from subtlest thought.
If some young girl clad in ivy and fawn
invites me to dance the bacchanal,
who am I to say no?
For in Dionysos' eyes we are all alike,
all his kith and kin.
So, no matter if we're young or old,
rich or poor, male or female,
we all must dance for him.
From each of us he desires his honorable share,
he exempts none from his reckoning.

CADMUS:
Teiresias, since you're blind,
I will be the prophet of your words.

Oh oh, Pentheus is returning to the palace
as fast as he can. How excited he looks!
What's on his mind?

(Enter Pentheus all a-bustle.)

PENTHEUS:
It just so happened,

while I was out of the country on a mission of state,
reports reached me about some strange goings-on back home.
Seems our women have left the city
to go running through the hills
on some flimsy pretext or other—
all about a god I never heard of.
He's supposed to have ordered them up there
to dance for him.
He calls this 'worship'—his 'divine service.'
He wants our women to pretend to go crazy,
whipping them up to a frenzied search for ecstasy.
Wait—there's more.
He's given each of these chorines
a bowl brimful of wine
which they're to drink until drunk,
then slip away to some convenient thicket or cave
and have a nice private little fuck
with whoever they like.
Maenad priestesses, devotees of Bacchus,
they're calling themselves now.
Want to hear their real name:
whores of Aphrodite!
And they'll pay for it:
rest assured, they'll pay.
I've already had some of them arrested
and chained up in the city jail.
As for the rest who're still up there
gadding about—I'll hunt them down myself,
every last one of them.
That goes double for my aunts, Ino and Autonoe,
and my mother—to think, gawd, my own mother's
out there too! *Noblesse oblige,* godamnit!
They owe me and this city a special responsibility
to act decently, becomingly—
as befits those born to the purple.
Just let me get my hands on them,

I'll put them away some place out of sight,
where it's quiet and dark,
where they'll be forced to stop
this Bacchanalian tomfoolery.

I've also been told by a reliable source
there's newly come to Thebes
some new model screaming wizard from Lydia
that rubs toilet water into his gold-coifed hair.
His face, I hear, shines as ruby red
as the cheap wine he drinks.
In his eyes you're supposed to see
Aphrodite's wine-dark Graces dance.
That's why—in case you haven't already figured it out—
day and night the women flock around him
like stupid cows while he pretends to unveil
for them the 'Secrets of Bacchus.'
Some Secrets! Some Bacchus!
Once I get him behind bars,
that's it: say by-by, fella,
to all that thyrse-waving and drum-pounding.
What a headache that stuff gives me.
And no more letting the wind ruffle
his blond mane so romantically:
I'll shear him bald as a lamb in spring.
Now get this:
here's what this self-styled priest
goes around preaching:

(in a mincing falsetto)

'Dionysos is a god
who got sewn in Zeus's thigh
because he and his mother, Semele,
were zinged by Zeus's thunder lightning.'

Well, gosh golly gee, what else were people

supposed to think was gonna happen to that little bastard?
specially after all the lies my former aunt,
god rest her simple soul, told
about how Zeus'd slept with her
and made her preggers—
because he loved—who?—her, Semele?!
Do we hafta wait for the lightning to strike twice
before we know what it's our plain bounden duty to do?
And that's hang that slit-eyed, zit-faced *fakir*
and shut his blasphemous mouth
before he gives all of us—think of your families, men!
his foul superstitious diseases!

*(A chorus of ragged cheers from the palace guards greets these last re-
marks of Pentheus. Then Pentheus turns his attention on Teiresias and
Cadmus.)*

My, my—what have we here?
Two old poopsies in search of some young god
to whore after? Just no end of miracles
is there today, hmmmm?

Grandfather—do you have to act like this
or what? Can't you see how you're humiliating me
in front of the people? 'No fool like an old fool:'
but I never thought you were that old or so foolish.
Please, take that ivy off your head
and drop that stupid thyrse. Remember—
no matter what, you're still my mother's father.
That means you have certain obligations
to me and the throne you gave me—
as well as maintaining a modicum of dignity
as the former ruler and founder of this city.

Teiresias, this is all your doing, I can tell
you put him up to this.
I'm wise to your game:

promote the first new god that comes along
and make a few fast bucks at the same time
from all the extra divining, prophesying,
bird-watching and oracle-chasing
that'll just happen to fall your way.
If it weren't for your grey hair,
I'd throw you in jail—
where you belong—
right with all those crazy women,
for having a hand in bringing
this mad religion to Thebes.
Soon as you see women drinking wine
and traipsing through the hills on holiday,
you know they're up to no-good.
Do I have to spell it out for you
in words of one syllable or less
or have I made myself sufficiently clear?

CHORUS LEADER:
Yes, you've made yourself clear alright:
you're the blasphemer,
not those two wise and holy men.
Have you no shame before the gods—
let alone in the presence of Cadmus
who sowed the dragon's teeth
to found your House and Lineage.
Know you disgrace him
and Echion, your father,
and everyone else in your family.

TEIRESIAS:
King Pentheus, whenever a wise man
has something to say,
you'd do well to listen.
The power in his words
contains nothing supernatural,

just the blunt force of truth.
But you—you talk like a salesman;
the words just slide like snake oil
off your tongue.
You pose as if indeed you're wise:
but anyone who talks the way you were just now,
reveals himself for what he is—
a poor citizen and a madman.

I tell you straight:
this god you find so funny
someday will be great and strong.
Everyone in Greece will honor him.
The gods, my friend,
have given people two fine gifts.
The first is the wheat Ge Meter Earth provides,
for that's the food that feeds us all.
The second is wine which Semele's son invented;
it's just as good and good for you
as Earth Mother's grain.
Dionysos gave us wine as his offering to us.
When we drink and fill ourselves
to bursting with it,
pain dies;
we remember not to weep
and so can sleep carefree nights.
Wine makes us forget
the troubles of our days:
what other medicine does this?
When we give the gods
something good to drink,
we offer them Bacchus,
the wine god himself,
in his liquid body,
hoping through him

to gain the kindly grace
of Those Who hold the Sky.
You thought that was some joke,
didn't you: that business
about Zeus stitching Dionysos to his thigh.
Now I'll tell you what really happened.
After Zeus'd saved his infant son
from his own thunders,
he brought him to Olympus.
Hera was heart-sick with jealousy,
she wanted to throw the baby
as hard as she could
back down to Earth.
Now Zeus's a better god than her,
he knew in advance
what she'd likely do.
So he broke off a tiny bit
of the FireAir that girdles Earth
and slapped it into a shape
resembling Dionysos.
Then he let Hera take
this counterfeit bastard hostage,
to do what she liked with it.
Meanwhile he brought up the boy
in the normal way.
That's the true story.
But people down through the years
got their facts all twisted up.
This explains why they tell that garbled tale
of Zeus sewing the boy to his thigh.

There's more to Dionysos
than wine, though:
he's also a god of prophecy.
Those who seem crazed—
the maenads, for example,

are actually empowered by him
to tell what the future holds.
When as god he enters man,
he breathes into him or her
prophetic tiding's gift.

Here's something else he does:
he can face down Ares, the god of war.
Sometimes you'll see an army
that's been formed up properly
into ranks and files
suddenly bolt and jump from panic and fear
before they've begun to fight.
Now that panic's Dionysos' doing,
and no one else's.

Sometimes you see him carrying a torch,
and leaping along the mountain ridges at Delphi,
racing over the green fields between the hills there,
waving, throwing that wand of his
that's made him so strong everywhere in Greece.

Pentheus, listen to me:
it's not a man's strength that makes him strong
but god's power flowing into him.
Don't make the mistake
of confusing what you think is going on
with what is really happening.
Welcome this new god to Thebes.
Greet your cousin happily, courteously:
put ivy in your hair,
and come with us.
Come and join the dance.

Bacchus never makes a woman chaste
against her will. Rather it's always the case
that it's what she is to herself—

how she views herself—
that keeps her modest and pure.
She can go to his holy orgies
and leave just as she came: intact.

Think about it.

You like it, don't you,
when the people stand outside the palace gates,
shouting and cheering—
when the whole city cries out in one voice
'Pentheus! Pentheus! Our great, our noble king!'
He wants his share of glory also,
his name sung in joy by your citizens.

Now Cadmus and I—
well, I see by that dopey look
on your face you still think
we're too funny for words—
we're going right on with it:
we'll crown ourselves with ivy
and do the dance of god.
Yes, we're old and gray,
but not so dumb in the head
that we'll take your advice
and start a war with the gods.
You're mad for thinking that.
And your madness wounds you to the heart.
For that there's no cure,
since it's a magic of your own mind
that's done this thing to you.

CHORUS LEADER:
Honored sir, your words
would not discredit Phoebus himself,
whose prophecies, as we all know,
are always fulfilled to the letter.

Your wisdom, as well, augments
Thunder Bacchus, our strong Lord.

CADMUS:

My boy, Teiresias has given you
the benefit of his best advice.
Abide with us. Do not stray beyond those paths
our fathers and our fathers before have walked.
Right now you're living a dream.
The thoughts you think you're thinking
are light and substanceless as air.
Just suppose for a moment
that Dionysos—as you maintain—
is not a god: call him one anyway.
All right—that's a golden lie,
if you like. But at least this way
our people will honor Semele
as Mother of a God.
That can only raise our House
higher in the ranks of honor.

Remember what happened
to your other cousin, Actaeon.
His hounds he'd raised by hand from pups
tore him apart,
then feasted on his flesh up there
in the high meadows. Why? because
he bragged he hunted better than Artemis.
If you don't want something like that
happening to you—here: let me place
this ivy wreath on your head.
Then come with us. Give the god
honorable service. You have been warned.

*(Cadmus attempts to put an ivy wreath on Pentheus' head but Pentheus
pushes his hands away.)*

PENTHEUS:

Take your hands off me, you old fool!
Go ahead, become a dancing slave of Bacchus.
See how far that'll get you.
Just don't, I repeat: don't try and tar me
with the madness that's touched you.
As for that self-styled clairvoyant over there
who's instructed you in this business,
I'll take care of him right now.
Guard!

PALACE GUARD:

Yessir!

PENTHEUS:

Go to the Seat where he holds Seance,
take a coupla crowbars and smash it,
level it to the ground—turn it
upside down if you have to—
but I don't want to see a trace of it left
after you've finished.
Confiscate the wool hangings
that supposdly sanctify the place,
tear them to bits
and scatter the pieces to the four winds.
That ought to squeeze his heart some.

*(The guard makes a snappy salute and leaves at a trot. Pentheus beck-
ons to the other guards.)*

The rest of you—
go, make a thorough search of the city.
Find the strange boy who looks like a girl—
that weird epicene who's been monkeying
with our women and stained our sheets.
I want him brought here in chains!
He'll rue the day he decided Thebes

242

was the place he could carouse in safety—
with our women, no less!
My sentence is all ready and waiting for him:
he'll die by stoning.

(The rest of guards salute and make a quick exit in a precise military formation.)

TEIRESIAS:
You fool, oh you poor fool!
Do you know what you're doing?
What you're *really* doing?
If you weren't crazy before,
you are now: and more— if that's possible.

Cadmus, let's leave for the mountains right away
and hope our prayers will convince the god
to spare him, wild as he is, and save
the city from paying for their king's madness.
Come, thyrse in hand,
and leaning on each other,
let's make our way into the wilderness.
If we slip and fall,
don't worry—
because it's to serve Bacchus Son of Zeus that we go
and he knows how to take care of his own.

Hear my final warning:

(Teiresias raises his thyrse and points its tip straight at Pentheus.)

*Pent*heus may hear his own name echoing
if your House falls apart,
re*pent*ing what it has done to the god,
your grandson and *his* cousin.

I speak of what must surely happen soon—
not in artful, riddling paradox

but in simple language
anyone, it seems, except him can understand.
Out of the mouth of this fool
only foolishness comes.

*(Teiresias and Cadmus, arm in arm, and starting to dance slowly, leave
for the mountains. Pentheus strides swiftly and rigidly back to the palace.)*

CHORUS:
Sacred Lady, Queen of Sky,
You Who fly on wings of gold,
You Who hover over Earth:
does what Pentheus says reach You?
Does his blaspheming the Prince of gods,
our Lord of flowering wreaths and regal feast—
does his ranting against Bromius, Semele's Son,
wound Your ears?

These are the gifts Bacchus gives:
laughter pealing
to the flute's sweet intonings;
sorrows lost
when gleaming wine
is poured at the banquet of the gods,
and the wine-bowl,
with flower petals floating on top,
goes its rounds
and makes the divine revelers drowsy,
our Lord's ivy braiding their hair.

A tongue its owner can't control:
obstinacy, stupidity:
we know that brings on ruin.
Therefore live in wisdom,
in the peace and tranquility it bestows,
accept what must be,

and so survive serene, untroubled.
This is the way
to uphold and preserve your House
and the generations you hope
it will unfold.

Far off in the skyey distance
the Children of Heaven dwell.
They watch over what we do.
What they determine is wise.
Alas, those poor, pitiable folk
who turn this upside down,
because they think their thoughts and acts
so upright, honest and strong
they can strain against and break beyond
those eternal limits
the gods have foreordained for us.

We live little lives,
die tiny deaths:
so go ahead—chase glory upon glory,
pursue those infinite, those more-than-human dreams:
instead of what you have
and may enjoy here and now,
you'll embrace a sudden, untimely death
and be forced to acknowledge
that this rewards your titanic striving.
You're mad, then, you'll find,
in the final instant of your life, that,
thanks to your self-deceiving schemes,
what you planned was wrong from the start.
You became the devious instrument of your own undoing.

I want to go to Cyprus, paradise isle,
where Aphrodite lives,
where her Cupids cast glamours
that enchant men's hearts,

where pastures bloom
in unheard-of flowers of gold,
where the stream that empties into Ocean
does so through a hundred mouths,
where rain never falls,
where clouds never cast their bleak spell.

I want to go where no Greek lives—
to Macedonia so beautiful
there is no place like it
any where in the world;

or else to Pieria
which the Muses have found
gives them everlasting delight;

or else to the holy mountain, Olympus,
where Zeus sits enthroned,
where I might also stand
and cast aside all my fear.

Bacchus Bromius Roarer Leader Joyous God—
take me where I want to go,
take me where happiness will be mine forever,
where lithe, slender Graces dance
in unisons of three,
where Desire will feed my hungry heart:
take me, take me!
where I will be free—
free to serve, honor and obey in holy bacchanal
you, the god I love.

Dionysos, Zeus's Son,
loves feasts and feastings,
loves the goddess Peace
who cheerfully gives all good things
since she mothers all who're young,
while our Lord supplies his basic gift

to every one, rich or poor, it makes no difference:
he extends to all the gospel of the grape.

Make fun of him,
spit on his blessing
that brings ease from care,
he'll return your hate
knowing you refused to live,
buoyed on the pleasurable wings of his grace.

If you long for days that give joy
and nights not cursed with loneliness,
choose wisely, choose well:
let your full thought
separate you from the proud, selfish conniving
of those who hold themselves better, therefore above
the likes of you and me.
Yes, keep distance between you and those
who dream of out-goding god:
for then Dionysos shares himself with you.

What ordinary people think and find
gives satisfaction,
what the man in the street holds true,
I honor by what and in the way I do,
I do.

(The guards return, leading the chained and manacled Dionysos in the center of their formation.)

GUARD:
King Pentheus, you see we've got the big game
you sent us out to catch. But doncha worry:
he's really very tame. Why, he didn't try
to escape. He just held out his hands
for us to cuff. Didn't blanch one bit either:
look—his cheeks are as rosy now
as when we caught him. He smiled and asked us

to tie him up and bring him here—
all without showing one ounce of fear.
The whole thing made me feel sorta
ashamed of myself, so I said to him:
'look, feller—we're just obeying king's orders,
that's all. Nothing personal about it.'

But you know what else happened in the meantime?
Those maenads you had safely tucked away
over at the city jail somehow slipped their chains.
They just took off, skipping and dancing
over the fields. They're still there,
singing and carrying on about this here Bromius,
their, unh, Thunder Lord. From what the jailer
told me, seems the manacles on their feet
loosened up all by themselves, cell doors
opened of their own accord—haunted or something.
Now I think this guy's come to Thebes,
loaded down with all sorts of miracles.
Anyway, here he is. The rest's up to you.

PENTHEUS:
What's the matter with you?
You all gone mad?
And you call yourselves soldiers?!
Once someone gets tangled up in my nets,
struggle hard as he likes,
he'll never get away.

(Pentheus addresses Dionysos.)

Well, I must say, you look pretty good—
for a gigolo. And that probably explains
why you came to Thebes in the first place.
Bet you've never wrestled a real man
in your life, have you? Just look
at your hair—how long and curly it is.
And my—sexy, sexy—all that cute peach fuzz

on your cheeks. I see you don't let
nasty old sun hammer away at your soft white skin
unprotected. You hide in the shade,
you stalk the shadows, hunting what Aphrodite
procures, using your beauty as a come-on.

But now it's down to business, eh?
Where're you from? What country?

DIONYSOS:
No place special. I was born on Tmolus,
that flowery mountain perhaps you've heard of?

PENTHEUS:
I have. It circles the town of Sardis, right?

DIONYSOS:
That's the one. Lydia's my homeland.

PENTHEUS:
Whose mysteries are you bringing to Greece?

DIONYSOS:
I reveal the Secrets of that Son of Zeus:
Dionysos, who showed them to me personally.

PENTHEUS:
You mean there's a Lydian as well as a Greek Zeus
who goes around fathering new gods?

DIONYSOS:
No, we honor the same Zeus as married your Semele.

PENTHEUS:
Did you become this god's slave
because he came to you in a dream
or did he show himself in a daylight vision?

DIONYSOS:
No, we met face to face: just as we're doing now.

That was when he gave me his Secrets.

PENTHEUS:
Yaz, yaz . . . now these mysteries:
what are they like?

DIONYSOS:
I'm forbidden to tell you a thing about them
until after you've been initiated.

PENTHEUS:
What profit or pleasure is there for those
who go off partying in the hills with him?

DIONYSOS:
Once again I am forbidden to say;
yet what they receive is worth knowing.

PENTHEUS:
Humph—trying to tempt me with fool's gold, no?

DIONYSOS:
No: the work we do for our god
makes the godless hate us.

PENTHEUS:
Now you claim you've seen your god clearly:
what'd he look like?

DIONYSOS:
The way he wanted;
that was up to him, not us.

PENTHEUS:
Well, you've used up a lot of words
and told me exactly nothing.

DIONYSOS:
When you talk knowledgeably to a fool,

of course he'll say you're the fool, not him.

PENTHEUS:
Are you the first person
to bring us this god?

DIONYSOS:
By now, everybody in Asia sings and dances for him
just the way his Secrets taught them to.

PENTHEUS:
Yeah—that's cuz us Greeks are smarter and tougher
than all you goddamn slopes put together.

DIONYSOS:
That's precisely where you're mistaken.
This is something they do better.

PENTHEUS:
When do they do this?
At night or during the day?

DIONYSOS:
Mostly by night.
They find the darkness more solemn.

PENTHEUS:
Ahh—yep . . . and I'll bet it's a whole lot easier
to finger up some nookie then—ey?

DIONYSOS:
You can do that just as well when the sun's up,
if you've a mind to.

PENTHEUS:
I see you're going to make it necessary
for me to teach you how not to lie.

DIONYSOS:

Makes no difference. You'll still have to pay
for being so stupid as to play games with god.

PENTHEUS:

Goodneth Graysheuth!! What a saucy little bacchant we've here:
a regular athalete with his tongue . . . when it comes to words.

DIONYSOS:

Let's get it over with. What's my punishment?
What dreadful things are you going to do to me?

PENTHEUS:

First off, boy, I'm gonna give you a haircut.

DIONYSOS:

Better not.
My hair is holy.
I grow it long to honor my god.

PENTHEUS:

Next, gimme your thyrse.

DIONYSOS:

You want it so bad,
you come and get it yourself.
Just remember it really belongs to Dionysos.

PENTHEUS:

Finally I'm going to lock you up
and throw the key away.

DIONYSOS:

Whenever I want him to,
Dionysos will set me free.

PENTHEUS:

Oh, I'm sure he will:
the next time he sees you

dancing with your crazy girlfriends.

DIONYSOS:
Yes, indeed: he's here right now,
watching what you're doing to me.

PENTHEUS:
Where? Where?
's a funny thing, you know:
your seeing a god I can't.

DIONYSOS:
He's standing here beside me.
And of course you can't see him
because you have this strange ability
of being unable to see
what you don't believe.
Unfortunately for you, however,
my god does exist and he does see you.
You'll find out I'm right—
but maybe by then it'll be too late . . .

PENTHEUS *(to the guards)*:
Seize him!
Get him out of my sight!
He's been making fun of me and Thebes
long enough.

DIONYSOS:
Watch it!
Here's a scrap of wisdom for you fools
and solemn warning too:
lay no chains on me.

PENTHEUS:
I give the orders around here.
Chain him twice and twice as tight
for that last remark.

DIONYSOS:

You don't know what life you live,
what things you do.
You even don't know who you are.

PENTHEUS:

In that case permit me to introduce myself:
I am King Pentheus, Agave's and Echion's son.

DIONYSOS:

So it's *Pen*theus, is it?
Well, you'll re*pent* yourself
soon enough.

PENTHEUS:

Enough of his jabber. Away with him!
Lock him in the stables.
Put him where it's darkest and smelliest.

(to Dionysos)

Go on—dance your head off
in that black 'solemn' hole
I'm putting you in.

As for those whores you brought here,
I'll auction them off as slaves.
Or maybe show them a little mercy
by keeping their dainty fingers
so busy spinning and weaving in the palace
they won't feel like shaking tambourines
or pounding drums anymore. Honest work
never hurt anyone—might do wonders
for their character, too—whaddayah think?

DIONYSOS:

I go. But I shall not endure
a destiny My Destiny denies.

Dionysos himself—whom you say does not exist—
personally will pay you back
for the crimes you've committed against him.
When you put these chains on me,
remember it's really him
you're hauling off to jail.

(Dionysos is led away by the guards. Pentheus re-enters the palace.)

CHORUS:
Dirce, sacred river, child of Acheloüs,
once in your sweet waters
you harbored god:
Dionysos Son of Zeus—
when he, the Father,
took his Son
from immortal flame,
crying out:
'Dithyramb FourStep Dance,
come to me,
journey up my male womb.
You are Bacchus the Shout.
I promise I will make
every Theban Shout out your Name.'

Dirce, sacred river,
now you drive me from your banks,
though I came to you,
bearing the vision of god
coiled in ivy
and dancing the Dithyramb.

Dirce, sacred river,
why do you send me away dishonored and disowned?
I swear by the close-knit clusters of the grape,
by the wine Dionysos invented,
one day even you will learn

the meaning of his name: *Bromius*, Thunder Lord;
one day your heart shall receive our King,
your mouth profess him with the words: 'my master and my god.'

Madness, madness!
Pentheus, Titan Echion's son,
reveals his flesh was formed by dying clay,
that in his veins there courses still
blood of that dragon with whose teeth
Cadmus sowed these fields.
In his mindedness he betrays
he is spawn of serpent's seed,
that Earth littered him like a sow,
for like his father he is no man
but a beast foaming at the mouth,
while he rages titanically
in the wilderness he calls his city,
to summon up storms
he recklessly believes will bring the Family of Heaven down.

The fool has said to us, handmaidens of our Lord:
'I will chain you up from head to toe,
with my law will violate your souls,
cage your loyal, loving hearts
in the darkness of my eternal dungeons.'

Master, Son of Zeus:
does your eye see—
Dionysos, Prince of Thebes and her rightful King—look!
how he binds me in links of steel,
how he thinks to hold me down in unbreakable compelling bondage?
how your prophets strain against the hoops of his tyranny?

Master, Son of Zeus,
leave Olympus and come here, waving your golden thyrse.
Stop with death this Pentheus
whom only the shedding, the returning, of his blood to Earth

256

can quell.

Lord Bacchus,
where are you now?
among what god-driven maenad bands
are you whirling, throwing your thyrse and dancing?
Do you leap in Corycia from crag to crag?
Do you race through the lonely forests of Olympus
where Orpheus, they say,
sang to his harping
to lead the trees to dance love's circle all around him,
while with his music he tamed the savage hearts
of the beasts who roamed free there?

Holy Pieria,
Bacchus Evoi graces you.
There he treads out his dance,
leading his Bacchai and leaping
across the chasm Axios' current carves.
Where he goes, his women follow—
they spin for joy;
their white feet flash rings about him
over the Lydias, spendthrift father of rivers,
who's known everywhere for his fine water
that quenches perfectly
the thirst of thorough-bred horses—

(The Chorus is interrupted by Dionysos, who is shouting at the top of his lungs from inside the palace.)

DIONYSOS *(inside the palace)*:
  ió Bacchai ió !
  Hear me—listen: I shout—
  ió Bacchai ! ió Bacchai !

CHORUS *(confusedly)*:
  Who's that calling us?

Where's it coming from?
It's the voice of our Shouting Roaring Lord!

DIONYSOS *(inside the palace)*:
ió Bacchai ió !
I shout again—
I, son of Zeus, child of Semele.

CHORUS:
ió ! ió ! Lord! Lord!
Come join our dance.
Lord! Ranting Roaring Lord!

DIONYSOS *(inside the palace)*:
Now! Earth, dance quake—
break land's floor.

(An earthquake occurs; portions of the palace topple.)

CHORUS:
See— see—
Pentheus' palace dances, shakes,
falls to the ground.
Dionysos is here!
He is with us still.
Kneel! Worship! Adore!
Do! Yes, we do, we do!

Look—
great stones slip their pillars,
crash to the ground.
Our Shouting Lord cries: 'I've won!'

DIONYSOS *(inside the palace)*:
Seize lightning's smouldering flame.
Smear it over Pentheus' halls.

(Halos of light appear, outlining the palace and Semele's tomb.)

CHORUS:
Ha! Ha!
See in clearest light
fire circling Semele's tomb—
flame from Zeus Thunder King.
On your knees, maenads!
Fall to earth.
The God our Master comes
to turn upside down
the proud facades of Pentheus' House.

(The Chorus kneels and bows as Dionysos approaches them from the palace.)

DIONYSOS:
Sweet Ladies, were you so afraid
you hurled yourselves to earth?
You saw the palace dance and fall
when Bacchus called the tune.
Arise.
Put away your fears.

CHORUS LEADER:
Hail! grandest light of god who cries *evan! evoi!*
to our reeling feet.
We see you and we're glad.
Without you we were sad and lonely.
I hope we never part again.

DIONYSOS:
Did you lose heart,
thinking I'd give way to darkness,
once I entered Pentheus' pit?

CHORUS LEADER:
Yes, I'm sorry to say we did.
Our faith, our fate hung in the balance
and wavered . . .

If you failed—who would protect us?
Tell me:
how did you escape that godless fool?

DIONYSOS:
I did it all by myself.
It was so easy.

CHORUS LEADER:
But didn't I see
Pentheus lock
you up?

DIONYSOS:
Ha! That was just me playing a little joke on him.
I let him think he'd caught me good,
then I cheated his eyes:
he couldn't so much as touch me or fence me in.
Instead of me,
you know what he found in my cell?
A bull—yeah, that's right:
it was a bull's hooves and fetlocks
he hobbled, grinding his teeth he was so mad,
the sweat just pouring off him.
I sat down quietly beside him and watched.
Then our Bacchus came and shook the earth,
knocking down the palace, outlining
the surfaces of his mother's tomb
with instant flame. Pentheus, the fool,
thought his house was on fire.
He ran around in circles,
ordering his men to start a bucket brigade—
not that it made any difference: it didn't.
Then he stopped for a moment and realized
I might have escaped. Immediately
he drew his sword and rushed back to the palace—

just at the moment Thunder Bacchus appeared.
To me he looked like a ghost
that suddenly materialized out of thin air.
Again and again Pentheus stabbed and hacked away
at the sheath of beguiling light
without affecting it in the least.
So our Lord humbled his pride another notch:
he broke his palace, smashed it to earth.

Look at it now:
makes quite a picturesque ruin, doncha think?
Folks'll come from miles around
just to see it and be thunderstruck with amazement.
Lo, how the mighty have fallen, dear oh dear . . .

Eventually Pentheus got tired
playing swords with god—
it was a pretty one-sided contest anyway—
and fainted dead away.

Ya see what happens when a Dier
fights a deathless god?

Then I walked out calmly to you.

Pentheus? wal, right now
I wouldn't give ya a fig for him.

But—hold it . . . just a second—
I think I hear him coming.
Watcha think he'll hafta to say for himself now, hunh?

(Pentheus comes stumbling out of the palace, obviously dazed and distracted, but making an effort to pull himself together.)

PENTHEUS:
  Oh my god . . . what's going on? . . .
  what's happening to me . . . that, uh, that wizard fella

... got away ... thought ... thought ...
I ... bound him hand and foot ... oh no!
there he is again ... still hanging around ...
Hey you!
What're you doing in front of my House?

DIONYSOS:
Just stay where you are. And calm down.

PENTHEUS:
How'd you escape? I had you in chains.

DIONYSOS:
I told you—or weren't you listening:
'someone would rescue me.'

PENTHEUS:
Who'd you mean? Your words get stranger and stranger.

DIONYSOS:
I was referring to the god
who grows the grape for man.

PENTHEUS:
[You mean—that devil who drove away our women!]

DIONYSOS:
Remember when you talk like that,
it's Dionysos you're blaspheming.

PENTHEUS:
I'll—I'll—Soldiers!
Seal every gate in the city wall.
We'll catch him yet.

DIONYSOS:
Why bother? Gods can walk through walls, you know.

PENTHEUS:

You're so goddamned smart. You know everything
except what you're supposed to.

DIONYSOS:

I am wise where my wisdom does most good.

(A herdsman arrives from the hill country.)

But first let's listen to what this herdsman
has to tell us about what's going on
in the mountains. And don't worry.
I won't run away. I'll be right here
when you need me.

HERDSMAN:

Your Majesty, I've just come from Mount Cithairon
where the white snow's clear bolts never cease—

PENTHEUS:

Cut the crap. Get to the point.

HERDSMAN:

Majesty, I've seen the wild women at their Bacchanals.
You know who I mean: the ones who ran light-footed and barefoot
from your city. I thought you and the rest of Thebes
would want to know what strange, impossible things they do.

First promise: do I have your permission to speak
freely? I'm afraid of your suddenly shifting moods,
of how your royal displeasure can too quickly
execute its wrath.

PENTHEUS:

Speak as you like. You have my word there'll be no reprisals.
We kings are never angered by honest men.
This I vow: the more sinister and ugly

you report the goings-on at these Bacchanals,
the more pain I shall visit on their leader
who taught our women these foreign so-called 'rites.'

HERDSMAN:
   Just about dawn when the Sun sends down his light
   to give Earth his life, we started herding our cows
   up the usual way to the mountain pastures
   where the grass'd be new and fresh. Suddenly
   I saw three bands of women dancing. Each was led
   by one of the Royal Princesses: Ino, Autonoe and Agave.
   Moments later they stopped—they looked so tired
   as if they'd been dancing all night. They just lay down
   and went right to sleep—some on beds of pine needles,
   the rest wherever they happened to fall—
   usually it was on oak leaves. Nicely dressed they were—
   their bodies fully clothed. They weren't acting like drunken sluts,
   their bellies full of wine, the way some people say, oh no.
   Weren't shaking their hips, or belly dancing either,
   seduced by forest flutes into chasing Aphrodite's pleasures
   in some nice woodsy spot—naw, that wasn't their game at all.

   Agave musta heard our cows mooing or sumpin.
   She jumped to her feet real quick and started shouting.
   That woke up the other girls. They rubbed the sand
   out of their eyes and looked all around. Lissome and straight
   they stood, stretching their arms and legs. Oh, wasn't that
   a sight for sore eyes! Then just like they were all one person,
   they all started letting their hair down: young and old,
   married and single. They let it fall loosely over their shoulders.
   The ones whose fawn skins had come undone tied them back
   together with real snakes: yep, that's right—I saw them
   wriggling and twisting in their hands. About these snakes, now:
   I watched some of them slither right up a coupla girls' necks
   and kiss them on the cheek. I also saw young mothers, their breasts

264

so full of milk it was trickling off their nipples in white tiny streams
(they musta left their little babies at home, I guess), that they
cradled gazelles in their laps, just so's they could give them
their tits to nuzzle. Other girls were weaving themselves crowns
for their hair out of ivy, oak and briony flower. I actually watched
one lady drive her thyrse straight down into a rock: out spouted
a fountain of live, bubbling water. Another one—she pushed
a fennel stalk into the earth. And where she did, all at once,
at god's stroke, a small gusher of red wine shot up. Any woman
who wanted milk—well, all she hadda do was scrabble at a patch
of loose ground with her bare hands and guess what? white milk came
like a spring and filled her cupped hands. Endless streams of
clear liquid crystal honey spilled like fine spun amber threads
from their wands. You should have been there yourself, Majesty,
and seen these miracles in person. You'd have sunk down
on your knees and prayed to the god you say does not exist.

Us—well, we're just poor cowboys and shepherds.
What do we know, anyway? We were standing around in twos
      and threes,
arguing, talking about this and that we'd just seen—about what
these women were doing. Looked to us more like the stuff dreams
are made of than what you see in ordinary, every-day life—
the witch-work, the marvels these Bacchai were performing routinely:
when up comes some city feller who sure had a way with words.
He said something like this—oh really pitching it to us, he was:
'Listen, boys, how'd you like to do something that'd make King
      Pentheus
happy—and pick up a little extra cash at the same time? Here's how:
he wants his mother to cut out all this Bacchus business. So why
      don't we
chase her out of the hills and right back to town? We'll just,
      as you say,
break her loose from the rest of the herd. Well, what do you think?
Is it a deal?' I dunno—but it seemed like a good idea at the time.

So we hid in the forest, burying ourselves in leaves, and waited
for the women to show up. We didn't have to wait very long. All
    of a sudden,
they started spinning their wands and dancing real fast. Yeah,
no doubt about it: their wild orgies were starting up again. All
    together,
they shouted: *'Iacchus! Zeus' Son! Bromius!'* 'til every living thing
and all the hills rang with the sound of god. The Bacchai began
    running—
so did everything else, creating a panic, a total rout, you might say,
    sir.
Agave loped past where I was hiding. I jumped and tried to tackle her.
But she screamed: 'Maenads, bitch-women, all who roam with me:
    help!·
Men use us for their game! Come! Come with me! Beat them with
    your thyrses!'
What else could we do? We ran away. They nearly tore us to bits—
although they didn't have any other weapons but their hands
and those damned sticks. Next they took off after our herds
that were up there in the pastures. And this is what I saw, so help me:
one woman, bare-handed, ripped open a big, fat calf while it screamed
    out
its life. Others tore apart whole heifers. Everywhere I looked,
I saw the ground covered with bits of fur, bones, guts, hooves,
I don't know what-all. Chunks of meat, dripping blood, dangled
from the fir trees. Our bulls lowered their horns, like they was gonna
charge—but the women got them first. They wrestled them to
    the ground,
then yanked them to pieces. Yeah, that's right, King Pentheus,
they'd peel the hide and strip the meat off an animal quicker'en
    a wink.
That's fer a fact, sir, a fact. By now they were really going at it
hard and heavy. They fanned out and swarmed like the biggest
    flock of birds
I ever saw, wiping out all those big farms down by the Asopus
    River: y'know

266

where the soil is thickest and blackest. Then like a regular army
    they hit
Hysiai and Erythrai, two little villages in the foothills of Cithairon:
smushed them up good, they did. Everything they saw they stripped,
    wrecked
or robbed: why, they even grabbed little children right out of their
    homes.
They stuck all this stuff on their backs and carried it away with them
when they ran back into the hills—without using so much as a piece
of twine to tie it on. And naturally they didn't lose a bit of it;
nothing made of iron or bronze fell off even one of their backs. Fire
jumped and sparked from the curls in their hair—but were they singed
one bit? nossiree, bub! Those poor people in the towns: you can
    imagine
how they felt. They went right for their weapons. Then, Majesty,
    something
so horrible happened I wish I could make my eyes unsee it but, no,
    I can't.
The spears the men threw or tried to jab the women with, didn't hurt
them one bit. Seemed like the Bacchai's flesh was made of hard rubber
or toughened leather: spear points just slid or bounced right off them.
They were practically invulnerable. But when the maenads turned
their thyrses on the men, they went straight through those fellows
like they was made of fresh butter. They cut them up something
    horrible.
That's how the women beat the men today. Now I say a god musta
    been there
all the time with them. Ain't no other way ta account for it. Anyways,
them Bacchai's gone back up Cithairon where they were before when
    we first
started watching them. Right now they must still be there, sitting down
beside those enchanted pools of water and wine, milk and honey
    their god'd
made for them, and washing up. Last I saw of them those snakes
    that'd been

267

in their hair all along was lickin away the hard, caked-on blood
that was still clinging to their cheeks like some funny kinda rouge.

Now, Your Majesty, I don't say I know
which god it was, or even if he has a name yet,
but whoever he is, let him in,
make him feel at home in Thebes.
He's got to be strong and great
and considerin what I saw today,
he must be able to do lotsa other things
we still don't know about.
But I do know for sure
he's the god who gave us Diers
the gift of wine to somehow see us through our troubles—
which, as you know—or oughta, never seem to end.
Besides, if we didn't have wine,
how're we gonna make love?
An iffen you can't drink or fuck,
what'd there be left to live for, hunh, bub—
you tell me?

(Pentheus dismisses the herdsman with a curt nod.)

CHORUS LEADER:
I am afraid in front of this tyrant king
to speak freely. But I shall anyway:
I will conquer my fears,
raise my voice,
shout it aloud:
'there is no god born less great than Dionysos!'

CHORUS:
Yes! Yes! he is! . . . there is no one else!
. . . he lives! he lives! . . . he is here now!

PENTHEUS:
So: that's how he operates:

268

first a tiny spark . . .
soon the whole forest's burning . . .

What these Bacchai are up to
will make us the shame,
the laughingstock of Greece.

(to the palace guards)

Men! we've got to act fast.
No time to waste!

You—go to Electra's Gate:
assemble the infantry,
call out the cavalry,
round up the slingers,
find me some archers:
we're marching on the Bacchai.
A fight they want—
a fight they'll get!
Lawless bitches—
no more Mr. Nice Guy—
time to stop being soft—
and indulging their fool antics any further—
the buck stops here—

DIONYSOS:
    Pentheus, you've heard every word I've said,
yet you won't budge an inch.
You're still trying to make me jump
through your quibbling hoops.
I warn you again:
do not declare war on god.
Stay here. Sit on your hands if you have to.
Bromius Thunder Lord
will not permit you
to chase his maenads

from the hills,
for there they perform
his essential dance.

PENTHEUS:

Oh shut up—
stop lecturing me like I was still a kid.
Just be glad you gave my chains the slip.
Watch out: if I did it once,
I can easily do it again.

DIONYSOS:

Give this new god gifts.
Feed him with sacrifice.
Don't kick against the pricks.
Man: don't fight god.

PENTHEUS:

So it's sacrifices you people want, hunh?
I'll make some sacrifices for you.
I'm gonna kill those women up there on Cithairon
and tell everybody I did it to honor Dionysos.

DIONYSOS:

They'll rout you, you know;
their thyrses beat down
your brazen shields.
You'll die the way
those villagers did.

PENTHEUS:

Why're we standing around,
wasting precious time
arguing with this nobody?
Nothing we do or say
seems to shut him up.

DIONYSOS:

Listen, friend—

there's still a way
we can all come out of this,
smelling like roses.

PENTHEUS:

Oh yeah—how?
by my becoming my slave girls' friend?
You must be out of your mind.

DIONYSOS:

I'll go up into the hills
all by myself and,
without using force,
bring your women back.

PENTHEUS:

Hey—that's smart, ya know, real smart.
Even I can smell a rat.

DIONYSOS:

No, no—this isn't a game: it never was.
I'm not trying to trick you—but save you,
if that's still possible,
by using my brains, not my fists.

PENTHEUS:

You've made some kind of deal,
haven't you, with our women—
to keep them up there partying forever?

DIONYSOS:

The only bargain I've ever struck
is with my god.

PENTHEUS:

Guards! my armor and sword.

(to Dionysos)

You—not one more peep out of you, hear!

DIONYSOS:
  Hey hey hey!
  How about this:
  how'd *you* like to go up there
  and see for yourself
  what they're doing . . .

PENTHEUS *(dreamily—as if starting to go into a trance)*:
  Ohhhh—yessss . . . for that
  I'd pay gold beyond telling . . .

DIONYSOS:
  Now what would you
  specially like to see?

PENTHEUS:
  If they're drunk!
  That'd make me so mad
  you wouldn't recognize me.

DIONYSOS:
  Lemme see if I got this straight:
  it'd make you genuinely happy
  to see something guaranteed to make you sad?

PENTHEUS:
  Yes! Yes!
  I wanna go creeping, crawling up there,
  quiet as a mouse and watch them,
  hiding unseen under the pines

DIONYSOS:
  No matter how little noise you make,
  they'd still hear and track you down.

PENTHEUS:
  Well, what's a guy supposed to do?
  just stand out in the open and watch?

DIONYSOS:

Guess so. Want me to take you there?

PENTHEUS:

Right—fast as we can!
Lolling around, jawing like this,
when I wanna be up and doing
makes me get all edgy.

DIONYSOS:

There're a couple of things you've to do
before we go. First, you have to wear
a long, white, diaphanous shift
spun of finest linen.

PENTHEUS:

How's that?
Am I going to turn into a woman?

DIONYSOS:

Listen—they see you up there
looking like a man,
they'll probly kill you.

PENTHEUS:

Awright already—
you maneuver me around with words
as if you're used to doing it
all your life.

DIONYSOS:

Whatever I know and do
Dionysos taught me.

PENTHEUS:

Now how're we going to translate
your words into deeds?

DIONYSOS:
Let me into the palace,
I'll dress you myself.

PENTHEUS:
In what? A dress?! Jeezus—
what if somebody sees me like that?

DIONYSOS:
You wanna see the maenads dance or not?

PENTHEUS *(sighing):*
O—kay . . . once more:
what am I supposed to wear?

DIONYSOS:
First I'll fix you up with a perfectly divine wig
with long, honey blonde curls.

PENTHEUS:
Then?

DIONYSOS:
You'll put on one of those ankle-length shifts
we've been talking about—next I'll fit
a cute little tiara on your head.

PENTHEUS:
That's it?

DIONYSOS:
Not quite: you'll have to drape a dappled fawn skin
over your shoulders and carry a thyrse.

PENTHEUS:
I just don't know if I can bring myself
to dress like a girl.

DIONYSOS:
Do it your way, then—the stupid way.

Call out the troops. Butcher your women

PENTHEUS:

Afraid you're right again—as usual.
It *is* up to me—it's my civic duty
to go up there first and spy on them.

DIONYSOS:

Yes, indeed. And it shows you're using your head.
Two wrongs don't make a right.

PENTHEUS:

But—how're we going to leave Thebes
without anyone seeing us?

DIONYSOS:

Leave that to me.
We'll take the backstreets and the alleys
I'll go first and make sure
the coast is clear.

PENTHEUS:

Right—you take care of little details like that.

(He points at the Asian Bacchai.)

But I don't want one of those dumb cunts over there
laughing at me.
Anything's better than that!

DIONYSOS:

A—men, brother. Now doncha worry about them:
They'll do whatever I tell 'em to.
Remember: whatever you decide, I'll be here,
ready, willing and able.

PENTHEUS:

Right! I'll either assemble the army
and march on the women
or . . . er, do as you suggest.

275

(With a surreptitious wink at Dionysos, Pentheus returns to the palace.)

DIONYSOS *(capering around joyfully):*
We've got him, girls: he's ours!
Oh, the fun we're gonna have,
watching him try to wiggle his way
out of the webs we've woven for him!
And to think all the while
he thought he was setting a trap for me.
Too bad he won't be around long enough
to appreciate the humor of it.
For, yes, indeed the moment's come
we've all been waiting for:
when Pentheus finds the Bacchai
and the Bacchai find Pentheus
and Pentheus finds Death ready and waiting for him.

Now we're gonna settle some old scores.

Hey, girls! how'd ya like the recipe for killing a king?
Goes like this:
first, stir until howling mad;
shake thoroughly for a coupla minutes;
then, bake in his own juices until done—oh, rarely done!
Garnish in skirts;
stick a sprig of ivy on top;
serve to his women piping hot and bubbling over.
Now that's a gourmet-treat sure to tickle his mumsie-poo's dainty
    palate.

Yes, Pentheus, put on that fine, long robe,
and while you're at it, be sure you remove your mind—
you won't be needing it anymore.

I'll make you the standing joke of Thebes:

(going into a high, adoring falsetto)

'All Hail to Thee!
Thy Closet Majesty,
My Most Seductive Monarch!'

There: that's for all those icky, nasty cracks
he made about you, my mother, and me.

Well, girls, I'll have to leave now
to go back to the palace
and do my duty as wardrobe mistress.
Wouldn't be right for Pentheus
to take up lodgings in Death's House
unsuitably clothed, ha! would it now?

Once his mother's finished with him, I'm positive
he'll confess I am Dionysos God Arisen Son of Zeus,
Fiercest and Gentlest to all!

(Dionysos enters the palace.)

CHORUS:
Shall I dance all night?
Once more,
my feet gleaming in moonlight,
gliding through those endless joys our god's dream brings?
tossing my head back and forth,
up and down,
while night dew falls?

I will be like that faun that lights for an instant,
then is gone,
who finds sweet delight in green fields,
now that she's out-run her hunters,
leapt over those who beat the grass in vain for her
and jumped high above the nets
they strung across her path to bring her down:
she will no longer be their game.

Hunters can shout on their baying hounds

until both burst their lungs:
I will be like that faun
who drives herself still faster, further, outstripping thought,
until she breaks cleanly away from her pursuers,
running swifter than storming wind,
pattering, bounding across marsh, prairie, river,
until I can hide, panting softly beneath the forest's branches,
containing myself in stillness in dim light under leaves
that hang down like my hair when I let it fall freely.
I shall be happy here
because no man will dare violate this—
my quiet shadowed retreat.

What is wiser or more lovely,
what greater honor can the gods give,
than to stretch out our hands in victory
over those who hate us?
This is a gift lasting forever.

Slowly, steadily,
gods' strength prevails,
breaking all who dishonor divinity,
all who brag they're free of god,
who say there's no need to believe.
Gods hide in subtle thickets,
waiting to ambush the hunters
who've now become the hunted!
Time's foot presses on,
tracking down the godless
until there's no place left them
to cover their shame with.

We have not gone, we will not go,
beyond those laws custom makes second nature to us.
This costs us nothing
while our reverence strengthens law.

God is strength; usages of time
our eternal law,
what age hands down to age,
nature embeds in us as our souls' bent.
What is wiser or more lovely,
what greater honor can the gods give,
than to stretch out our hands in victory
over those who hate us?
This is a gift lasting forever.

You that escape the unrepentant sea,
sail under a kindly spirit:
you know the happiness the gods provide those
who've passed their lives untouched, unhurt.
Everyone wants strength and riches his way and no one else's.
A thousand hopes are answered a thousand separate ways.
In their strivings only a handful find happiness.
Most discover despair greets their journey's end.
But the happiest meet with joy every hour they are alive
and eternal delight crowns their day.

(Dionysos re-appears from the palace.)

DIONYSOS:
Ah, Pentheus, you fool—you fanatical, puritanical fool!
still burning, aren't you, to behold the forbidden.

*(Dionysos makes a pretense of looking all around. Then he hollers
back at Pentheus, who is peeping out nervously from behind the palace
gates.)*

Hey—it's alright—no one's looking.
You can come out now if you want.

*(Pentheus, nervously and hesitantly, leaves the palace and approaches
Dionysos. He is dressed like a bacchant exactly like Dionysos. In fact
they bear such a close physical resemblance they might almost be taken*

for twins. Pentheus moves awkwardly, tripping over his robes, acting as if he's more than just a bit tipsy. He also has trouble focusing his eyes and watching where he's going.)

That's it, Your Majesty . . . you're getting the hang of it all right
. . . now sashay back and forth in front of the palace—I want to get
a good look at you from every angle . . . yes . . . yes . . . hold it
. . . just a moment . . . hold that pose—don't even blink!
There, girls—whaddayah think?
If that isn't the cutest bacchant I ever laid eyes on,
why—I'll eat my thyrse!
Ummm-ummm! Pentheus—what a perfeck lil lady you've become!

Now—all set to go spying on your mother and her friends?

Lass, Ah declahr—if'n Cahmus udda hahd hisself ahnudder dawter,
she'da lukt jes lahk yew dew naow . . .
kitchy-koo—sweet stuff—itchy-kitchy-koo!

(Dionysos makes a mock pass at Pentheus and pinches him playfully on the cheek.)

PENTHEUS *(still groping and stumbling about, his speech slurred):*
Oh . . . oh . . . I think . . . I see . . . two suns shining today.
Thebes—why, Thebes, my seven-gated city—
you're really two cities, no?

(looking at Dionysos)

Friend, you look just like a bull!
Jeez—are those really horns on your head?
Say, you always been an animal—
cuz that's what you are now.

DIONYSOS:
Dionysos himself walks with us.
Before, when he was angry,
he wouldn't let you see him.

Now that he's composed himself—
behold him as he really is.

PENTHEUS:
How do I look?
like Ino? or my mother?

DIONYSOS:
I see both of those gracious ladies
charmingly combined in you.
Unh-oh: what's this? a curl out of place?
Let me fix it. There—how's that? Better?

(Dionysos playfully re-arranges Pentheus' wig.)

And to think I did your hair myself.
Well, it just goes to show you: nobody's perfect.
Oh, darling, if you could only see yourself:
how perfectly divine you look!

PENTHEUS *(patting his hair back into place):*
Guess I must of messed it up,
dancing and twirling for Bacchus.

DIONYSOS:
No harm done. Now just remember:
let me take care of everything.

PENTHEUS:
Right: I put myself entirely in your hands.

DIONYSOS:
I won't let you down.
Hold still a moment: these straps need tightening.
The dress doesn't quite hang right.

PENTHEUS:
Yeah, it droops some on the left;
looks ok, though, on the other side.

DIONYSOS:

Once you see how sober and decorous
the Bacchai really are, you'll tell
everybody I was the best friend you ever had.

PENTHEUS:

Now in which hand would a real bacchant
hold her thyrse: left or right?

DIONYSOS:

With the right.
So that when you lift your right foot
to dance the Dithyramb,
you can raise the thyrse and keep time with it.
Watch—you go like this:

(Dionysos shows him how to dance the Dithyramb in slow motion.)

Oh, whenever someone new decides to join our little fold,
it positively makes my heart skip a beat for joy.

PENTHEUS:

You think I'm strong enough now
to lift up Cithairon and put it on my shoulders
while maenads're still dancing on it?

DIONYSOS:

Why, of course you can! If you want to.
You see, up 'til now,
your soul was cramped, warped out of shape,
but now that you've seen the light,
its natural balance has returned
and so, sure of yourself,
there's no limit to what you can do.

PENTHEUS:

Maybe I should get a good strong lever
and pry up the mountain . . .

or I could always just use my hands
and lift it that way,
wedging an arm or shoulder underneath . . .

PENTHEUS:

Why do you want to do it in the first place
and destroy those lovely places where the nymphs live,
those soft groves that ring so sweetly
when Pan blows his pipes?

PENTHEUS:

Yeah, that's right. And besides,
we don't want to use force on the women.
Wait—I know what to do:
I'll just hide behind a pine tree.

DIONYSOS *(semi-aside):*

Hide all you want:
no matter where you are,
going up there to spy on my Bacchanals,
Death will still discover you.

PENTHEUS:

In my mind's eye I can see them already: the Bacchai
like love-birds twined in nests of sweet delight.

DIONYSOS:

That's why the god has chosen you to watch:
could be you'll catch them at it . . .

(semi-aside)

Unless, that is, they catch you first.

PENTHEUS:

Guide me invisibly through Thebes.
I'm the one real man left in this town of sissies
with enough guts to risk going up there.

DIONYSOS:
Yes: you and you alone work and suffer for Thebes.
Agony and ordeal await you—
the man on whom Destiny depends.
Follow me. I'll get you there all right.
But someone else will bring you home.

PENTHEUS:
You mean my mother, don't you?

DIONYSOS:
Yes, I did.
How'd you figure that out?!
And what's more—
she'll make you an example to everyone in this town.

PENTHEUS:
That's why I'm dying to go—

DIONYSOS:
—so you can return,
head held high—

PENTHEUS:
—raised in splendor?

DIONYSOS:
Yes! Lifted aloft in your mother's arms
like a splendid banner!

PENTHEUS:
You mean—you'd actually
give me all *this*!

DIONYSOS:
And *more*! Such pleasures—

PENTHEUS:
Yes, yes—I know:

are no more than I deserve.

It's plain to see,
you are no ordinary man.
What you go now to experience
will be as awesome and extraordinary as you.
In the end you will find your glory
mounting high beyond the stars' roof.

(Almost totally in a daze, Pentheus leaves for the mountains.)

Agave, Ino, Autonoe,
daughters of Cadmus:
be my instruments,
use your hands well for me.
I send this wilful boy
to contend with you
until death do you part.
I will win,
Bromius triumph.
The rest
time will disclose.

(Dionysos hurries out to catch up with Pentheus.)

CHORUS:
Up! bitch dog devils who drive men mad—
go into the forests on the hills
where Cadmus' daughters dance for god:
bite! chew! tear! rend!
that fool in woman's clothes
who comes to spy on you and your Bacchanals.

How madness races through him now:
his mother will be the first to see him—
either on some rock the wind has scoured
or on a tree bent back by storm—

where he'll be peeping, peering.
What Agave shouts
the sky will amplify:
'who goes there?
who walks this mountain trail
to watch Cadmus' girls
and the choruses they each lead,
flashing as they fly across these rough stones?
Tell me, I must know, what kind of mother
tendered his seed deep within her body,
for I think no woman took part in his spawning;
he must be brood of lioness who stalks the jungle
or some mutant those devils, the Libyan Gorgons, hatched.'

Justice, we need you here.
Come, unsheath your sword, avenge us:
slay this godless, god-cursed child of Echion Earth gave birth to.
Tear out his throat.
He has no fear of god or law.
Though we were all born to die,
we shall live and not weep,
if we keep our souls attuned to the gods,
moving swiftly to comply with their commands
without whining or whimpering.
It does not lie within us
to press our luck
beyond the limits the gods have drawn,
or force a passage
past that death
destiny has appointed each of us.

I will not be wise beyond my days.
My choice remains what it's always been:
to achieve that wisdom which then becomes my fate.

I seek, I search, I am
a huntress of righteous joy—

for a flash of that sure knowledge
that beams down to me
from the gods' eternal, brilliant day:
to give my life's flux form and plan,
making me sacred and unblemished,
allowing me to choose
what those who would walk with the gods
have traditionally chosen.
From life's dawning to the evening of my years
I will honor the gods
in the ways they require.
I refuse to go by that road
that brings me in harm's way
to evil and devious act.

Justice, we need you here.
Come, unsheath your sword, avenge:
slay this godless, god-cursed child of Echion Earth gave birth to.
Tear out his throat.
He has no fear of god or law.

Dionysos, the hour of your Epiphany strikes.
Come to us in bull's body.
Bring your dragon coils that bear a thousand heads.
Appear before us a lion rampant in sheath of glowering flame.
Bacchus, come—
laugh at this king who hunts your Bacchai.
Lay your chains on him.
Surrender this mighty hunter to us, your maenad girls,
and so let him discover he ends
our quarry and your game.

(A messenger arrives from Mount Cithairon.)

MESSENGER:

Weep for the ancient House of Cadmus all Greece knew
for its great fortune and still greater luck!

Weep for this noble family
Cadmus, patriarch of Sidon, founded
when he planted dragon's teeth in that same serpent's soil.
Listen—and you will understand my tears.
Although I am only a slave,
what has overwhelmed my master,
touches my heart's core
and will do the same, I think,
to the heart of every slave of this once-great clan.

CHORUS LEADER:
What's happened?
Anything to do with our Bacchai?

MESSENGER:
Pentheus's dead! Echions's son is gone!

CHORUS LEADER *(chanting melodiously):*
Bromius Thunder Lord!
You showed them what it means to be god!

MESSENGER:
How dare you sing, woman—
because my master's dead!
Death makes you shout for joy?

CHORUS LEADER:
I'm not from here—this isn't my home.
I was singing a happy song of my people
because now I don't need to fear
your dead king's chains.

MESSENGER:
You think there aren't enough men left in Thebes
[to take care of noisy sluts like you?]

CHORUS LEADER:
Dionysos, Lord of the Vine:

288

he is my King—no one else.

MESSENGER:
I could forgive what you've said—
except it's not right
to take such blatant pleasure
in other people's misfortunes.

CHORUS LEADER:
How did he die?
that fool who left here
with evil in his heart . . .

MESSENGER:
There were just the three of us
who went up into the mountains:
Pentheus, myself and the foreign priest
who was supposed to guide us.
We'd made our way past the outlying farms
and had forded the Asopus,
we were just starting to climb
the withered wastes at the bottom of Cithairon
when we stopped for a moment
in a little stand of trees
where the grass'd barely begun to come out.
We didn't move or say a word.
We wanted to watch without being watched.
Then we saw what looked like the ideal spot:
a small cave cut into a sheer cliff face.
There was a small water fall in front;
below it the pines grew so thick
you couldn't tell which branch
went with which tree.
Shadows completely enclosed the area.
From there we watched the maenads
who were sitting down, happily keeping busy
doing various sorts of things.

Some were wrapping fresh ivy around their battered wands;
others danced, kicking up their heels
like fillies that'd just been unharnessed.
All were singing hymns to Bacchus in antiphony.
But for Pentheus, poor fool that he was,
this wasn't good enough. He had to get closer.
He told the stranger: 'from here
I can't quite make out what those fake maenads
are up to. I'd like to climb that tall pine down there
that hangs over the river. Then I'd get a better look
at the degenerate filth that're these women's stock in trade.'

Then that strange priest did something—
I'm not exactly sure what or how—
but he reached up and grabbed the highest branch
of that big pine tree and bent it all the way down
until it touched the dark ground.
He'd arched it like a bow strung taut
or a wheel rim forced to curve around an axle pole.
Yeah, that's what he did—don't ask me to explain.
He made the top of that pine tree bow down to earth.
I don't think any of us could've done it.
Then he told Pentheus to sit right on top of the topmost tip
of that tree. And very slowly, very carefully,
using his hands just right,
he let that tree rise up again just like it was before
without Pentheus losing his balance.
The pine shot up gently, almost brushing the sky—
our king holding on right at the top.
Then the maenads saw him—
saw him more clearly than he saw them.
And the next thing I knew the stranger'd disappeared!
We heard a giant voice bellowing from the sky—
it could only have been Bacchus.
'Girls!' he said, 'here he is. He's all yours:
this man who played his little games with you and me,

who thought our religion was just for his private amusement.
You know what to do. Do it!' He spoke.
A pillar of fire, writhing like a snake, united heaven and earth.
The upper air grew still.
The leaves in the forest ceased their whisperings.
Animals hushed. A great silence fell.
The Bacchai'd heard this huge voice.
The meaning of the words escaped them.
They jumped to their feet
and looked around:
The voice shouted once more.
Now they understood.
What the god wanted from them came clear.
They broke like pigeons rousted from their perches,
they ran through the woods, waded through creeks,
clambered over edged boulders, charged—
the god's wind breath flaming at their feet,
driving them mad.

Soon as they saw my lord sitting on that tree,
they scampered up a cliff that went as high as where he perched.
They started throwing stones and pine wood spears at him;
some hurled their thyrses.
Every one of them missed.
Poor Pentheus in that cat bird seat of his held on for dear life,
keeping just out of range of their weapons.
But treed like a 'coon he'd no hope of his ever getting away from
    them.
Finally they ripped thick branches off oaks.
Using them for levers, they tore away the roots,
trying to topple that pine.
That didn't work either.
So Agave shouted: 'girls! join hands, let's make a ring around this
    tree.
Hold on tight right up against the bark.
We've got to kill this slithery thing now—

or you know what he'll do:
tell everybody our god's Secrets!'
That did it. Thousands of hands gripped the tree, shook it,
tore it out by the roots from earth.
And so down, down Pentheus tumbled
from his high chair back to the ground,
weeping, screaming as he fell.
He knew he was dead before he died.
His mother, now high priestess,
poised for a moment over her victim—
then was the first to grab him.
Pentheus tore off his wig and hair net
and tried to hold his mother by the cheeks,
so she'd get a close look at him
and recognize her son. He shouted:
'No, mother, no! It's me, Pentheus!
Your son! whom you bore for Echion!
Stop! Don't! Please, mother! I was wrong!
Wrong! I know now! But don't kill me for it!'
Too late: she was already foaming at the mouth.
Her eyes went white. They rolled back into her head.
Bacchus owned her. His madness was hers.
She couldn't hear a word her son said.
She took hold of his left wrist,
planted one foot firmly against his left shoulder
and gave a good yank. Out popped his whole arm.
right down to the arm pit. She wasn't strong enough
to do this by herself. Bacchus had lent her
divine strength. Ino was next in line:
she ripped out chunks of his meat by the hand-full
from the right side of his body.
Then Autonoe and the rest of the maenads went to work.
They finished the job.
god! the screams . . .
He didn't stop screaming and yelling

292

until he'd exhausted all the breath in his body.
The Bacchai kept on singing and chanting at the top of their voices.
They never stopped.
For them it was a great victory.
One wrenched out the other arm;
another pulled off a foot.
His face showed the pain, the agonies they were putting him through.
He lived long enough to see them gnaw and suck
the flesh right off his ribs until they were long, white, clean sticks.
Their hands were slippery, slimy with blood.
They played catch with the tatters of his corpse.

What's left of Pentheus
is scattered everywhichway;
some of him's crammed between rocks
or loosely covered by dead leaves.

Agave picked up the head
and stuck it on the tip of her thyrse.
She wants to think it's a cougar's head
she's parading triumphantly through the forest.
She's left her maenad sisters who're still up there dancing.
She's headed this way to show everybody what she caught.
She brags what a grand trophy that head,
once properly mounted,
will make up on the palace roof.
Right now she's calling for Bacchus, her fellow hunter.
She says things like: 'Dionysos hunts with me:
see how lucky we were.
Look what I've caught—
thanks to him.'
All she's won,
all she brings home,
is grief.

Before she arrives,

I intend to be gone.

Bow down: honor whatever Sons the Sky sends down.
Do that, knowing there's nothing more or better,
we who are slated to die,
can do to please the gods and their Children.
This is wisest and best.

(The messenger leaves.)

CHORUS:
Dance!—Dance!—Dance!
for our Lord who Roars Shouts Screams

Fallen!—Fallen!—Fallen
the king
who rose from serpent fang:
whom dragon's blood made live—
The king who hid in women's clothes
is dead!
The king whose hand held the bacchant's wand
is dead!
The king who wound ivy around the thyrse
is dead!
These are the crimes that killed him!

eván! evói!

The king the Bull made a fool of
died!
The Bull who lead him up the mountain
gored him and
he died!
Led by the Bull straight down Death's pocket,
Yes! he died!

eván! evói!

You: women of god,

294

daughters of Cadmus,
have slain your king.

How nice to win—
how lovely, nice, and sweet it is to win!
What a change—
what a fine difference winning, killing makes!
    how lovely,
    nice and sweet
    it feels
    to kill a king!

        eván! evói!

What you have won
will make you weep—
your tears fall—

grand game! good hunting! fine sport!

His mother holds
her son's head—
she dips her fingers
in his blood—

grand game! good hunting! fine sport!

        eván! evói!

Agave's running here—
I see her coming—
her eyes are rolled back up into her head—
her eyes are white and blank—
she stares—
she does not want to see—

Dance!—Dance!—Dance!
    for our Lord who Roars Shouts Screams

(Screaming, Agave runs into the middle of the Chorus of Asian Bacchai, with Pentheus' head impaled on her thyrse, which she holds as high as she can.)

AGAVE:
Asian Bacchai!

CHORUS LEADER:
Why arouse us further
for the Lord we share?

AGAVE:
See what I brought from the mountain?
See this ivy clump
I cut to hang in the palace?

CHORUS LEADER:
Yes!
Now dance—
dance with us!

AGAVE:
I caught him—
I killed him all by myself—
look at this lion cub
I killed bare-handed!

CHORUS LEADER:
Where did you do it?
In what wild wood?

AGAVE:
On Cithairon—

CHORUS LEADER:
Why there?

AGAVE:
—I killed it!

CHORUS LEADER:
And who struck first?

AGAVE:
Me! Me! The honor's mine!
As they danced and whirled,
my friends cried:
'Happy, lucky Agave!'

CHORUS LEADER:
Who else came in for the kill?

AGAVE:
My sisters—
they hit him hit him hit him.
'Good hunting!' they said.
Now eat eat eat eat—
Share with us!

CHORUS LEADER:
Share what?

AGAVE:
Why—this sweet, juicy cub.
Look—
see the soft down feathering his cheeks—
look at his fine golden mane.

CHORUS LEADER:
Yeah, by the hair
I can tell
he must be some wild thing from the forest.

AGAVE:
We sprang to the chase—
we ran him down smartly—
just as our wise god ordered.

CHORUS LEADER:
Yea, a mighty hunter is our Lord Bacchus.

AGAVE:
　Then—you approve?

CHORUS LEADER:
　Of course. What else?

AGAVE:
　Soon the sons of Cadmus—

CHORUS LEADER:
　—including your son, Pentheus?

AGAVE:
　Yes! Yes!
　They'll all approve what I've done.
　My boy especially'll be proud
　his mother caught and killed
　a lion's son.

CHORUS LEADER:
　What a magnificent catch!

CHORUS LEADER:
　So you're glad?

AGAVE:
　Oh—glad glad glad—
　how glad you don't know
　it makes me to show the whole world—

CHORUS LEADER:
　Then, creature of sorrows—
　show the Thebans
　what you killed in the mountains.

AGAVE:
　My people!
　Come and see for yourselves what wild thing
　we, the daughters of Cadmus,

tracked down and slew—
barehanded—
no spears—
no nets—
just with our delicate, white lady fingers!
Is there one man among you
who dares say the same—
that he can catch his game
then shred it limb from limb
without using knife or spear?
Well—is there? Is there?

(Agave exhibits the head to the Chorus, the palace guards and a crowd of Thebans attracted by all the commotion. Once they realize whose head it is, they turn away and cover their heads. At this point, Cadmus returns, with slaves carrying the rest of Pentheus' body on a covered stretcher.)

Father—come and see what I've got!
Pentheus, you too!
And bring a ladder, someone, will you?
I'm going to climb up and nail this lion's head
on our palace roof.

CADMUS *(to the slaves):*
Follow me into the palace.
Bring Pentheus' remains with you.

(Cadmus now addresses the Thebans and the Chorus.)

We searched up and down the mountain sides
for this body's broken fragments.
We found no two in any one place,
because the women had scattered him
all over that impenetrable forest.
Yes—I heard what my daughters did,
just as Teiresias and I were coming back
from dancing with the god. At the city gate

I turned around and went back up the mountain
to retrieve what I could of my grandson.
In the oak glades I saw Actaeon's mother,
Autonoe, and her sister, Ino, still jerking
their bodies in time to the divine music.
One girl said she saw Agave dancing her way here.
So I followed: and I heard what I wish I hadn't.
Then I saw her and knew what I'd heard was true.
All that was left of my happiness simply melted away.

AGAVE:
Daddy, tell the world!
Make it your proudest boast:
about what strong, good, brave daughters you have—
each of us—but me, most of all.
Tell them how I left loom and shuttle
to do high deed—to hunt lions and tigers weaponless
with only these small hands.
I bring you proof: see this head
I'll mount as a trophy on our roof.
Here—you take it

(She lowers her thyrse and offers him Pentheus' head.)

and share with me my kill
and the honor it confers on us all.
Hey—I know what:
let's have a big party tonight—
invite all our friends
so they can see how happy I've made you:
how happy all your girls—

CADMUS:
Is there any end of grief in this world!
This tears out my eyes.
Woman—you have murdered your son!
Now you want to give the gods
his noble corpse? and summon

300

all Thebes to our house
to dine on what you've killed?
Ye gods—this surpasses belief!
Agave, dear child, my heart goes out
first to you, then to me.
Girl, do you see the justice of it:
a god, blood of our blood, flesh of our flesh,
Bacchus, Lord of Thunder, ruins his family—
each and every one of us
because of what we did to him and his mother.

AGAVE:
Pops—that's the trouble with you old folks—
always cranky and crabbing away about something—
if it's not one thing, it's another—
moan, moan, moan all day long: I can't take it anymore.
No wonder you resigned as king. Why can't you
ever find anything good to say about your children?
Always picking on us like we was still little girls.
Look—it's about time you realized it: I've grown up.
I'm my own woman now—and a mother: I'm not your little girl
any more—stop treating me like one. And I want my son
to grow up and be boss—be the greatest hunter in Thebes!
I hope he's always first to drive home the spear!
It's too bad, though, all he ever does these days
is get into fights with the gods. He won't get ahead,
behaving like that, that's for sure.
Daddy, you *must* try talking some sense into him sometime;
tell him what's likely to happen if he goes on like that much longer.
He's such a big boy now, he never listens to his old ma.

(She addresses the palace guards.)

Hey—won't one of you good-for-nothings
run into the palace and bring Pentheus out here?

I want him to see for himself
just how happy I am!

301

CADMUS:

My child, when you finally wake up
and see what you've done—
the sorrow, the pain,
that will then be yours . . .
Although it could be,
if you persist in this dream
until the day you die,
I suppose you'll think yourself 'happy.'
But for what it's worth—
know now:
your luck's run out.
You're living a curse.

AGAVE:

Why, daddy, what's wrong?
Why am I supposed to weep?

CADMUS:

First—take a good look at the sky.

AGAVE *(reverting to a little girl's voice and humming a few bars of a familiar song out of key):*
Why? La-da-la-da-dee-dee-dum . . .

CADMUS:

Just look. Take your time.
Now tell me carefully:
does it look the same as always
or do you notice any changes?

AGAVE:

Well . . . La-da-la-da-dee-dee-dum . . .
it does seem . . . brighter . . . la-da-la . . . than before
. . . fuller somehow . . . dee-dee-dum . . . like—like
DayFather Zeus was up there in person . . . smiling . . . la-da-la
. . . shining down on us. . .

302

CADMUS:
Those clouds swirling in your head—
they've started to disappear, haven't they?

AGAVE *(using her normal voice):*
Yes, I . . . I hear you but I don't understand.
Yet what I was feeling just moments ago—
it's vanished—gone!

CADMUS:
Now pay strict attention to me
and answer my questions.

AGAVE *(shaking her head as if coming out of a trance):*
Daddy, what were we just talking about?
Everything seems to have gone clean out of my head.

CADMUS:
You remember that tune you were just humming?
Well, it was a marriage hymn.
Now who did you marry? Whose house
did you go to, singing that song,
when you got married?

AGAVE:
I, unh . . . was going to Echion's house.
You recall him, don't you—
you arranged for me to marry him
because he was one of those titanic heroes
who sprang from the earth
where you sowed the dragon's teeth.

CADMUS:
That's right: it was Echion you married.
And you went to live in his house
where you gave birth to a son named . . .

AGAVE:

  . . . Pentheus!

CADMUS:

  See—it's all coming back, isn't it?
  Now slowly, slowly—
  look at the head you're cradling in your arms.
  Whose is it? Whose?

AGAVE:

  A lion cub's . . . at least that's what the girls
  who were hunting with me said.

CADMUS:

  Please, look again.
  That's not asking too much, is it?

AGAVE:

  No . . . no: you're right. It's not a lion cub's.
  What is it, then? What am I holding?

CADMUS:

  Look very, very closely this time. And make sure.

AGAVE *(screams):*

  I see! I see! But why? Why?

CADMUS:

  Dear heart, you still say that's a lion's head?

AGAVE *(screams again):*

  No! No! It's Pentheus's!

CADMUS:

  For whom I wept before you knew why.

AGAVE:

  Who killed him?

Why am I holding his head like this?

CADMUS:

It's always too soon
to tell the truth that wounds.

AGAVE:

Tell me! Tell me before my heart bursts!

CADMUS:

You killed him: you and Ino and Autonoe.

AGAVE:

Where? Here in the palace
or someplace else?

CADMUS:

Up there in the forests—
the same place where
Actaeon's hounds tore him to bits.

AGAVE:

But why did my poor boy
go to Mount Cithairon
in the first place?

CADMUS:

To make fun of your nephew Dionysos
and what you were doing for him up there.

AGAVE:

What exactly *were* we doing?
I don't remember a thing about it.

CADMUS:

Divine madness laid hold of you—
yes, you and everyone in Thebes.

AGAVE:
Now I'm beginning to understand:
it was Dionysos all the time.
He ruined us.

CADMUS:
That's right. You wronged him.
You did not believe he was god.

AGAVE:
Father, where's the rest of my boy—
my Pentheus, whom I loved so very, very much?

CADMUS:
Here on this stretcher.
I went out myself and found the remains.

AGAVE:
Is all of him there—every last bit?
Does he look recognizably—human?

CADMUS:
[Yes—all except for his head which you're holding.]

AGAVE:
But what part did he play in my madness?

CADMUS:
He was like you in this respect:
he did not believe Semele's boy
was really a Son of Zeus.
Now you know why Dionysos destroyed
all our House: you, your sisters,
our young king—and myself as well,
since except for Pentheus
I leave no legitimate heir to the throne.

What does the sum of my years amount to but this:
to see Pentheus, flesh of our flesh, torn apart,

306

eaten by the very flesh that bore him?
Pentheus, it was to you we looked to prop our dynasty,
you to rule the city we built.
While you were king, no one dared strike an old man
like myself—lest you turn on him the stern majesty
of your all-seeing eye.
Now it's my turn: time for me who sowed the dragon's teeth
and reaped the noblest crop of heroes the world has ever known:
time to leave in shame, cast out,
exiled from the House and City I began.

Pentheus, my child,
whom I loved best
of all who live on earth,
though now you live no more
you I shall rank forever closest
among those dearest to my heart.
Son, never again
will you run your fingers
rippling through my hair and beard,
never again take me in your arms
and call me 'grand-dad,'
wanting to know:
'Cadmus, who has done you wrong?
dishonored you in your years,
thereby thrusting pain in your heart?
Tell me, Cadmus, my lord,
and I will attend to him.'
Now it's my turn to suffer,
now that you have endured
all that death has to offer,
while your mother earns
our pity and our tears.
If there's one person here
who thinks he can out-think the gods:
look well upon this king
and so learn to believe.

Cadmus, we share the anguish you feel.
But remember: though his death lies heavy upon you,
he received just sentence from the god.

AGAVE:

Father, you see what change has come over me—

[At this point there are about fifty lines missing from the original Greek text of the *Bacchai*. However, E. R. Dodds, drawing on material from the *Christus Patiens (Christ Suffering/Enduring)*, a medieval Passion Play from the twelfth century, which in part its unknown author adapted from a more complete text of the *Bacchai* than we now possess, offers the following summary in his edition (Oxford, 1960) of the play of what very likely took place in this lacuna: "Agave, flung in a moment from ecstasy to despair . . . and conscious of being a polluted creature . . . begs permission to lay out [Pentheus'] body for burial . . . and to bid it a last farewell. Cadmus consents, warning her of its condition . . . Over the body she 'accuses herself and moves the audience to pity,' embracing each limb in turn and lamenting over it . . . Dionysos now appears above the [palace] . . . and first addresses all present . . . speaking of the Theban people who denied his divine origin and rejected his gift [of wine] . . . and of the outrages for which [Pentheus] has paid with his life . . . He then predicts the future of the survivors, each in turn . . . The Cadmeans will one day be expelled from their city . . . they have themselves to blame for it . . . Agave and her sisters must at once leave Thebes for ever, 'for it is against religion that murderers should remain.' Finally the god turns to Cadmus . . . the description of whose fate survives almost complete." Using Dodds' remarks about the opening of the apotheosized Dionysos' speech, I offer the following version:]

(Dionysos appears in a puff of smoke on top of the palace in his divine body. He is a tall, swarthy, well-muscled figure with thick black hair and a short, pointed beard and mustache. A pair of short, turned-up bull's horns sprout on either side of his head. He is still dressed as a bacchant and carries a thyrse. Light radiates from all of him. Except

308

that he lacks a tail and possibly cloven goat's feet he might be taken
for the Devil Himself.)

DIONYSOS:

[Yes, I really am Dionysos,
Son of Zeus, child of Semele,
come back to Thebes,
known as god to man.
You denied me—blasphemy!
You cursed me.
You said I was just like one of you,
only worse—not a Greek,
and that like you one day I would die.
Now you know differently.
And—as if all that wasn't enough—
you terrorized my women,
you tried to jail me and beat me:
you who I loved—my family—
you did this—
because you hated and feared me both at the same time.
My crime: that I wished to help
and give all of you
the benefit of my gifts.

Well, as far as my family's concerned,
that's all over now.
From this moment on
I consider you my enemy
and will treat you accordingly.
First I cast you from this land and city,
to go where you'll wear the collar of slaves
and waste your remaining years
performing dull, meaningless tasks.

Pentheus achieved what he worked so hard to earn:
death and dismemberment on the razored slopes of Cithairon
at the hands of his women.

You all saw what he did—
yet made no move to stop him—
how he came at me, evil in his heart,
thinking he could chain me up
and curse me before the people.
His death was just:
his murderers those
without reason to murder.
What he got
he got deservedly.
Now, Agave,
hear the sentence I decree for you and your sisters:
leave this city at once.
You are tainted.
It violates divine law
for you to live in peace
next to the tomb of the boy you've slain.

Cadmus,] here's what's in store for you:
you will become a dragon snake—
yes—you and your wife, Harmonia, Ares' daughter,
will both be turned to serpents.
Together it will be your doom
to journey on an ox-cart,
leading a great, barbarian horde.
This is the future Zeus's oracle lays down for you.
The army that follows you
will be so big no one can number it.
With it you'll wreck many cities.
But after you've attacked Apollo's Home at Delphi,
your way will become hard and dangerous.
In the end, though, Ares will save Harmonia and you
and give you eternal life in the Land of the Blest.

You have my word on this—

the word of a god
whose father is immortal Zeus.
If only you had listened to me before
and not inflicted your madness on me,
I would have been your friend—not your judge.

CADMUS:
Dionysos—please!
I know we've done wrong.

DIONYSOS:
Too late, too late.
You came to know me
long after the hour had tolled
for you to divine who I am.

CADMUS:
Yes, that's true, yes!
But your punishments
far exceed our crimes.

DIONYSOS:
I am a god.
You declared war on me—
all of you.

CADMUS:
It is not just for gods
to vent their anger like men.

DIONYSOS:
Long ago Father Zeus consented
that what has happened here
would take place exactly as scheduled.

AGAVE:
Father, it's useless.

You can't argue with him.
We're exiles now.

DIONYSOS:
What are you waiting for?
Your future is now.

CADMUS:
My child, is this sorrow, this pain
all that remains
for you, your sisters and myself?
Am I really to wander in old age,
a stranger among strangers,
destined to lead a motley horde
against the Greeks, my own people?
Shall Harmonia, my wife,
indeed put on a serpent's body
and be led by me, a snake her husband,
while I marshall foreign troops
to attack the altars and graveyards of Greece?
And when I die,
does that end my suffering?
Once I cross Acheron, river of death,
that forever channels deeper into earth:
there I will find peace?

AGAVE:
After today, father, I'll never see you again, will I?

(They embrace.)

CADMUS:
Poor thing—you hold me so tightly,
like a white swan hoping to bring life back
to her dying lord.

AGAVE:

Because I have nowhere to go . . .
Because I've been driven from my home . . .

CADMUS:

Don't ask me for help—
I'm of no further use to you.

AGAVE:

Home—good-by.
City of Seven Towers—good-by.
Marriage, Family—all good-by.
I leave you now.
I enter exile.
I begin despair.

CADMUS:

Try the house of Aristaeus . . .

AGAVE:

Father, my tears go with you.

CADMUS:

And mine with you and your sisters.

AGAVE:

King Dionysos is to blame.
He brought this misery and disgrace
on all our House and Family—

DIONYSOS:

—because thanks to you
I suffered much
and never received
but a bastard's name
here in Thebes.

AGAVE:
Father—farewell.

CADMUS:
And god speed you, child of sorrow:
though you'll find no way easy to go.

AGAVE *(to the guards):*
Take me to my sisters
so that we can share our fate together.
I hope Cithairon never casts
its hateful eyes on me again,
or that I see that fearful place
once more. For there I leave
no thyrse to remember me by—
though I pray some other Bacchai will.

CHORUS:
Gods come in many shapes and sizes.
What you think they'll do,
you find they most often don't.
By paths you didn't even know were there,
they bring to term what you hoped would never be:
just what you've seen happen here today.

(Agave and Cadmus each go their separate ways;
Dionysos and the Chorus remain.)

Peace

Aristophanes

Translation by

Tim Reynolds

The thought of what America,
The thought of what America,
The thought of what America would be like
If the Classics had a wide circulation—
  Oh, well:
It troubles my sleep.
                    E. Pound

Introduction

The aims were movement and relevance. By movement I mean control of movement, relation of line to line, chorus to context, interaction of dramatic, musical, choreographic structures. Relevance explains itself. These stresses mean serious losses: The lyric beauty of Aristophanes' chorus, his delight in complex wordplay (regularly hashed by most translators anyway).

In places this version is not Faithful to the Text. I felt, doing it, involved in deeper fidelities to the play: to the whole play as it was first presented, crimsom tryglyphs and purple metopes and all, a structure in which music and movement were no less important than the words that are all we have left; to the play's absolute contemporaneity, made to be presented once, for a specific audience, in a specific theatre, on a specific afternoon, once; to its function as celebration, its vision of Peace not as some pale absence-of-war, but as metaphor for the concrete pleasures war denatures and corrupts: drinking, eating, fucking. (Isn't the play most summed up in the conclusion of the beautiful strophe at 856, "securely/to screw, to sleep"?) The peace/piece pun is an act of God, leading at last to a sort of double vision, the vanished, wordless, never-quite-real Peace absorbed in the actual Prosperity, distortedly echoed in Abundance, wistfully recalled in the Old Man's "young pussy."

Hsuntse says:

Therefore man is the product of the forces of heaven and earth, of

317

the union of the yin and yang principles, the incarnation of spirits and the essence of the five elements. Therefore man is the heart of the universe, the upshot of the five elements, born to enjoy food and color and noise . . .

Time after time (would God more often) I believe I've hit on a way, a bridge across.

That there are valuable things over there, things we need, in that squiggly writing; that it's like the man who has to get the goose, the fox and the corn across the river in a boat that will carry only two things at a time; that I've had to leave things others have ferried across—but want to think I've translated (= metaphored) things they had to leave behind, over there where none of us are entirely at home, across the river, in the squiggles.

Additional Notes

"For the lyric, I see each stanza as spoken by a separate chorus member—and would like to see the whole thing held together with music, flute probably; a single simple series repeated for strophe and antistrophe. (I think I can bring out the structures on paper, but I'd like to see them show up in performance too, particularly when they're separated, as 856 ff. and 909 ff.)

"What I'm doing here is trying for a clear line (vocal, verbal and potentially musical) over *anything* else; the prettiness of the opening of each section contrasted with what Platnauer would call the coarseness of the rest of it.

"For the hexametre passages, I think now it would be best not to worry about metrical effects much—it should move fast enough and freely enough so they'd be lost any way. The emphasis here would be on the lunacy of the sound-patterns and wordplay (like specific puns or lines like 900 can't be reproduced *in situ* often, I suppose, but the translators might watch for a chance *anywhere* to do something Aristophanes might have enjoyed).

"The slaves might seem a little peculiar; but they might bring the slave-jokes to life again, where otherwise they'd simply be archaisms, not very funny. (This occurred to me while watching the San Francisco Mime

Troupe do a minstrel show.) But I'm not going ahead with this until I get a tentative green light from you, in case you think it's *too* strange. (Lets not worry about anachronisms, OK? If they're good enough for Shakespeare they're good enough for us. They can call us naifs too if they want.)"

(from a letter to John Herington dated c. 15 December, 1966, Veracruz)

"In defence of the mélange that results—and the most obvious is pervasive anachronism—I can only say that Aristophanes seems to enjoy this sort of approach to language and structure, the brutal juxtaposition of comic and tragic terminology and metres, the abrupt transpositions between obscenity and divinity, the most gorgeous lyrical choruses in the middle of the most prosaic hexametre. And if there seemed no way *out* but the use of Hubert or Adlai, I used them here. (Other pretty strange—and sometimes funny, I think—businesses developed through my trying to *avoid* flatout anachronism . . .)

"Oh, hey. I've been keeping away from metrical problems, figuring that if anyone was unhappy, they'd bitch. But with the really long line I've been using as a rough hexametre equivalent, I've been sweating blood as to what to do about the parabasis. In the version I'm working on now, it's prose; I suppose I could plead *Murder in the Cathedral* as precedent, but it seems more important that, again, it's a drastic tonal change (these lines may seem chopped-up prose to you, but if you want to experiment, type a passage out *as* prose; the line-endings are doing a lot.) (I'm not happy with any approach to the parabasis I've hit on yet, but I *do* strongly incline to prose—is that OK?)"

(from a letter to John Herington and Bill Arrowsmith, 20 April, 1967, Mexico, D.F.)

A Final "Thing"

"I was writing this as if the Community, all the American people, was going to have a big festival, a Greater Dionysia, and this play would be one of the things we'd do. Everybody would be there, the people that initiated things, at all levels, and the people that carried them out and the

319

people that profited and suffered from those things, and the Weathermen would booze with the generals and the rednecks would dance with the spades, etc. The thing that got me about Aristophanes was his incapacity to hate any Athenian, and God knows I didn't hate anybody.

"I haven't seen the manuscript for years, it must be far more dated than the original already, it was for that festival in the fall of 1967, and the festival never came off. The end was sodden and inconclusive and meaningless as the whole war. Nobody danced in the streets when the radio said it was officially over. Probably a lot of us everywhere cried a little, but it didn't mean anything. No one forgave or was forgiven. Not one single opportunity for grandeur or imagination or magnanimity or even good sense in two decades not thrown away or botched or corrupted and dirtied. I liked it better my way."

(from a letter to Charles Doria dated 25 July, 1974, Oxford)

Tim Reynolds

SCENE: mostly at the house of Trygaeus, a gracious ante-bellum (i.e. pre-Peloponnesian War) mansion in Athens.

(Antebellum housefront. A large mailbox labelled: TRYGAEUS. To the left a large gate into the beetle's stable; to the right a shed with a half moon cut out in its side.)

(The stage is empty. Then Liza enters from the stable, a greatly exaggerated Aunt Jemima, in blackface, carrying a silver tray with great dignity. She walks to center stage.)

LIZA:
ANUDDER SHITCAKE FO' DE BEETLE!

(Rastus enters from the shed, a greatly exaggerated blackface field-hand, wooly poll, much given to footshuffling and headscratching. He is carrying the shitcake on a large shovel, and transfers it to Liza's tray.)

RASTUS:
Hyar she am.

(And, as Liza carries it into the stable:)

An' I sho' hopes dat ugly mutha never get no *better'n* dat too.

(A horrible gobbling noise from the stable. Liza re-enters.)

LIZA:
Anudder shitcake. He say he want pigshit dis time.

RASTUS:
Liza, I jes' *gib* him one! He didn' go
an' eat dat whole thing already?

LIZA:
      Sho' did Rastus,
jes' kin' ob roll it aroun' in his paws a little an'
GLOM.

(Rastus goes into the shed. Liza calls after him:)

Y'all better make a *bunch* mo', he like dem
roun' an' firm an' fully packed.

*(Rastus re-enters and the new shitcake is transferred to the tray. Liza
takes it into the stable. The horrible gobbling noise again.)*

RASTUS:
Ain't dey no garbage collectors out dere
to help me out befo' I ups an' asFICtionates?

(Liza returns.)

LIZA:
Come on now. Dis time he say he want a *fairy*-shitcake,
so it's good an' pounded down.

(Rastus exits to the shed, returns:)

RASTUS:
                                    Hyar she am.

(Liza carries it to the beetle. Gobbling.)

Folks, dey is only one good thing about dis yere job:
Massa cain't say I's swipin' de scraps off de table.

(Liza returns.)

Good gawdamercy, *mo'*?

LIZA:
                              Yep, anudder shitcake.

(A truly ferocious gobbling from the shed.)

                                              Better
make dat two. Dat dere's a mighty gobbledy beetle in dere.

322

RASTUS:

No, ma'am. I done had dis yere copry-fagëous job up to *heah.*
Maybe I ain' no house nigger, but I an' no *shit*house nigger.
Y'all let Brer Bug fetch his *own* food fo' a change.
O' y'all kin fetch it yo'self. Cause I is *through.*

(Leaning on his shovel, he turns to the audience.)

I wisht one ob y'all out dere could tell me
where I kin buy me a nose widout dese yere holes in it.
Cause dey ain't no job in de terasseral globe mo' obnocerous
den to fetch an' carry de puticullar kin' ob food dat dat bug eat.
Y'all take a hawg, o' a dawg, he eats it where you drops it;
but dis yere bug won't touch turd number one
lessen you mash it up fo' him an' serve it on a silver plate
like he was Queen ob de May.
                                 I guess I jes' peek in dere,
so he doan see me, an' see is he finish eatin' yit.
                                 Whooo*eee!*
Go on, mutha, eat! Stuff yo'self till you bust!
                                 Liza,
look at him. He got all dem little arms jes' aworkin'
like a whole fiel' ob cottonpickers, jes' astuffin' dat stuff
in his mouf. An' look at dem *teef* go chompety, chompety,
like pistons on de Midnight Special. Dat animal am de most
nauseratin' and *disgusterbatin'* an' STINKIN' animal I ever seed.

(Turning to Liza, nervously:)

Y'all doan think dey's no god minds what you says about
shit-eatin' bugs, Liza, does you?

LIZA:

                                 No god I'd let in *my* house.

RASTUS:

Some god got to watch out fo' dese yere shit-eatin' bugs, Liza.

323

(An immense fart from the stable.)

LIZA:

Den it got to be Zeus, de god ob de thunder!

(They laugh, poke one another in the ribs, etc. Then Liza turns to the audience. Entirely without accent:)

About now some bright young critic in the audience
is going to start wondering: "But what's the *symbolism*
of this beetle? I mean, what does it all *mean*?"
And Someone ingenious sitting next to him will explain:
"It obviously refers to the Chief Executive; you know him by
his diet."

RASTUS:

'Scuse me, Liza, de beetle need a drink.

(He stands, back to the audience, urinating into the stable during her speech.)

LIZA:

So let me explain the situation to you toddlers and youngsters,
you teens, you young marrieds, you junior executives and executives,
and you senior citizens, so you can follow the plot.
Through excessive concern with the international situation,
our master's developed a set of pathological symptoms
unique in clinical literature—not the usual neuroses,
like yours, something brand new. All day he wanders around
with his eyes turned up to the sky, calling and calling:
"God*damn* it, God, what do you think you're doing?
Lay off, before these cretins push the buttons!"

(She listens a moment; in accent again:)

O lawdy, lawdy!
I thinks I hears him now!

(Trygaeus enters from the house and, during the following, crosses to

and enters the stable, his eyes turned upward. He is wearing a cowboy suit, chaps, sombrero, etc.)

TRYGAEUS:

Oh GOD! What in hell are you *doing* up there in heaven?
When are you going to wake up and *stop* these maniacs?

(After his exit Liza resumes, again without accent:)

LIZA:

See? That's exactly what I was talking about.
And that's only a sample. When this paranoia first started
to get serious, he used to say: "If there was just some way
to *talk* to God and get this mess straightened out."
And then he built some little ladders and set them up
against the shed there, to try to climb to heaven;
he was lucky he only sprained his ankle.
And so yesterday he came home with this monster beetle,
God knows where he got it, and put it in the stable
for us to feed, and spends half the day
currying it, and stroking it, and talking to it:
"Ah, my little Pegasus, oh, you noble beast,
you'll get me up to talk to God, won't you?"

RASTUS:

What he up to in dere now?

(He peeks into the stable.)

                    Great Gawdamercy!
Liza! Help! Liza! Massa's RIDIN' de mutha!

(The stable doors fly open. Trygaeus bursts forth, mounted on a huge beetle which is bucking and crowhopping all over the stage. Trygaeus spurring and waving his sombrero à la rodeo.)

TRYGAEUS:

WAAAAHOOOOOOOOOO!

325

(Gradually the beetle tires, and finally stops in center stage. Trygaeus dismounts and walks around him, talking to him, stroking him, readjusting stirrups, cinch, etc.)

> There, baby, easy, easy.
> Don't wear yourself out before
> we start, you'll sprain a wing.
> Start off slowly, let your muscles
> relax, warm up, let the sweat oil you.
> We've got a long way to go.
> Yecchh! And don't blow your
> rotten breath in my face
> or the whole project's off.

(He walks behind the beetle, who farts. Trygaeus falls over backward.)

> Lethal at both ends.

(Resolutely he gets up and remounts. Nervously, Liza and Rastus emerge from the hiding-places.)

RASTUS:

> Boss, dis ol' darky fears yo' mind am
> destroyed.

TRYGAEUS:

> Shhh, I'm busy.

LIZA:

> Massa, y'all gwine *fly* on dat dere bug?

TRYGAEUS:

> I'm making one last, desperate, heroic
> attempt, for the sake of all the Greeks.

RASTUS:

> Whuffo' y'all gwine do dat fo', boss?

TRYGAEUS:

Don't stand around asking stupid
questions. Just wish me luck.

(To the audience:)

And you too, out there: keep still,
and plug up your toilets and board up your
outhouses and keep your assholes corked.

RASTUS:

But massa, massa, how kin I keep still lessen y'all tells me
where y'all gwine to?

TRYGAEUS:

Where do you think? To Heaven,
to get things straight with God.

RASTUS:

What y'all gwine say to de Lawd?

TRYGAEUS:

I just want to ask him what he plans to do about
genocide and nuclear fallout and the population explosion.

RASTUS:

But massa, spose de Lawd doan wan' to tell y'all?

TRYGAEUS:

I'll turn him over to the Unhellenic Activities Committee.

LIZA:

Massa, I jes' cain't *bear* to see y'all fly off like dis.

TRYGAEUS:

Try and stop me.

LIZA:

O lawdy, lawdy, lawdy.

(She calls into the house:)

Chillen, y'all come here.

(Trygaeus' two little girls enter.)

> Honies, you pappy done gone crazy,
he tryin' to sneak off to Heaven on dat dere bug. Po' babies,
y'all ask him real pretty-please an' maybe he gwine stay.

(The girls speak in chorus, violins in the background:)

GIRLS:

> O daddy daddy, we can't believe our ears;
> we always knew you were a little queer;
> but can you really go and leave us here
> like orphans, all in tears?

GIRL 1:

I mean really, Daddy, are you getting senile or something?

TRYGAEUS:

I'm afraid I've got to go. Try to understand how it hurt me
when you'd ask me for food, and call me 'Daddy,'
and I didn't have a nickel in the house. Look, kids,
if I can negotiate some kind of deal with God,
I'll buy you the biggest cake in Athens, all for you.

> And
a knuckle sandwich right now if you don't quit pawing at me.

GIRL 1:

But Daddy, *nobody* just goes and *talks* with God.
You don't even know where he is, or how to get there.

TRYGAEUS:

Here's my transportation. And the direction's up.

GIRL 2:

Daddy, you must be *crazy* to think you can get to Heaven
on a beetle.

328

TRYGAEUS:
          In Aesop's Fables it says a beetle flew
to Heaven and talked with God.

GIRL 2:
                              Oh Daddy, you don't
believe that stuff? It's just a bug, and it's dirty,
and it *smells.*

TRYGAEUS:
               Says it right there in the book,
in black and white.

GIRL 1:
                    Daddy, couldn't you get a Pegasus,
or something *nicer*, so the neighbors won't make fun of us?

TRYGAEUS:
     Use your head. If I had a horse, I'd have to carry supplies
for both of us; this way, I just take enough food for me;
after I'm through with it, *he* eats it.

GIRL 2:
                              But Daddy,
suppose you fall in the ocean?

TRYGAEUS:
                         I come equipped
with a rudder.

(He exhibits his phallus.)
               And this model's amphibious,
he's got enough gas in him to float a battleship.

GIRL 1:
  But where would you sail to?

TRYGAEUS:
                         To Liverpool, where else?

329

If I don't get a medal, at least the beetle ought to.

GIRL 1:

Just don't fall off. You could scramble your psyche
and end up in some play of Genet's or Ionesco's; or even
injure your you-know-what, and Albee might make you a star.

(Trygaeus clutches his phallus:)

TRYGAEUS:

Oh, I'll be careful of *that*, don't worry.

                                                    Wish me luck.

(To the audience:)

And you out there, I'm doing all this for you. So remember,
no defecation or urination for at least three days;
because once we're airborne and he gets a whiff of some tidbit,
he'll take the bit in his mandibles and goodbye, Trygaeus.

*(The beetle starts rising slowly. A hard spot follows it up as the lights
dim to blackness. Liza, Rastus and the children call 'Goodbye,' 'Good
luck.')*

                        Hiyo Pegasus, we're off! Ah, the creak
                        and groan of leather, the sunlight
                        glancing from your bit and bright wings, the . . .

(The beetle suddenly starts down again.)

                        Hey, hey, hold it! Keep your mind
                        on your business, ignore that latrine!
                        Keep your head up!

*(The beetle, with much hauling of reins, is persuaded to resume his
flight upward.)*

                                Here we're off to see God,
                        heading into the wild blue yonder,

and all you can think of is shit!
Consider heavenly sustenance and . . . .
                                    HEY!
You! Yeah, *you* down there! *You*,
taking a crap in the alley back of
Joe's Bar, you could get me killed!
What are you trying to do? Look, bury that,
and dump a lot of dirt on top, and plant
roses and violets on it; and do it quick,
because if Pegasus here gets a noseful of *that*,
the world might blow itself to pieces, just
because *you* couldn't keep a tight asshole!

(The beetle jerks. Trygaeus grabs the saddlehorn.)

Whoops! To be serious a moment . . .

(The beetle jerks again; Trygaeus grabs the saddlehorn.)

                        Hey, damn it, wake up,
you up there! You on the winch! I could break a leg,
I'm a long way up . . .
                        Lousy stagehands and their lousy union . . .
But here I am, approaching Heaven.

*(The beetle is gradually settling down to the lower stage again, as the
lights gradually come up on heaven.)*

                        And here's God's house,
It looks just like I'd always imagined it somehow.

*(God's house is Trygaeus' house, although the mailbox in front now
reads ZEUS. At one side of the stage there is an immense rock buried
in the ground. At the other a balcony rail facing the audience.)*
(The beetle settles slowly to the stage. Trygaeus dismounts.)

No doorbell?
            Hey!
                    HEY!

Anybody home here?

HEY!

(Hermes enters, middleaged, effeminate to the point of absurdity. He is curlyhaired, a sort of Apollo gone to seed, wearing sandals strapped up to his calves, a wreath of ivy, and a mini-chiton.)

HERMES:
I could have *sworn* I smelled something perfectly . . .

OOO,

What is *that*?

TRYGAEUS:
A horsefly.

HERMES:
Ooo, you *filthy brute,*
how *could* you bring that simply *nauseating* object here
to *Heaven*? How *revolting*! How utterly DISGUSTING!
Who *are* you?

(The beetle farts. Trygaeus, standing behind it, recoils.)

TRYGAEUS:
Oof, disgusting . . .

HERMES:
Where did you *come* from?

(The beetle farts again, more loudly.)

TRYGAEUS:
Oof, disgusting!

HERMES:
Well, who's your *father* then?

(The beetle farts thunderously. Trygaeus falls over backwards.)

TRYGAEUS:

UGH! DISGUSTING!

(He kicks the beetle ferociously and repeatedly; finally it begins to move and crawls ponderously offstage. Hermes is almost in tears.)

HERMES:

If you don't tell me your name right this very minute,
I'll give you such a *smack*!

TRYGAEUS:

Who, me? I'm Trygaeus,
And I live in Athens, Greece, at 1065 Olive Oil Avenue,
and I'm sick and tired of war!

HERMES:

Well, why are you *here*?

(Trygaeus holds one hand behind his back, coyly.)

TRYGAEUS:

To bring you a little surprise.

HERMES:

Why, you *nice* man, how thoughtful of you. What?

(Trygaeus brings his clenched fist out and waves it under Hermes' nose.)

TRYGAEUS:

THIS!

And you get it if I hear anything more about "nauseating"
or "disgusting" and especially "filthy brutes," right?
Now get in there and tell God I'm here.

HERMES:

Oh, oh dear,

but I *can't*. I mean *you* can't. See God, I mean.
They're gone! They all moved out yesterday, all the gods.

TRYGAEUS:
Where in the world *to*?

HERMES:
Not in the *world*, silly.

(Trygaeus brings out his fist again.)

TRYGAEUS:
WHERE?

HERMES:
As far away as they can get, at the other end
of the sky.

TRYGAEUS:
How come *you're* still here?

HERMES:
Oh, me?
They left me behind to take care of the house; you know,
all the little knick-knacks and odds and ends of things
they didn't pack.

TRYGAEUS:
Why on earth have they moved out?

(Hermes starts to protest his usage: the fist again.)

HERMES:
Because they were simply *furious* with the Greeks. So now
they've turned just everything over to War
and told him he can do whatever he likes with you,
and they've gone away, as high and far as they can,
so they don't have to watch you fighting all the time
and be bothered with all those nasty explosions
and children screaming and people praying for peace.

TRYGAEUS:
  But *why?*

HERMES:
           Well, they *tried* to stop the war, but you
ignored them. I mean, if the Spartans got some little
advantage, they'd say: *"Now* we've got them by the . . . "

(He giggles:)

Well, *excuse* my *French!* But you know what I *mean.*
And if you Athenians got ahead a little, and the Spartans
sent out peace feelers, *you'd* say: "It's all a trick!
Who ever heard of a godless Spartan keeping a treaty?
Besides, we'd have to disassemble all our catapults!"

TRYGAEUS:
  I've got to admit it sounds familiar.

HERMES:
                      And *that's* why
I don't know if any of you will ever see Peace again.

TRYGAEUS:
  Where is she?

HERMES:
           War, that simply *impossible* God, buried her
  in a hole.

TRYGAEUS:
           In a *what?*

HERMES:
                In that hole, over there;
  and you can see the rock he put on top, so no one
  can *ever* get her out again.

TRYGAEUS:

But what's War
planning to do with us, now he's in charge?

HERMES:

I don't know.
All *I* know is, last night he brought back a sort of a
bowl, well, simply *immense*, I never saw anything *like* it.

TRYGAEUS:
And what's he going to do with this bowl?

HERMES:

Well, he *says*
he's going to put all the different countries in it and . . .

(A noise of squeaking wheels inside the house.)

Oh my goodness! I think I hear him now. If I were you,
my dear, I'd hide.

(Hermes hides behind a column.)

TRYGAEUS:

Oh-oh. Where's my trusty beetle?
I hear the thunder of enormous wheels inside the house.

*(He hides behind a column next to Hermes'. Enter, pushing a gigantic
toilet mounted on tiny wheels, General Disorder. The general, almost
a dwarf, is further dwarfed by his elaborate parody of a general's uniform, great quantities of gold braid, huge circles of stars on his epau-
lettes, a monstrous bank of combat ribbons, a hat with an immense
eagle, and a diminutive ceremonial sword. Behind him walks War,
dressed in a neat and conservative business suit, rimless glasses, ap-
pearing a thoroughly conservative bank official or insurance adjuster.
He walks with his eyes down, his hands clasped before him, something
like the stance one imagines a prison chaplain adopting as he follows
one of his parishioners to the chair.)*
(Trygaeus' eyes follow General Disorder; he ignores War following.)

336

WAR:

Poor mortals, poor mortals, you've endured such misery,
and now it seems you've only begun to suffer.

TRYGAEUS:

My God, what a bowl! It's terrifying! And just the look
of War sends shivers up my spine, so fierce and evil!

*(Hermes indicates, by gestures, that War is not General Disorder but
the man behind him. A spirited exchange of gestures, Trygaeus looking back and forth between Hermes, War and the General, unbelieving.)*

That's the God of War? The ferocious bloodsoaked
terrible God we've feared so long? I can't believe it.

*(General Disorder has finally wrestled the toilet to the center of the
stage; he turns, salutes, and stands at attention.
War sets down his attaché case. With great care he removes his coat,
folds it tidily, and hands it to General Disorder, who salutes, and carries it offstage. War then opens his case and removes a white coat, like
that of a chemist in an aspirin advertisement, which he puts on. During
the following scene, War removes various flasks, test-tubes and retorts
from his case, mixing their contents with great care until he has arrived
at a mixture that satisfies him.)*

WAR:

Poor Sparta! Poor miserable Spartans! Ashes to ashes,
dust to dust . . . Oil of Sparta . . .

(He pours the mixture into the bowl of the toilet.)

TRYGAEUS:
                                          Well, it's only Spartans.

WAR:

And Megara, ah, you poor doomed city! What a shame!
But duty drives me on. Tincture of Megara . . .

(Into the bowl.)

337

TRYGAEUS:
Hard luck for Megara. They'll be yelping *there* tonight.

WAR:
And Sicily . . . Farewell, you golden land! Farewell,
my dear dear friends. Sicily capsules . . .

(He pours these from a large bottle, the capsules plopping loudly into the water.)

TRYGAEUS:
Now that's a shame! Some of my best friends are Sicilians.

(War removes a handkerchief from his pocket, delicately wipes his eyes, refolds it and returns it to his pocket.)

WAR:
And last—oh, it breaks my heart to have to do this—
Essence of Athens . . .

TRYGAEUS:
HEY!

(He is stifled by Hermes and prevented, after a brief scuffle, from interfering as the Essence is poured into the bowl.)

But that stuff costs four obols an ounce! Can't he
use something else? How about Essence of Thessaly?

(Solemnly, War pulls the chain hanging above the toilet. There is a clanking noise, but nothing happens. He pulls it again, waits a moment, then yanks at it repeatedly. Still nothing.)

WAR:
GENERAL DISORDER!

(The General rushes on, leaps to attention, salutes.)

GENERAL:
                    Yes, *sir!*

338

(War puts out his hand for General Disorder's sword, which the General hands him. War pokes about in the toilet with it, stirring things up, then hands the sword back to the General. As War tries again to flush the toilet, still with no success, General Disorder looks about for something to wipe his sword with, holding it with distaste. He eventually notices Trygaeus behind his column and wipes the sword on his neckerchief. Trygaeus attempts to protest but Hermes quiets him again, pointing at the toilet, holding his nose, making chainpulling gestures. The General is replacing his sword in its scabbard when:)

WAR:
GENERAL DISORDER!

(The General leaps to attention again, salutes repeatedly.)

GENERAL:
Yes, sir!

WAR:
You have nothing better to do,
I presume, than stand there?

GENERAL:
Yes, sir.

(A pause.)

Ah, no, sir.

(War rips off the General's left epaulette. The General's face crumples up as though he is going to cry, but with great effort of will he recovers himself.)

Yes, sir. Your orders, sir?

TRYGAEUS:
That's what I like to see,
civilian control of the military establishment.

WAR:

General Disorder, you will secure the plunger.

GENERAL:

But sir,
we don't have a plunger! We only moved in yesterday!

WAR:

Then I suggest, General, that you commandeer a plunger
from the Athenians.

GENERAL:

Yes, *sir*!

(And adds, aside:)

Or I won't have a star
left on my shoulders.

(Exit General Disorder. Trygaeus addresses the audience:)

TRYGAEUS:

Friends, we're in a jam.
Do any of *you* have any ideas? Because if he comes back
with that plunger, we *all* go down the drain. Together.
If any gods are listening, I pray he breaks a leg.

(Re-enter General Disorder, out of breath. Salutes.)

WAR:

Well?

GENERAL:

Yes, sir.

WAR:

DID YOU GET THE PLUNGER?

GENERAL:

Well,

no sir, Plumbing has been raised to such a fine art
in Athens, they don't need them now.

TRYGAEUS:
Thank *some* god!
I guess they're not *all* of them out of earshot.
Because once he'd got that machine unplugged
our chances would have been worth . . .

WAR:
General Disorder!
You will commandeer a plunger from the Spartans.

GENERAL:
Yes, sir.

WAR:
And with all deliberate speed.

GENERAL:
Yes, sir.

(He leaves.)

TRYGAEUS:
Oh my God,
we're off again. Look, if any of you out there
have a direct line to God, any DAR's or SDS's or Birchers
or Rotarians or NAACP's or even Baptists,
now's the time to put in a good word.

(He mimes pulling a chain, holding his nose.)

Or WHOOOOOOM!

(Re-enter General Disorder.)

GENERAL:
Sir, I'm sorry to report, sir, that logistical . . .

WAR:

The plunger?

DISORDER:

No plungers in Sparta, sir.

WAR:

What?

GENERAL:

Sir, I'm sorry, sir,
but the Spartans have no toilets, sir. Just holes
in the ground, sir.

TRYGAEUS:

Somebody's getting through out there.
We may survive yet. Don't you people lose heart.

WAR:

We'll have to make other arrangements. General Disorder!

(He gestures for the General to follow with the toilet and walks off-stage as he entered. The General follows, struggling with the toilet. Trygaeus emerges from behind his pillar.)

TRYGAEUS:

It must have been a day like this that Datis,
jerking off, just for the pure joy of it,
in the marketplace, at noon, was heard to exclaim:
"What fun! What delight! What extradelectation!"

So now's the time, and maybe the last time we'll have,
to forget the diplomacy and police actions and protocol,
and get together to haul Peace out of that hole
before they find a plunger and unplug that thing and
pull the chain on all of us. So come on! Everybody!
Everywhere! Come on, come on, come on, come on!

(A very light percussion begins to be heard behind his words; it will build, during the following, to the chorus' work rhythm.)

342

If we want to get her out we've got to work together!
Bring shovels, pickaxes, crowbars!
If you don't have anything, bring hands!

*(The chorus straggles in from the audience as a hint of the Marseilleise
is heard behind the work rhythm.*
*The chorus is composed of distinct individuals, each a parody—in
speech and appearance—of his or her stereotype. There are six:*
*SLICK is hippy cum Hell's Angel—beard, long hair, leather jacket,
cycle boots. ALICIA is drab, a housewife, bridge on Wednesday
nights, PTA Friday. LILY is a middle-aged semi-pro, a contemporary
Mae West but seedier; trussed-in, bleached, much madeup. VIVIAN is
(say) the Lady Editor, the professional woman; hornrimmed glasses,
tailored suit. HANK is the jovial JC member, usedcar salesman,
flabby. SETH is the oldest; he preserves, with some difficulty, a certain gentility. As they come on stage they address the Audience,
Trygaeus, one another; although their first lines ought not to be inaudible entirely, the effect is loud and confused.)*

SLICK:
Hey, come on, let's move it out, let's *move!*

ALICIA:
Well, it's about *time* somebody did something!

LILY *(a little wistfully):*
It was getting like the Big One all over again,
soldiers in all the bus stations.

VIVIAN:
Mr. Trygaeus,
just tell us what to do. We'll take care of the rest.

HANK:
And I'm not about to quit till we get this job *done.*

SETH:
I just want to see Peace again, just see her face,
I practically forgot what she looks like.

343

TRYGAEUS:

SHHHHH!
War's just around the corner! And if he finds out
what's going on, we're done for. Stop gabbling!

ALICIA:

How can you blame us for shouting, now that our men
won't get those "Greetings from the Athenian State"
in the mail any more?

TRYGAEUS:

But you people holler like *this*
and you'll wake the ghost of some old soldier Down There
who just faded away.

SETH:

Just let me get my hands on Peace,
just once before I die. Wow!

TRYGAEUS:

I'm serious, damn it,
War's in there! Keep it down!

VIVIAN:

Mr. Trygaeus, this
is a day of international celebration; if War wants
trouble, just let him try!

TRYGAEUS:

What's *wrong* with you people?
You'll screw the whole thing up if you don't keep *QUIET!*

*(Behind the steady work-rhythm of the drums a counterbeat begins to
be heard, and to this Slick and Lily, who have been engaged in private
conversation, begin to frug. Lily's heels and Slick's boots make quite a
racket. Trygaeus attempts to pry Lily loose and although Slick continues
dancing by himself, Lily stops.)*

LILY:

I just can't *help* it, honey. I just hear the word Peace
and it gets my legs to going. And he does it so *good* too!

(Trygaeus talks to Slick, who stops. Lily starts again.)

TRYGAEUS:

Look, will you cut the dancing? We've got to be quiet.

SLICK:

Don't sweat it, baby.

(Trygaeus turns to Lily; same business.)

TRYGAEUS:

WILL YOU *QUIT* IT?

(She stops.)

LILY:

I've stopped.

(Trygaeus turns to Slick.)

TRYGAEUS:

You said you'd quit, and here you go again.

SLICK:

Man, just let us *move* a little taste.

TRYGAEUS:

Thirty seconds,
and that's *it*.

*(They burst into a frenzy of dancing. Trygaeus times them with a stop-
watch, glancing anxiously between the watch, them, and the house.
After thirty seconds he attempts to separate them but they continue.)*

LILY:

Honey, for you I'd *love* to stop, but I'm so *happy*!

TRYGAEUS:
   But you *promised*!

SLICK:
                              Man, thirty *seconds*!

TRYGAEUS:
                                        Thirty seconds,
   but then no more dancing and no more noise.

SLICK:
                                        My man!

(Same business; at the end of thirty seconds;)

LILY:
   Baby, this thing is bigger than the both of us.
   Can't you see we're dancing because we're happy, just
   for pure joy? Why, I've lost thirty . . .
                              lost five years today!

*(Trygaeus finally succeeds in separating them, firmly leading each to
an opposite end of the straggly group.)*

TRYGAEUS:
   Now look, partying is premature. We're not safe yet.
   But once we get her out, friends, out of that hole, THEN
              laugh and holler
              as much as you like,
              free to travel
              or stay home,
              free to nap
              or fuck or shoot
              craps or feast or
              go to the opera,
              I don't care!
              Free, friends, *Free*!

CHORUS:

HOORAW! HOORAW!

(Trygaeus frantically urges them to be quiet.)

Hooraw!

Hooraw.

(hooraw)

(During the following choral passage, the members of the chorus are half addressing one another and Trygaeus, half the audience.)

SETH:

I never thought I'd live to see the day.

HANK:

I guess we'd kind of got to think it was
a sort of breakfast cereal: 37 SPARTANS DEAD
WITH MINOR ATHENIAN LOSSES.

VIVIAN:

Maybe it didn't bother me because it hadn't touched me really.

TRYGAEUS:

Meaning your Fiat or your schnauzer or your 21 grand a year?

ALICIA:

Things change. People
change. We're changing.

SLICK:

Maybe you don't like the kind of life I choose
to live; but I don't ask you, man, to die for mine,
and I'm damned if I'll die for yours.

LILY:

Talk, talk! Let's
get to work. Mr.

Trygaeus, you look like the one who knows
what's going on. So tell us what to do.
Somebody's got to be boss, and it looks like you're elected.

TRYGAEUS:
Well, let me get a look at this rock. Looks pretty big.

(Re-enter Hermes.)

HERMES:
You *rude*, nauseating, simply *filthy* animal, *who*
are these *humans*? And What are you *doing*?

(Trygaeus brings out the fist again.)

TRYGAEUS:
Hermes,
didn't I once mention something concerning your use
of words like "filthy animal"?

(Hermes cringes, but:)

HERMES:
I assure you, Mr.
Trygaeus, your threats don't concern me in the least. Because
you're as good as dead.

TRYGAEUS:
As good as *what*?

HERMES:
As dead.

TRYGAEUS:
When?

HERMES:
Right this very *minute*.

TRYGAEUS:

But that's ridiculous, I didn't
bring along any sandwiches or Cokes or anything
for such a long . . .

HERMES:

Since *you* brought up the subject of
length, sweets: you're screwed.

TRYGAEUS:

And I never even
noticed it? What a waste!

HERMES:

It's kind of you to mention it.
But really, didn't you know God has ruled that anyone
who tries to dig Peace up *dies*?

TRYGAEUS:

Well, actually, no.
Is it absolutely indispensable?

HERMES:

Well, the law's the law.

TRYGAEUS:

Then could you lend me five drachmas? I'd like to
get me a *little* piece, at least, before I pass away.

HERMES:

GREAT GOD ALMIGHTY . . .

TRYGAEUS:

Couldn't you leave God out of this
for just a minute?

HERMES:

Sorry. I have my job to do.

HERMES:
I've left doves on your altar, right?

HERMES:

Right.

TRYGAEUS:

And COCKS?

HERMES:
Look, I *remember*! But God would thunderbolt me if I didn't call his attention to flagrant transgressions of his laws.

(Again he opens his mouth to yell; Trygaeus holds his hand over it.)

TRYGAEUS:
Now hold *on*! Just a minute. *Quiet, that's* a good Hermes.

(He turns to the chorus.)

So what's wrong with you people? You stand there like stones. If he tells God, we're finished. Talk it up!

(In this chorus the members address Hermes, still held by Trygaeus with his mouth stopped, and one another.)

LILY:
Don't do it, Mr. Hermes, please don't do it!

HANK:

You can't pretend *I* haven't gone to church
and dropped my drachma in the plate like everybody
every Sunday.

ALICIA:

So now when it's a
matter of life and death, remember our little contributions.

TRYGAEUS:
See! See how good they've treated you! You can't just . . .

SLICK:

> That's not the point.
> The point is, things
> are changing, and we're changing them, like it
> or not.

SETH:

> Don't get him all riled up, son
> We won't get nowheres that way.
> Let's just get her *out*.

VIVIAN:

> Now *that's* sensible!
> Mr. Hermes, we have you outnumbered; but
> we'd rather have you with us than against us.
> And think what a *hero* you'll be on Earth, what *offerings*!

TRYGAEUS:

Listen to them, Hermes! They've always worshipped you,
and now you'll be a sort of patron saint to them.

(Aside:)

What I mean is, they seem to be kind of a queer bunch . . .
And look, you let me off, and I'll warn you of a plot
they're working up down there against all you gods.

HERMES:

Well, *try* me, honey. I mean, I *can* be persuaded. Try!

TRYGAEUS:

Look, have you noticed how the sun goes out sometimes
when it's not night?

HERMES:

> Umhmh.

TRYGAEUS:

> Well, that's part of the plot.

And have you noticed how the moon changes size, gets
bigger or smaller?

HERMES:
> Well, of course, silly.

TRYGAEUS:
> *That's* part
>
of the plot too.

HERMES:
> Whose plot?

TRYGAEUS:
> The sun and moon; they want
to kill all the Greek Gods and run everything themselves!

HERMES:
But *why*?

TRYGAEUS:
> *Think*! Nobody but a barbarian would worship
the sun and moon, right? So they only get sacrifices
from barbarians, right? So what they want to do
is kill *you* and get everything for themselves!

(Hermes ponders.)

HERMES:
So *that's* why thirty days hath September, April, June
and November, and all the *rest* . . .

TRYGAEUS:
> *Right*!

HERMES:
> They've
>
been stealing days from us!

TRYGAEUS:

Right! And *that's* why
you should co-operate with us, not fink to God; and
humans will make you a hero and celebrate your birthday
with parades like we do for Aphrodite and the Mysteries
and all. And not just Athens, *all* the countries you've
freed from war will sacrifice to you as Hermes the Savior,
everywhere.

*(During this speech Trygaeus has been engaged in swiping a large bottle
from Lily's purse, which he now hands to Hermes.)*

And, as an indication of our good faith,
permit me to present you with this small token of our esteem.

HERMES:

I've got to admit I've always had a soft spot in my heart
for little gifts . . .

*(But his tone is not conclusive. As all watch intently, he opens the bottle
and takes a sip; then a swallow. Rolls it around in his mouth. Another.
Roars:)*

OK, you mortals, let's get this show on the road!
For a start, see if you can move that rock if you shove
together.

SETH:

Let's go!

(Lily, vamping wildly, sidles up to Hermes.)

LILY:

You're really a nice god after all.

*(Hermes backs off distastefully. Lily shrugs and walks with the rest to-
ward the rock.)*

353

You just be foreman, Mr. Hermes, and tell us what to do,
and watch our smoke!

(Lily looks dubiously at the rock, which is very big.)

LILY:

                    I guess it can't hurt to try.

*(While the chorus members are shoving and hauling at the rock, get-
ting nowhere, Trygaeus and Hermes pay no attention to them, engaged in their own business, although Trygaeus yells to Hank and Lily:)*

TRYGAEUS:
That's the spirit!

(He takes the bottle from Hermes and has a drink.)

                  But we ought to toast the gods
before we start, right?

*(Hermes jealously grabs his bottle back, drinks again. He becomes
more and more obviously drunk as the scene progresses.)*

HERMES:
                  A toast! That's the stuff!
Got to pro*pish*iate all the other Olympians, huh?

(He drinks again, raises the bottle:)

A TOAST TO GREECE! And all you Greeks. And may you
live happily ever after! And may whoever lays a hand
to this job today never have to touch a sword again!

*(Trygaeus takes the bottle, drinks. Although he becomes tipsy during
the scene, he never becomes as sloppy drunk as Hermes.)*

TRYGAEUS:
I'll drink to that: a long life, and a peaceful life.

And a hot girl so once in a while you can whip out the old
poker and poke up the fire.

*(At this point, and during the following exchange, he assumes the
stance of a quite pompous minister; the chorus, in unison, respond like
a congregation's "responsive readings.")*

AND IF, O ALMIGHTY GOD,
THERE BE THOSE WHO DESIRE BATTLE . . .

CHORUS:

MAY THEY YANK
ARROWHEADS OUT OF THEIR ELBOWS THROUGH ALL
THEIR DAYS.

TRYGAEUS:

AND SHOULD THERE BE ANY, MOST GRACIOUS GODDESS,
WHO,
THIRSTING AFTER MILITARY EMINENCE, HARBORS RAN-
COR IN HIS
HEART THAT WE FREE YOU . . .

CHORUS:

LET HIM BE CALLED BY
HIS FELLOW-
CITIZENS UNCONSCIENTIOUS OBJECTOR, AND BE MADE
LESS
THAN THE DUST OF THEIR BOOTSOLES.

TRYGAEUS:

AND IF SOME
MAKER
OF MUNITIONS, FOR LOVE OF GAIN, SHOULD DESIRE WAR . . .

CHORUS:

MAY HE FALL AMONG THIEVES AND BE NOURISHED WITH
HOG-SLOP.

(Hermes now notices the chorus, who have succeeded in attaching the ropes and are preparing to haul on them. As Trygaeus and Hermes watch, they pass the bottle back and forth.)

HERMES:

Hey, y'gotta pull onna rope, rope's no good you don't pull on it . . . Huh, Trygaeus?

(These pulling scenes which follow are generally of the Keystone variety; the members of the chorus trip over themselves, the ropes, one another, engage in personal argumentation, pratfalls, etc.)

CHORUS:

HEEAAVE! HEEAAVE!

(Hermes echoes them drunkenly, waving his bottle in time to the basic work-rhythm, which becomes continually louder now—although at first the members of the chorus are by no means working in harmony with it.)

HERMES:

HEEAAVE HEEAAVE

CHORUS:

HEEAAVE HEEAAVE

HERMES:

Assa way HEEAAVE

(Trygaeus approaches the chorus to straighten out the muddle.)

TRYGAEUS:

AND IF THERE BE THOSE WHO, CRAVING GENERALSHIP, SHOULD
REFUSE US THEIR AID OR PLAN IN THEIR HEARTS TO FLEE
LIKE SLAVES IN THE NIGHT . . .

CHORUS:

LET SUCH BE PLACED IN

ZOOS
FOR THE WARNING AND EDUCATION OF FUTURE GEN-
ERATIONS.

HERMES:
Byooful prayer. Nothing to say but HOO RAY. Mean AH MEN.

(The chorus returns to the project and, during the ensuing, mostly under Vivian's direction, attach two ropes to the rock, making them secure, etc.)

TRYGAEUS:
If we can get *her* out, us *men* can take care of ourselves.

HERMES:
OK, no Amen. Just Hooray. Gonna say it again, HOORAY.

TRYGAEUS:
And hooray for Hermes first of all

(Hermes attempts to bow in response, almost falls)

                              and then hooray for
the Graces, 'nen hooray for Aphrodite, 'nen hooray for . . .

HERMES:
But not hooray for War.

TRYGAEUS:
                    uh-*uh.*

TRYGAEUS:
Hey, hold up. You're not working together. You there,

(Addressing Hank:)

you're not getting your back into it. Now try again.

CHORUS:
            HEEAAVE HEEAAVE

TRYGAEUS AND HERMES:
HEEAAVE HEEAAVE

SLICK:

Hey, what's the matter with *you* two? Too good to dirty
your hands?

HERMES:

Gotta be sup'intenets, don't they?

ALICIA:

But we're not
getting anywhere.

TRYGAEUS:

You really want to know why? Look,
you two,

(Indicating Slick and Hank)

you spend half your time tripping each other up.

(To Lily:)

If you'd care to step behind a rock and take off your girdle,
maybe you could *pull.*

(To Vivian:)

Miss, I have no objection to tidiness;
but did you have to do your nails just *then*?

SETH:

Me,
I'm pulling.

TRYGAEUS:

I'm afraid you don't carry much weight.

(Hank points at Slick.)

HANK:

He makes more *noise* than anybody, but he obviously doesn't know what's happening.

SLICK:

You could tell me maybe?

HERMES:

HEY!

Same thing alla time, all Greeksh do ish talk, lesh
shee shome acsh'n here, huh? Wayya say, huh?

(The members of the chorus, a little abashed, return to work. Trygaeus too taking an end of one rope. But the two ropes, during this attempt, diverge first into a V-form and finally are totally opposed.)

CHORUS:

HEEAAVE HEEAAVE

HERMES:

Atta boy HEEAAVE

CHORUS:

HEEAAVE HEEAAVE

HERMES:

HEEAAVE HEEAAVE

(Lily drops her hold on the rope and walks away:)

LILY:

It just won't *move.*

TRYGAEUS:

A*maz*ing! With your side pulling
East and us West, I suppose it'll just pop right out,
huh?

Lady, you can use the exercise, believe me.

Again!

359

CHORUS:

HEEAAVE HEEAAVE

HERMES:

Woops! Gotta . . .

CHORUS:

HEEAAVE HEEAAVE

(Hermes dashes behind his pillar again; when he returns shortly later he is somewhat more subdued and sober. Meanwhile Slick drops his hold on the rope and walks away.)

SLICK:

God*damn*, you got to have *some* co-operation.

ALICIA:

Just *pull.*

SLICK:

They keep getting in my way.

(Trygaeus drops the rope as well and stands a moment, hands on hips, surveying them all. Finally:)

TRYGAEUS:

You people can all shove it.
I come all the way to Heaven to try to clear this up
and all you can do is squabble. Let me just say now,
anybody who has any doubts about this project, get out;
the rest of us'll handle the job. I've noticed a lot
of *talk* about Peace around here, but damn little effort.

(All drop the rope and stand. There is a long pause. At last Seth steps forward toward Trygaeus.)

SETH:

I got a boy in the service.

(He picks up a section of rope. Another pause.)

ALICIA:

My husband was reported
missing in action.

(She takes hold of the rope beside Seth. And Then Slick joins them, saying almost furiously:)

SLICK:

I don't *know* why. And *you* don't *have* to.

(There is an extended stasis. Vivian and Hank look at the ground, at anything but the others' faces. Lily is caught between the two groups; starts to join the workcrew; then slowly withdraws to stand with Hank and Vivian to one side. Trygaeus grabs the rope.)

TRYGAEUS:
Now maybe we'll get somewhere.

ALICIA:

Sure we will, Mr. Trygaeus.

SLICK:
We got to.

SETH:

OK, all of us now. All together. Pull.

(Gypsy fiddles, Volga boatmen song (which also fits the basic rhythm). Hermes and Trygaeus call out over the chant, which is never interrupted. The music builds. The relation of movement to rhythm has changed; now sound and work are in harmony. Very slowly, not loud:)

SEMICHORUS:

Yo heave ho
Yo heave ho

HERMES:

(Hey! It's moving! Look! It's moving!)

361

SEMICHORUS:

> Pull to-geth-er

TRYGAEUS:

> (It's coming, coming! Don't stop! Don't stop!)

SEMICHORUS:

> Forward we go

HERMES *(awed):*

> (Will you look at that? Will you look at that?)

(The rock rises slowly from its hole, huger and huger; the four continue to pull and chant:)

> Yo heave ho
> Yo heave ho
> Yo heave ho

(The rock emerges with the sound of a cork popping and crashes loudly to the stage. All sound stops. Everything stops. The four who were pulling sprawl on the stage, the three to the side have not moved, Hermes stands motionless as well; and all eyes are directed, in total silence and immobility, at the hole now revealed.
Peace and her attendants, also noiselessly, rise, seated on a platform.)

(PEACE is most like the Girl Next Door, a touch of the young June Allison. This is not a matter of parody (gingham and freckles) but a general freshness and openness of bearing. Very attractive sexually but not sexy. Her clothing is tasteful, practical, ordinary.
Of her two companions, PROSPERITY is far more elaborately groomed, coiffeured, etc. A certain dignity, and of course that aura reflecting the self-confidence coming from wealth and beauty; but she can be had.
ABUNDANCE is a Bunny from a Playboy Club, in dress and personality—or non-personality. She is simply a trained sexual object. Abundant in every respect.
Trygaeus rises, approaches, inspects them. All remain motionless. He

362

is not in the least confused as to who is who. In a moment, he addresses himself directly to Peace.)

TRYGAEUS:

Peace . . . It *is* you. And here I am without a word
in the house to welcome you, not one I haven't cheapened.
I've said "love" to human women, just to get laid, even
"adore" and "worship." What can I say to the thing most
precious in life, goddess, but "Welcome home"?
*He*llo,
Prosperity, nice to have you back; and Abundance . . .
and
Abundance . . . My *goodness,* how nice to see *you* again,
Abundance! You haven't changed a bit! And what's that
perfume you're wearing?

(He starts sniffing around her bosom; it has become a matter of centimetres when Hermes finally speaks up.)

It smells so *good*! Like *Evening*
in Lesbos mixed with smoke rising from burning draftcards.

HERMES:
Don't you smell just a touch of the barracks about her too?

TRYGAEUS:

Barracks? No, I'd recognize that stench of stiff socks
and sweat and secret sperm and despair. No, Hermes,
she smells to me of Spring when violets and hearts

(He moves closer and closer to her, begins to fondle her absently, his phallus rising; but his eyes are far away.)

burst into bloom, of drunkenness with friends, of music,
of Jeffers' grave, noble odes, or maybe
James Dickey's . . .

HERMES:
You don't have to *insult* the poor child.

TRYGAEUS:

    . . . ivy, maybe, and lots to drink with friends, and birds twittering, and music half-heard in a canoe by moonlight drifting over the water, and drinking, and . . .

HERMES:

                                        Trygaeus!

(Trygaeus starts, takes his hands from Abundance and starts to join Hermes at the balcony of Heaven; and then, as though being pulled by a magnet, starts to drift back again.)

Trygaeus!

(Trygaeus joins him at the balcony. They gaze out over the audience.)

        Look down! All the people in all the cities running around . . .

TRYGAEUS:

                the ones that have legs . . .

HERMES:

                                  and
slapping each other on the back . . .

TRYGAEUS:

                        the ones with arms . . .

HERMES:

No one afraid to look in another's eyes . . .

(Then anticipates Trygaeus, stops him with a gesture.)

                            But Trygaeus,
really, can't you see how happy everyone is?

TRYGAEUS:

                    Not everyone.

Isn't that the chairman of the board of Dow Chemicals
on the window ledge over there? Napalm's gone the way
of the bustle.

HERMES:
But look at that tractor-and-combine
salesman!

TRYGAEUS:
The one farting in the general's face?

HERMES:
Yes! And look! There's somebody from the War on Poverty
program!

TRYGAEUS:
Why, he seems to be giving the *finger* to the chief
of Central Intelligence of Athens!

HERMES:
So it's clear enough
you've done what you came for.

(With a reappearance of his initial distaste for the chorus:)

So you can tell *them*
they can leave now.

(Trygaeus turns to the chorus.)

TRYGAEUS:
I guess that wraps it up, friends.
You've all got jobs in the world to do. But I think
you'll find it a different place when you go back; you
can be proud of yourselves.
Or some of you.

(He resumes the pastoral tone:)

But before
we part, Brethren, let us refresh our hearts with a Hymn
of Thanks. Please turn to page 157 of your hymnals.

(He marks the beat: 1, 2, 3. A full band accompaniment blares forth as Trygaeus and the chorus sing:)

> Oh beautiful for spacious skies,
>   for amber waves of grain,
> For purple mountains' majesty
>   above the fruited plain:

(More slowly, more emphatically:)

> Athenia, Athenia,
>   God shed His grace on thee:
> And crown thy good with brotherhood
>   from sea to shining sea.

TRYGAEUS:

Fine, fine. You might stop to say a word of thanks
to Peace as you pass out. She's been good to you.
And then run home and see what's happening.

(During this last, Lily's wandered over to the balcony and has been looking down. She now calls to the rest:)

LILY:

It looks kind of nice to see all those people down there,
just going about their business.

(The rest join her.)

SETH:

Looks *mighty* nice.

TRYGAEUS:

Look at that little country over there, for instance.

It's looking better these days; things starting to grow
again, and blackbirds and mockingbirds instead of
whirlybirds. And nothing but water falling out of the sky.
It's real pretty

(Explosion offstage. All flinch and look away.)

                    except when some little kid
steps on a leftover landmine . . .
                           But look at *Greece*!
                      And think of all we're grateful
                      to the goddess for: for figs
                      dried in bunches, or picked
                      ripe from the tree, and sweet
                      wine, wells of clear water,
                      the olives we missed so much . . .
Maybe we could just try to tell her how grateful
we are for all she's done for all of us.

*(All turn to the goddesses. Peace turns her face to them. A faint echo
of the earlier work rhythm can be heard. Vivian begins, hesitantly and
formally. As each speaks, Peace's head turns slowly to face the speaker directly.)*

VIVIAN:
                    We want to say we're grateful for all you've
                    done for us.

ALICIA:
                            When they killed my Frank,
                I almost went out of my head . . .

HANK:
                      I can tell you, goddess,
it'll be good to get back to work again without all that.

TRYGAEUS:
All what? All those extra taxes? And taxes on the taxes?

367

SLICK:
It don't make much
difference to me.
Unless it makes it more of a world you don't
have to hide from or be ashamed of.

SETH:
It makes a difference to *me*!
They'll send my son
home in one piece.

LILY:
I never wanted anybody to get hurt. I never
knew what was happening. I don't read the papers
much, except the TV Guide. But I'm glad it's over. Thanks.

(Peace nods, almost imperceptibly. After a moment, as though out of
embarrassment, Trygaeus turns to Hermes.)

TRYGAEUS:
Hermes, how did this whole business happen? I mean,
how did she get *into* the hole in the first place?

HERMES:
Oh,
the usual thing.

TRYGAEUS:
What do you mean, the usual thing?

HERMES:
Oh,
to put it briefly as possible, the Chief Executive
was in trouble; and *I* mean *trouble.* He had become Head
of State under—shall we say?—Questionable Circumstances,
and almost immediately a Close Associate of his, in a
Previous Position, turned out to be in a—well, say—a
Compromising Relation with, ah, Certain Persons who . . .
Well *you* know what I mean, you read the papers; or

(A glance at Lily.)

most of you read the papers. So he needed a Distraction,
of course; and there it was ready to hand. And *that's* how
the military advisers became soldiers and . . . Well, the rock.

TRYGAEUS:
Nothing's as simple as that. But I've got to admit
you've kept your eyes open up here in Heaven.

LILY:
                                                    It makes
good sense to me.

HANK:
                    It would. You don't read the papers.

SLICK:
You believe the *papers*?

SETH:
                    Be quiet now, let him go on.

HERMES:
Well then, *if* I may continue. So what was *supposed* to
be a quiet sort of skeetshoot off in a country nobody'd
heard of and *some* couldn't even pronounce, provided
a kind of *Cause* for all your Imperial Subjects who felt
unhappy—for other reasons, of course, but subjects
are always unhappy. I'm a God, I know. And worse,
you were getting beaten as badly as you beat the Persians,
for the same reasons, only reversed of course, so
you couldn't shut it off when it got embarrassing. And so
it became a matter of Honor, and so forth, and the little
people suffered, and so forth, and so forth, and so forth.

ALICIA:
Gods take life pretty lightly, Mr. Hermes. One of those
little people of yours was my Frank.

VIVIAN:

                                 And then what?
    Go on.

HERMES:

        Well, if you *people* would only stop inter*rup*ting . . .

(He pauses. No response. Satisfied:)

Now, Peace had always had a soft spot for Athens; and so
she'd show up at public hearings and demonstrations; but
they'd shout her down, or arrest her. And meanwhile, of
course, the Imperial Subjects were chafing; they'd support
your Persian policies, or whatever, and get nothing for it.
And some, inside *and* outside, claimed that Athens
would never treat a *Greek* state like that, that it was a
matter of *race*. And after all . . . Well, you read the papers;
or most of you. And there's always somebody making money
out of war, and they had their ways of making themselves
felt where it counted. Not that they'd started it,
but why stop a Good Thing? And so . . .

TRYGAEUS:

                                 Stop it! *Stop* it!
    I can't bear to see Athenian foreign policy based on
    scandals in men's rooms and vicuna coats.

LILY:

                                 But *you*
    made your mind up, and *stopped* it.

TRYGAEUS:

                                 That's nice of you.
                    But if any of you would care to
                    make some formal statement about
                    those cocksuckers, those heifer-
                    fuckers and boilers of babies'
                    blood who'd put a blowtorch

to their own daughters' tidy
assholes or order another Hiroshima
to keep political pressure off,
spit it out now.

(A pause.)

SLICK:

I guess that takes care of everything.

(Another pause. Seth looks again at Peace.)

SETH:

Won't *she* say something? Anything?

HERMES:

She's afraid;
when she looks out at the audience she sees so many
people with a financial interest in her death.

TRYGAEUS:

But maybe
she'd *whisper* to you?

(Hermes leans over to Peace.)

HERMES:

Is there anything you'd like to say,
dear?

(He listens as she whispers.)

You *what*?

They *what*?

I see your point.

She says
she's lost hope in a democracy that fights more than ten
years to prevent democracy somewhere else. She quotes some

371

barbarian: NOT IN ONE COUNTRY ALONE. She says you should be ashamed.

ALICIA:

      I am.

HANK:

          When she puts it that way . . .

VIVIAN:

                        The situation
was different then.

TRYGAEUS:

          I hope it's different now.

(Hermes has been listening again.)

HERMES:

                    Hey,
fellas, she has more questions for you.

(All turn to listen.)

                 Of everybody
you know, who hates her most? and who can she *trust,*
to help her keep this stopped?

HANK:

          Well, *I* can tell her who
loves her most, those chickens that burned their draftcards.

SETH:

      Some burned themselves.

HERMES:

          She wants to know, is *that*
any way to love the goddess Peace?

SLICK:

The only way they had.

HERMES:

She wants to know, what were these people like?

ALICIA:

Silly,
and braver and more honest than all of us put together.

HERMES:

Where can she find them now?

SLICK:

In jail.

SETH:

And a few dead.

(Hermes listens again.)

HERMES:

Now what she wants to know is, who's in charge of Foreign
Policy these days?

TRYGAEUS:

Nobody knows.

HERMES:

Well, who's *supposed*
to be in charge?

(Trygaeus shrugs disgustedly.)

TRYGAEUS:

You're the one who reads the papers;
you tell her.

*(Hermes whispers to Peace. Peace, without altering her expression,
slowly turns her head from chorus and audience.)*

LILY:

                  Why is she turning her head away from
the audience?

HERMES:

                  Disgust. She can't understand how
so many of you can choose small unimaginative people
when you have the *freedom* to choose.

VIVIAN:

                                I don't believe
it's going to happen again.

HANK:

                      Honest, it was any port in a storm.

TRYGAEUS:

How can it *not* happen again? Have you seen what we'll have
to choose from *next* time around?

ALICIA:

                           But the people are
catching on.

TRYGAEUS:

                The *system's* not. And the system's under-
ground, and we grope in the dark; let's lift *that* stone
and take a hard look at what you find under stones
most of the time.

    (Hermes is listening again.)

HERMES:

                (She's *simply* wearing me to a *frazzle.*)

TRYGAEUS:
What now?

HERMES:

Well, first she wants to know what became of an old friend of hers, some "Hubert."

TRYGAEUS:

He seems healthy. But she might not want to know him now.

HERMES:

And she asks how "Adlai" is?

TRYGAEUS:

Dead.

HERMES:

But stayed her friend?

(Trygaeus is suddenly very angry:)

TRYGAEUS:

Tell her there might be *some* questions she wouldn't want to have answered!

(And then, addressing Peace directly:)

Goddess, I'm sorry. It's just that so many have died so strangely, or changed suddenly, and nobody understands anything, or trusts anyone. I'm sorry. Just never leave us again, goddess, and we'll be all right.

(More whispering between Hermes and Peace.)

HERMES:

She understands. She says to take Prosperity for your wife, and live in the country, and be happy, and raise lots of cotton.

375

TRYGAEUS:
Prosperity? And not . . .

(Hermes shakes his head. Trygaeus inspects Prosperity.)

Well, she's a little
classy for country life. But we'll get something straight
between us, eh, Prosperity?

HERMES:
And the Goddess also says
Abundance must be given to the world.

TRYGAEUS:
Oh, lucky world!
World, you'll have a ball tonight! There's plenty of *her*
to go around

(Wistfully:)

and maybe a piece left over . . .
Well, Hermes,
it's been fun. You take care now.

HERMES:
You too, Trygaeus; and
honey, think of me sometimes.

TRYGAEUS:
Here, beetle, beetle! Here,
beetle, beetle, beetle!

HERMES:
He's been called to higher things.

TRYGAEUS:
Where is he?

HERMES:
He's pulling the Chariot of God Himself.

TRYGAEUS:

He'll die of starvation! What's he going to live on,
with nothing but gods around?

HERMES:

Honestly! What did you *think*
happened to all that nectar and ambrosia?

TRYGAEUS:

So how do I
get home?

HERMES:

Everything's been taken care of. Just
step up here with the girls.

TRYGAEUS:

Come along now, girls.

*(Trygaeus, seated, clasps one hand of Abundance and one hand of
Prosperity about his hugely erect phallus, throws his arms around their
buttocks. Peace is standing behind the chair.)*

Hang on! The world awaits you! AND IT'S A HARD WORLD, KIDS!

*(Blackout. Whistle of falling bomb. Tremendous explosion. Cries from
the chorus: "Goodbye," "Good luck," etc. Lights come up again
after a moment, but now ordinary stage worklights. Trygaeus and the
goddesses have vanished.)*

OFFSTAGE VOICE:

STRIKE THE SET!

*(The remaining characters immediately lose all element of stereotype;
they relax, become themselves, their costumes and makeup irrelevant
to the real people underneath. They talk, light cigarettes, at last wander
offstage or into the audience.
Meanwhile a stagehand has effortlessly removed the rock; others remove
the castle façade, the balcony rail, until the stage is entirely cleared.)*

(They then carry on a lecture podium, which is placed facing the audience. Electricians hook up and test a microphone.)

(Then all exit. For a moment the stage is empty.)

(The lighting now changes to a stagier affair, mostly footlights; simultaneously sound effects of a large audience shuffling into place, gradually quieting coughs, rattling of programs.)

(Hermes enters and steps up to the podium. He is now dressed very modishly in mod clothes, brilliant flowered vest, etc. He carries a small sheaf of papers in his hand, which he arranges before him on the podium.)

(His personality has essentially not altered; he's still queer, but a different sort; any pompousness previously present has now taken over entirely. He has acquired a rich (and overdone) British accent, much throatclearing and such. Although he seems to be the director of the play, or possibly the author, he parodies the very worst sort of bad professor. He is intolerably dull.)

(As he climbs the podium, the sound of great applause.)

HERMES:
Thank you, thank you. *(The applause diminishes.)* Thank you.
(It disappears.) Thank you.
    Although I don't, of course, intend to spend the evening praising our own production—I shall leave that to the critics and personal friends—I should like, in case I should seem overly pleased with this evening's entertainment, to read you precisely what Aristophanes himself, through his Chorus, of course, this being the so-called parabasis of EIRENE, or PEACE, has to say of his own work at this point in his play:

ε'ι δ'οὖν ε'ιηός τινα τιμῆσαι, Θύγατερ Διός, ὄστις ἀριστος
ἠωμωδοδιδάσηαλος α'᾽θρω᾽πων ηα'ι ηλειηο᾽τατος γεγε᾽νηται,
ἄξιος εἶναι᾽ φησ᾽ ε᾽υλογι᾽ας μεγάλησ᾽ο διδα᾽σηαλος ᾽εμῶν.

Aristophanes, *Peace,* 736–738

That is to say, "But if it be proper, daughter of God, to praise the finest and most acclaimed comic dramatist—*komodidaskalos*—in the world—*anthropon*—, your preceptor (that is, Aristophanes himself) claims to be worthy your applause."

And there's quite a good bit more of that, of the 'Exegi monumentum' sort, later on in this same parabasis.

Now this estimate may well be accurate. But it has seemed to us, in presenting this version of Aristophanes' comedy, that precisely that phrase *"didaskalos emon,"* a teacher or instructor of *you,* the audience, representatives of the *polis,* or people, was that which Aristophanes most prided himself upon, and that it is precisely that element— of instructorship—that is lacking in most attempts to present Aristophanes on the contemporary stage. (You are all, of course, familiar with Mr. Eliot's celebrated essay concerning Gilbert Murray's translations of Euripides; I take that as my starting point.)

Now. What you will *not* find in this presentation of Aristophanes are references to historical events or personages unknown to, shall we say, *"l'homme moyen sensuel,"* the general theater-goer. No references, that is to say, to Pylos, or Brasidas, or Cleonymus—a fat person known to history only because Aristophanes delighted, upon every possible occasion, recalling the fact that he had thrown away his shield upon the field of battle. Such persons seemed to us precisely the *'idiotas anthropiskous,'* the "unknown little chaps," unknown at least to *our* audience, upon which Aristophanes prides himself, in line 751 of this same parabasis, on *not* attacking; attacking, rather, as he puts it in his somewhat highflown verbiage, *"to kharkadonti ou deinotatai"* . . . Well, to put it in English—although perhaps I shouldn't—"the sharptoothed animal itself, surrounded by the hundred heads of ah, 'Yes-men' (if I may so translate it, *kolakon*), with the voice of a thundering cataract, the stench of a seal, the—ah— private parts of—well, of a Lamia, you may not understand the reference, and the, ah . . . the, ah . . . the Hind End, shall we say . . ."

Well, you see my point, certainly: that Aristophanes, in his capacity as *didaskolos,* that is to say, teacher, took great pride in his willingness to attack persons who, although they might possess great personal or political power,

379

(A large hook begins descending slowly from the flies.)

were, in his opinion, harmful to the people, the *polis,* without regard to his own personal welfare.

It was on these grounds, then, in his capacity as *didaskolos,* or teacher, that he desired, at the end of the parabasis of the Eirene, or THE PEACE,

(The hook catches him up and carries him slowly upward. He notices nothing and continues. The footlights begin to dim slowly as he rises.)

that the audience should vote him first prize in the dramatic competitition, in these words: "For these reasons it is proper that both young and old vote for me; and even the very old, with bald heads, I invite to share in my feast of victory." Now this, as you will see developed

(He is drawn out of sight, and the footlights dim to blackout. The voice continues a moment longer, fading out.)

Aristophanes' own baldness, much celebrated in antiquity . . .

(Silence. Darkness. From this silence, from this darkness, the chorus is heard. Each stanza of the first strophe is recited by a different voice; the same order is preserved in the second strophe. Each strophe is accompanied by the same melody—odd but very simple—on a single flute.)

Muse, darling, war was a bad
dream, come out and
dance with us

> Be brides-
> maid at the gods'
> weddings and guest our
> banquets and bless us
>> BUT don't let
>> Karkinos come around with his
>> sons, Muse,
> even if he begs you, ignore them all

entirely, those yammering chihuahuas, those
stumpnecked androids big as a parakeet's
dingleberry
(Karkinos claims he finally
finished a play; but unfortunately
a polecat ate it by
accident, and strangled)
Muse, most goddess, the good
poets will sing
your songs
        to us come spring,
        when swallow-blood and
        bones and cells call
        'Sing' to him
            BUT no songs from
            Morsimos or Melanthios,
            please, Muse,
        those monsters bloated with pheasant
        under glass, gulpers of caviar, swollen
        scarecrows to paralyze octogenarians,
        all armpit
Muse, darling, drench them with your
spittle, it's
spring, come out and play with us

*(Flute and voices die. Again silence, darkness. Then the lights come up
on the original scene. Trygaeus is center stage, supporting himself on
the shoulders of Prosperity and Abundance. He addresses the audience:)*

TRYGAEUS:
    I'll tell you right now, it's *work* getting up to Heaven
    and back. My legs are about shot.
                    Hey, you people
    looked pretty tiny from up there; if I hadn't
    retained my human perspective, I might have thought

you were pretty small in *lots* of ways. But I was right;
now I see you close up, you're *actually* microscopic.

(Liza and Rastus rush from the house.)

RASTUS:
Massa, massa, you is back!

TRYGAEUS:
You better believe it, boy.

LIZA:
Well, what-all *happen,* massa?

TRYGAEUS:
I about wore my legs off.

LIZA:
Massa, would y'all tell me . . .

TRYGAEUS:
What, Liza?

LIZA:
Did y'all see
any other humanity-type people floatin' aroun'
way up in de middle ob de air?

TRYGAEUS:
I had a little trouble
with a bunch of Messerschmidts—I mean F-105's—in the
lower ionosphere.

RASTUS:
What-all was dey *doin,* up dere, boss?

TRYGAEUS:
Kind of anti-planting, you could call it; seeding clouds
with chemicals, to poison the rain.

LIZA:

Massa, am it true
what I heerd a man say, dat all of us turns into stars
when we dies?

TRYGAEUS:

True as you're standing there.

LIZA:

What kin' ob
a star am Massa Eliot now?

TRYGAEUS:

First he was a nova, and later
a red dwarf.

LIZA:

An' Massa Crane?

TRYGAEUS:

He's a white giant of the
second magnitude.

RASTUS:

What about dem *shootin'* kin' ob stars,
Massa?

TRYGAEUS:

Those are the headlights of souls from Orange
county, driving home from Minutemen practice.

RASTUS:

An' massa . . .

TRYGAEUS:

That's enough now.

(To Liza:)

Take this goddess here inside and let

her take a bath, and dress, and put her face on; we're getting
married. And when that's taken care of, bring her back.

(Resignedly:)

This one I've got to turn over to the world.

LIZA:

                                        Where'd y'all
git dese ladies, massa?

TRYGAEUS:

                        In Heaven, naturally.

LIZA:

                                        I wouldn'
gib a nickel fo' no god what pimp aroun' like Rastus do.

TRYGAEUS:
There're always a few bad apples in every barrel, Liza.
Now get everything ready.

LIZA:

                        Massa, does y'all want I should
fix de lady somep'n to eat?

TRYGAEUS:

                        No, Liza. It'll take her
a while to get used to hoecake and grits. Up in Heaven
the gods just nibble ambrosia all day long.

*(Liza and Prosperity start inside; Rastus follows them, flourishing his
phallus.)*

RASTUS:

                                        I reckons
we kin gib her a little somep'n to nibble on here too.

TRYGAEUS:
RASTUS!

(Rastus returns.)

RASTUS:

Yassuh, massa, yassuh, massa boss, suh.

TRYGAEUS:

Let's go.

*(Trygaeus claps his hands. Five other slaves enter; they will function as
chorus later and are as follows:*
*The OLD MAN is an old man, very old, woolly poll, etc. PAPA JOHN
is stout and comfortable-looking.*
LUKE is lazy, lackadaisical.
*SAM is the youngest; there is a trace of Harlem in him; he's not as
country as the rest, and less a parody.*
HOP is much like Luke, except with a guitar in his hands.)

(All are parodies of standard types of slaves.)

*(Great activity. The slaves sweep, dust, fumigate, string pennants,
etc., during the following chorus. Luke brings on a large wicker armchair for Trygaeus, who sits in it, fondling Abundance and occasional-
ly brought mint juleps by the Old Man, as three Veracruz-type musicians
(harp and two small guitars) serenade him à la veracruzano:)*

MUSICO 1:

Lucky Trygaeus, he fly to Heaven
On a big black beetle with her motors revvin';
He come back down all safe and sound—

MUSICO 2:

With the prettiest little women in all the town.

ALL:

Lucky Trygaeus, lucky he,
Lucky Trygaeus, lucky he,
Lucky Trygaeus, you can see
Trygaeus lucky as a man can be.

MUSICO 2:

>Think he lucky now, y'ain't seen nothing yet,
>Wait till he get that pretty woman in bed;
>Gonna touch that stuff with all of his organs—

MUSICO 1:

>And climb inside and not come out till morning.
>(CHORUS)

MUSICO 1:

>He deserve what he get, for he preserve the Peace
>Of the whole wide world and not just only Greece.

MUSICO 2:

>He arrange with the Lord, and he arrange it right—

MUSICO 3:

>So I can get my*self* a little piece at night.
>(CHORUS)

(Enter Liza. The other slaves leave. The three musicians remain, accompanying the following scene with quiet background music.)

LIZA:

Massa, she gittin' ready.

(Privately, with a wink:)

>I give her her bath, massa,
>'n I kin tell y'all, y'all got yo'sef a *bunch* o' woman.
>Turkey's in de oben, de veg'tables is comin' along fine,
>we jes' about ready. Doan need nothin' now but de groom.

TRYGAEUS:

Okay. Just let me finish this business of turning Abundance
over to the world.

RASTUS:

>What y'all mean, boss? Who dis one?

TRYGAEUS:

Her name's Abundance, and after all the trouble I took
to find her, they tell me I have to give her to the world.

RASTUS:

Massa, dis am sho' gwine to be one night de worl'
won't *never* fo'git.

(Trygaeus turns to the audience.)

                    So, who can I trust out there
to take good care of Abundance here, and keep her safe
for the world?

*(Rastus, with an erection, is dancing around like a small boy needing a
bathroom. Trygaeus turns to address him and he stands still immediately, covering his erection with the towel he carries over his arm.)*

TRYGAEUS:

            Rastus, what in the *hell* are you up to?

RASTUS:

Nothin', boss, nothing' . . . Hey, boss, Is *I* a part
ob de worl'?

(Trygaeus' look is answer enough. To the audience:)

TRYGAEUS:

               Nobody?

(To Abundance:)

                   Come up and let them get a good
look at you.

(He leads her to the very front of the stage.)

RASTUS:

           Massa, massa, somebody got his hand up
down dere.

(Rastus points; Trygaeus peers.)

TRYGAEUS:

Who is it?

RASTUS:

Dat's Massa Heffner, suh.

TRYGAEUS:

Forget it.
She's not a *toy.*

(To Abundance:)

Let them see what they're getting.

(Abundance strips. Trygaeus unzips her when she presents her back to him. This is not burlesque, but also without embarrassment; the essential is the matter-of-factness of her response. She stands naked, either awkwardly nor provocatively, facing the audience.)

Gentlemen, I ask *you!* I can't understand such suspicion.

(He gestures to Abundance, who turns around slowly.)

No blemishes, gentlemen. Nobody's trying to con you; she simply needs a guardian for awhile.

(Rastus can no longer contain himself:)

RASTUS:

Massa, massa!
Please, boss, I'll take care of her!

TRYGAEUS:

Rastus, Abundance
can be stretched only so far.

(He turns back to the audience.)

Gentlemen, are you so

entranced by your TV? TV can't *begin* to compete with
Abundance! The World Series? Try nine innings with
Abundance here. Indianapolis? Nothing. Take a couple
of laps around *this*! The Rose Bowl? Nothing, gentlemen,
nothing; tackle Abundance, there's a Rose Bowl worth bucking
the line for. Or basketball? *Here's* a hoop to dump
your balls in, boys. Or wrestling? Well, what *is* it?
Gunsmoke? Man from UNCLE?

(A long pause. Finally Trygaeus shrugs.)

Well, I'd heard the stories
about Athens too; but I never really believed it was this bad.
OK, Rastus:

(Rastus leaps forward eagerly.)

give her to Mr. Warhol. Sixteen millimetres
is better than nothing.

*(Rastus, dejected, follows her offstage. Trygaeus addresses the
veracruzanos:)*

Little wedding music, boys.

*(Again he sinks into the armchair and is brought mint juleps during the
following.)*

MUSICO 1:

Trygaeus fall in the Sea of Shit,
Have to swim five mile to get out of it.
When he reach the shore and struggle up on the land—

MUSICO 2:

He find he have a tit in each of his hands!

ALL:

Lucky Trygaeus, lucky he,
Lucky Trygaeus, lucky he,

Lucky Trygaeus, you can see
Trygaeus lucky as a man can be.

MUSICO 2:

The reason why Trygaeus so lucky,
Is he love drinking an' he love fucking;
He drink so hard that when he come

MUSICO 1:

He don't come jizzum, he come Jamaica rum!
(CHORUS)

MUSICO 1:

We owe a mighty big debt to Lucky Trygaeus,
Flew up to heaven on a bug to save us.

MUSICO 2:

But now that we saved and happy and free—

MUSICO 3:

I hope some of that luck rub off on me!

(They sing the last chorus a little more slowly:)

ALL:

Lucky Trygaeus save the world,
Lucky Trygaeus he get the girl.
It seem real fair he get all that stuff—

MUSICO 3:

But I sure hope *some*thing rub off on us.

(Trygaeus exits, followed by the musicians, strumming. Enter Liza and Rastus.)

RASTUS:

Well, Liza, what-all we got lef' to do fo de prema*rish*ial
preparation?

LIZA:

Ain' got nothin', Rastus, 'cep de sacerfice.

RASTUS:

Dat's it, I know'd dey was somep'n. I'll run right
inside 'n git some o' dem little sacerfice kin' ob
cakes.

LIZA:

You talks like a simple fool. You talks like dis
was jes' Sunday o' somep'n. De massa's gittin' hisself
MARRIED.

RASTUS:

I reckon you's right, Liza. How about a cock?

LIZA:

De massa got his *own* cock to sacrificate tonight, y'all
let *him* worry about de cocks.

RASTUS:

Cow mebbe?

LIZA:

Y'all be careful:
dey gits a cow mixed up wif a coward and dey'll have us
right back in de War agin.

RASTUS:

Damn, *I* doan know, Liza . . .
How about a boar?

LIZA:

I'd sho like to sacrificate ever' Boer
in Souf Aferca, Rastus, but we got to take things slow.

RASTUS:

Well,

what *y'all* think we oughter sacrificate? Bein' as how
de massa's gettin' married an' all?

LIZA:

                                      Well, long as how
y'all ask *me* . . . Rastus, is dey any bulls lef' down in de
big fiel'?

RASTUS:

                    Dey is. But Liza, why y'all spesifi*si*cally
think she oughtter be a bull what we sacrificate?

LIZA:

                                            Rastus,
de massa's done took care of a *lot* of bull today, an' I
doan reckon dey's gwine miss one mo'.

RASTUS:

                              I got to admit,
y'all got *somep'n* up in dat kinky haid. I'll go an'
git de bull, y'all git de thing to sacrifice him on.

*(They leave. Trygaeus enters, now in white tie and phallus, followed
by the five slaves, now functioning as a Chorus. Papa John, the baritone, sings the chorus as fakily as possible, to the tune of "Swanee
River":)*

CHORUS:

                    Way down upon de ol' Plantation
                          Where Trygaeus live,
             All his faithful darkies want to wish him
                     All de luck dat dey can give.

(They hum through the verse again. Liza enters.)

LIZA:

Hyar she am, de altar! Massa, has Rastus got dat bull yet?

(Trygaeus shakes his head, Liza leaves, the Chorus sings:)

> All de dark am changed to sunshine,
> All de war to peace.
> Lay yo' swo'd an' shiel' beside de ribber
> Long side de prods ob de Police.

(Liza returns as the chorus hums again.)

LIZA:

Hyar de basket, massa, an' de water y'all got to sprinkle
on de bull what y'all sacrificate. Where *am* dat damn bull?

(Exits again. The Chorus sings:)

> All you darkies lif' yo' hearts up
> Everyplace you am:
> Jes' don' fo'git to call de massa massa,
> An' call de mistress ma'am.

(Rastus brings on the bull, as Liza enters with a nurse's cap and mask, wheeling an operating table with surgical instruments. The Chorus continues humming a sort of Stephen Foster medley as the sacrifice proceeds. Trygaeus plays the part of a surgeon, extending his hand for the desired sacrificial implement, Liza that of assistant.)

TRYGAEUS:
Gown!

(He is helped into it by Liza.)

Mask!

(Same play.)

Lustral water!

(Liza holds it as he washes his hands, à la Kildare. Liza then hands the bucket to Rastus, washes her hands.)

Gloves!

(Liza helps on with gloves: over shoulder, to Rastus:)

LIZA:

Gloves!

(Rastus looks for somewhere to put the bucket of water as Liza helps Trygaeus into his surgical gloves. Liza turns with her hands extended for her gloves.)

RASTUS:

Gown! Mask! Lustral water! Gloves! Gloves!
Massa! What I do wif dis yere luster-water?

TRYGAEUS:

Sterilize something.

(Rastus looks at the bucket, shrugs, tosses it out over the audience, helps Liza on with her gloves.)

LIZA:

Ever'body git a little?

RASTUS:

Sho did.

LIZA:

De women git a little too?

RASTUS:

I doan know about de women. But dey husbins'll give em
a little tonight.

TRYGAEUS:

If you people don't get moving, the patient
will *live*. Or die of old age. Scalpel!

(Liza and Rastus hunt for the scalpel on the "altar." Animated whispered discussion. Liza runs off. Trygaeus is furious at the delay:)

TRYGAEUS:

Scalpel!

SCALPEL!

(Turns to Rastus:)

God*damn* it, boy, where's the knife to sacrifice this bull?

RASTUS:

Boss, Liza done fo'git it, she gone off to git it now.

TRYGAEUS:

Well, maybe we can get the prayer over while we're waiting.
Rastus, will you do the honors?

(Rastus addresses the Chorus. There is real dignity in his prayer, and the rhythms are those of the great Negro Baptist preachers, a very high form of rhetoric. The Chorus murmurs "Yes Lawd," "Amen," "Ain' it de troff," etc.; as Rastus gets warmed up, the cries get louder; and toward the end Papa John and Luke fall to the ground and begin speaking in tongues.)

RASTUS:

Brudders an' sisters,
I is now gwine to pray to Peace, fo de sake ob all ob us.
Peace! I calls upon you name!
Peace! Widout you, Peace, de Worl'
am a living Hell. Peace! Widout you,
we was chillen los' in a dark fores'.
Peace! Now you's back, doan be like
dem harlots in de town, that when dey man's
gone off, dey opens dey do' an' peeks out
fo' some other man. An' if somebody
see 'em dere waiting, dey goes back inside;
but when dat person gone, dey peeks out
agin! Peace! Doan do us like dat!
Be like a hones' woman wif us, Peace!

And what y'all say yo' all gone do, y'all do dat!
We is like bridegrooms awaitin' de bride!
Peace! Thirteen years we ain' had you!
Put a end to war, Peace! Put a end to
tumults an' battles, put a end to de
suspicions what we had ob one anudder,
so's we kin live togedder wif de hand
ob fellowship. Peace! Teach us we is one
fambly, one man blessèd fo'ever.
An' let dey be melons, agin, Peace, an'
hoecake an' grits an' sowbelly an'
gator tails and chitlins an' a chicken
in de pot sometimes. But Peace,
let dey be *melons* agin, an' if Gen'ral
Wes'mo'lan' come to git him a melon,
Peace, tell him dey's all gone! Amen.

TRYGAEUS:

Listen to him, Goddess. He's a colored man, but his soul's
as good as white, and his heart's in the right place.
Is that damn knife here yet? Let's get this over with.

LIZA:

I got de knife, Massa. But I doan think y'all oughtter
sacrificate dat bull right here.

TRYGAEUS:

And why not, Liza?

LIZA:

Dat dere's a altar fo' Peace, an' I reckon she doan wan'
no blood on it, massa.

TRYGAEUS:

That makes sense. Rastus,
take the bull inside and sacrifice him there. And bring
the parts we have to cook for the goddess back outside.

396

(While Liza kindles a fire in a charcoal grill, Trygaeus is helped into a suburban chef's uniform—tall white chef's hat, apron with Silly Sayings—by Rastus. The Chorus, meanwhile, serenades him to the tune of 'Wild about my loving' (as recorded in 1932 or thereabouts by Furry Lewis, not Lovin' Spoonful version): Hop sings lead this time, accompanied by the others on jug, washboard, comb-and-paper and kazoo; Hop plays guitar.)

HOP:

               Trygaeus scramble to de top ob' de sky
               To git a little Peace befo' he die:
                    Cause he's wild about his lovin',
                    An' he like to have his fun:
                    You wanna be a friend of his, baby,
                    Bring it wif you when you come.

TRYGAEUS:

You there! Go on inside and get the table, the big one.

HOP:

               He ain't no iceman, lady, nor no iceman's son,
               But he can keep you cool, lady, till de iceman come:
                    Cause he's wild about his lovin',
                    An' he like to have his fun:
                    Wanna be a friend of his, honey,
                    Better bring it wif you when you come.

TRYGAEUS:

That fire burns like a lacquer factory. Can't you fix it?

HOP:

               He ain' no Avis man, lady, nor no Avis man's son,
               But he kin move you around, lady, till de Avis man come:
                    He's wild about his lovin',
                    An' he like to have his fun:
                    You wanna be a friend of his, baby,
                    Bring it wif you when you come.

*(Rastus returns with a platter of steaks, from which a bull's tail is dan-
gling. Liza has the fire going. Trygaeus looks around:)*

TRYGAEUS:
Shaping up.

(Addressing Rastus:)

Why don't you start on these, then, and you

(To Liza:)

run inside and see how everything's coming along there?

(Exit Liza.)

RASTUS:
Yassuh, boss.

TRYGAEUS:
And let's hurry things up.

RASTUS:
Yassuh, boss.

TRYGAEUS:
Because there's somebody coming along with his collar on
backwards.

RASTUS:
Who y'all think it am, massa?

TRYGAEUS:
I don't know;
but he walks like he has a bayonet up him.

RASTUS:
Some preacher,
boss?

TRYGAEUS:

Afraid so, Rastus. It looks to me like the Reverend Hierocles, come to pay us a little visit.

RASTUS:

What-all *he* want?

TRYGAEUS:

It's not Peace, I'll tell you that.

RASTUS:

*No*suh, it de smell ob dis steak fryin', is what it *am*.

TRYGAEUS:

Pretend you don't see him.

RASTUS:

Yassuh, boss.

TRYGAEUS:

Or hear him.

TRYGAEUS:

Yassuh, yassuh.

(Enter Hierocles, pontifical as hell, but hail-fellow.)

HIEROCLES:

Good afternoon, friends. Seems to be a little sacrifice going on. Might I ask, to whom are you sacrificing?

TRYGAEUS:

Get this sacrifice right the first time, now, Rastus; and don't mess up the omens.

HIEROCLES:

Ah, to, ah, which God are you preparing this sacrifice?

TRYGAEUS:
Tail looks good. Tail's always a good omen.

RASTUS:
                                                    Ain' dat
de Lawd's troof, massa.

HIEROCLES:
Then let us commence the sacrifice, friends. If I might . . .
ah . . .

(Taking a platter from the table, he stretches it towards the grill.)

TRYGAEUS:
Better turn this one.

HIEROCLES:
                              NO, *no*! I prefer my sacrifices
rare.

TRYGAEUS:
         You're a *god*awful pest, friend, whoever you are.

(To Rastus:)

Fine, start cutting.

RASTUS:
                        Where de table?

(He looks for it, finds it, and begins piling the steaks on a platter on the table. Trygaeus claps his hands:)

TRYGAEUS:
                                          A little
liquid refreshment!

(Slaves come running in with bottles, cocktail shakers, icebuckets, which are also set on the table. Trygaeus helps himself.)

HIEROCLES:

Friend, you're being extremely rude,
if I might venture to point it out.

TRYGAEUS:

Go on and venture.
Do you know, even, what we're *up* to?

HIEROCLES:

Well, now, I hardly
can unless you tell me, can I?

TRYGAEUS:

It's nothing you'll want to get
mixed up in, reverend. We're sacrificing to the goddess Peace.

HIEROCLES:

I've got to say it almost does my heart good to see
such childlike innocence.

TRYGAEUS:

Get out.

HIEROCLES:

How can you hope
for peace with the godless Spartans, friend? They're more
like packrats than human beings, they'll . . .

(Trygaeus laughs)

I said something humorous?

TRYGAEUS:

I guess not; I liked the part
about the packrats, is all.

HIEROCLES:

Now, I'm trying to talk to you

seriously, man to man. No one but a fool would trust
a country that has broken, in the past twenty years . . .

TRYGAEUS:

It's
an occupational disease with God-people, you love to talk.

HIEROCLES:
Look, you know yourself, they've sworn to *bury* us. Will you
let yourself be talked around by bleeding hearts until
you *let* yourself be buried?

TRYGAEUS:

That's enough burials
for now.

HIEROCLES:
Try to be serious, friend. This is a serious
question. And don't feel, because I'm a minister, I'm
necessarily biased—although it was Lenin himself who said
'Religion is the opium . . .'

TRYGAEUS:

Marx, actually.

HIEROCLES:

That's irrelevant.
What I'm trying to say is, there's no way of living
peacefully with . . .

TRYGAEUS:

nine-tenths of the world starving, and us
with striped toothpaste.

HIEROCLES:

But coexistence between . . .

TRYGAEUS:
The used and the users? Impossible, padre, I agree.

402

HIEROCLES:

                                        But you . . .

TRYGAEUS:

Maybe just rub a touch of garlic into those steaks. Just a
touch, now.

HIEROCLES:

                Son, you just don't understand. We've got to
tighten our belts, resist this godless Spartan conspiracy
to the last . . .

TRYGAEUS:

                Bomb. I know. Go away. You want to live
in a cave, go live in a cave; why do I have to come?

HIEROCLES:

Cave . . . Cave . . . Caveman . . .

*(And suddenly he is in the middle of a hellforleather sermon, perhaps
frothing a bit at the mouth, accent suddenly Southern Baptist. Trygaeus and Rastus watch and listen, fascinated, Trygaeus taking an
occasional drink from the portable bar, Rastus taking a slug when
Trygaeus isn't watching.)*

So this here Cro-magnon man was just a fake, just a fraud they went
and put together to buttress their untenable theory of Evolution, just
like that Cardiff Giant I told you about.

Now if this Evolution sounds like Revolution, maybe
it's not just a co-incidence. It just so happens that Marx,
that German that invented Godless Communism, lived in London
in the 19th Century, and he used to study at a place called the
British Museum. And it *also* so happens that Russian named
Kropotkin, who was head of the Anarchists, *also* lived in London
in the 19th Century, and *he* used to study at the British Museum.
And this Charles Darwin, that invented Evolution, *he* lived in
London in the 19th Century and *he* studied at the British museum.

403

Doesn't that seem like a strange co-incidence to you, these
three people from all over the world meeting in just that one
building? It kind of makes you wonder *what they were studying.*

Because if there's one thing that Marx and Kropotkin feared and
hated, it was the Christian Religion. And if there's one thing
this Evolution does . . .

(Trygaeus suddenly roars:)

TRYGAEUS:
Now God*damn*! I don't mind a little anachronism, but
this is ridiculous!
> Rastus, fix me a mint julep.

*(Hierocles blinks a moment and looks around him, coming unposses-
sed. Then he becomes aware of the smell of the meat again and drifts
toward the platter.)*

> I *told* you,
don't come messing around with our sacrifice to Peace.

HIEROCLES:
As a priest, I have certain privileges.

(Rastus gives Trygaeus his drink.)

TRYGAEUS:
> Not here you don't.

(He raises his glass.)

A toast to Peace. May she be a permanent guest in Greece.

RASTUS:
Amen.

HIEROCLES:
> You can't do this without a priest!

TRYGAEUS:

                                        You watch us.
Rastus, take the meat inside for the guests.

HIEROCLES:

                                        What about *me*?

TRYGAEUS:
Try a bite of bible.

HIEROCLES:

                    This is blasphemy! And it's not *fair*!
Sacrificial food is for everybody!

(He makes a dive for Rastus, retreating with the platter of steaks. Try-gaeus calls:)

TRYGAEUS:

                                Rastus!

(Rastus wheels about smartly. Somehow his foot gets in Hierocles way as he plunges past him; Hierocles goes sprawling.)

                                    Why don't we
twist his neck around a little, so it fits his collar better?

(The two advance slowly on Hierocles, who retreats slowly.)

RASTUS:
Boss, is it true what dey says about de doowhackeys on
preeses, dat dey dangles down in dere an' gits all bigger'n
what de res' of us got?

HIEROCLES:

                    I protest! Sacrilege!

(He continues to retreat as they advance.)

405

TRYGAEUS:

                                        Well, Rastus,
we can sure find out.

(Hierocles breaks and runs, hitching up his voluminous garment to reveal his argyle socks, gartered.)

RASTUS:

                        Hoo*oeee*, Boss! He fly
like a angel, jes' look at him go!

TRYGAEUS:

                        He looks a little like
my trusty beetle from here, little and black and *flying.*

*(Laughing, they exit.
The Chorus members enter from both sides of the stage, and seeing no
one, squat down along the stable wall with Rastus. The following is an
alternation of two rhythms; when the Old Man speaks, all listen respectfully—his speech is slow and dreamy. When he drifts off into
silence the others begin speaking and behaving more animatedly.)*

OLD MAN:

            Well, I guess we kin be pretty
            happy now . . . Yep, pretty happy.
            Tell y'all what I likes, I never
            did like no wars, what *I* likes
            is jes' sit in de co'ner wif my
            friends, in de winter-time, wif a
            big fire a-goin', an' jes' put my
            feetses on de hob, an' mebbe git me
            a little taste ob squirr'l, o' coon,
            o' possum onct in a while, o' a little
            taste ob young pussy when my old lady's
            up to de Big House, dat's what I likes . . .

(He goes off into a dreamy silence, imagining the scene; the others begin talking among themselves.)

LUKE:

Ain' dat de Lawd's troof? Jes sit aroun' after de cotton's
all to de gin, an' outside it rain an' snow, an' mebbe
one o' yo' buddies come by an' say, "Luke, what y'all
fixin' to do?"

HOP:

An' *you* say, "Woman, fetch down de white
lightnin'," cause *you* is a drinkin fool!

LUKE:

'Nen *I* says,
"Woman, fry us some grits an' chittlins to go wid de juice."

RASTUS:

Sho' ain' nuthin' like de winter when dey ain' nuthin to do,
an' de fiel's is all jes' mud so y'all cain' work.

PAPA:

'Nen
Rastus, *he* say, "Well, I got me a couple of birds down to
de house, an' mebbe some possum lef' over . . ."

RASTUS:

Dat's unless
de cat didn' git it, cause I heerd a pow'ful thumping aroun'
out to de kitchin las' night.

LUKE:

'Nen *we* say, "Well, Rastus,
why doan y'all run over an' git dem birds an' dat possum . . . "

HOP:

"An' stop to Papa John's an' tell him bring over some o' dat
good drinkin' likker what he keep roun' fo' de arthur-itis."

OLD MAN:

An' summer's nice too, mighty nice;
I likes to hear de crickets an' walk

down by de ribber, when she good an'
hot, an' walk through de cawn an' see
is it comin' along, an' maybe take me
a couple of cobs fo' de ol' lady
to cook up fo' me, o' maybe git me
a melon . . . Man, in de summer I jes'
eats an' eats. I jes' sit dere
in de shade an' I *eats*. Fo' a ol' man,
I gits purty fat some summers . . . I
got to say dat I do like de summer . . .

(Again he fades away; a pause, and the others begin:)

RASTUS:

Well *sho'* he like de summer! He too ol' to pick cotton!

LUKE:

Dat jes' how it is wif de war, de people what likes de war
doan have to fight in it.

SAM:

                               Man, you got to *know* it. I seen
dem white folks on de TV: "We will never cease our struggle
against aggression until an Honorable Peace is attained." 'Nen
dey drops mo' bombs on de black people over dere.

PAPA:

                                             Dem ain'
black people, Sam, dey's some kin' ob Chinese. Deys yaller,
ain' dey?

SAM:

                         So's Muhammed Ali, an' he ain' *about* to fight
in no white folks' war.

RASTUS:

                         I doan know now . . .

LUKE:

Now look here,
Rastus, Sam talkin' some sense. He mean it ain' white folks
dey killin' *here,* an' it ain' white folks dey killin *dere,*
dat's all he sayin'.

RASTUS:

Well, I doan . . .

SAM:

An' when us *black* people
starts gittin' *together,* man, all over de *worl'* . . .

PAPA:

My Gawd!
Y'all hesh up now, nigger, is you crazy?

HOP:

Hush now! De massa!

*(As Trygaeus enters the slaves scatter, some slipping out, others stand-
ing more or less at attention and awaiting orders.)*

TRYGAEUS:
Hey!
The guests are starting to arrive for the wedding feast,
I see some coming already.

(To a slave:)

Brush off the table with this,
a little souvenir I brought back from Heaven. No use now.

*(He pulls from his pocket and hands to him General Disorder's epau-
lette. To two other slaves:)*

Run in, make sure the drinks are out, and potato chips and
pretzels in all the bowls, and that dip Liza was making, and
cigarettes, don't forget the cigarettes!

(They go indoors. A Lawnmower-salesman enters with a Potter; the first a small business man with a thick yiddish accent, the second an arty bearded type. The lawnmower salesman pushes a lawnmower ahead of him, the potter carries two rather fearful products of his kiln. The lawnmower salesman speaks for both.)

SALESMAN:

Where's Mr. Trygaeus?

TRYGAEUS:

Over here, barbecueing.

SALESMAN:

Mr. Trygaeus, we only want to say thank you for making peace.

TRYGAEUS:

Hell, I didn't even make Abundance.

SALESMAN:

A week ago, I couldn't sell a lawnmower for love or money, and now they're lined up outside the store, they'll pay *any*thing. And even this man here's selling his pots for a dollar apiece. So we brought you these for presents, absolutely for free, because you're getting married and because we're making such a profit we can afford it.

TRYGAEUS:

That's real nice of you. Just stick those in the shed, and go on inside and have a drink and maybe a bite to eat: I see some *mean*-looking people coming along now.

(The two leave. Various businessmen enter, dressed very much like Izvestia cartoons of Wall Street brokers. Each carries, incongruously, a product of his industry: the general spokesman for the group (LEADER) a large bomb, #2 the object described below, #3 a large airplane wheel, #4 and #5 jerry-cans, and #6 a very elaborate rifle.)

410

LEADER:
Mr. Trygaeus, you've destroyed the economy.

TRYGAEUS:
You drop that
son-of-a-bitch in here and we're *all* destroyed.

LEADER:
But we're
ruined! I'm ruined, and here's a senior vicepresident
of General Motors, and *he's* . . .

TRYGAEUS:
Hey, what would you take
for a couple of those bombs?

LEADER:
What are you offering?

TRYGAEUS:
Well,
it might be a comedown for you from high finance, but beggars
can't be choosers, right? So I'll give you half a buck for
two like that. I have these glass ashtrays and they break.

LEADER:
Well . . . Fifty cents is fifty cents.

(He extends the bomb.)

I'll bring you the other
tomorrow.

(To the man next to him.)

Better than nothing, I guess.

TRYGAEUS:
No, it might blow up
or something, and I have all these guests around.

411

LEADER:
                                                    Thirty
    cents.

TRYGAEUS:
        Nah, I guess not. Sorry.

LEADER:
                              Fifteen.

TRYGAEUS:
                                        Nah, I got
    a couple of pots in the shed there I can use.

(#2 approaches him, almost in tears, and carrying an utterly incomprehensible, very complex and shiny, part of a machine.)

#2:
                                        Mr. Trygaeus,
    what am I supposed to do with *this*? I don't even know
    what it's for, and they cost me three thousand apiece to
    machine, and now they've stopped the contract and left me
    with *one hundred twenty thousand* of them.

(Trygaeus squats down to look at the object, showing a real interest in the problem.)

TRYGAEUS:
                                        Hmmm . . . Maybe
    you could work out some kind of gimmick, like a hula-hoop . . .

LEADER:
    Mr. Trygaeus, we came here in good faith . . .

TRYGAEUS:
                                        I got it! Look,

(He inverts the object, in which position it looks something like a toilet with odd protruberances. He sits on it.)

412

A little modernistic, but there are people who go for
that kind of thing. And besides, look, you don't have to
lean forward to wipe yourself, just do it right through this hole!

(He demonstrates.)

#2:
Wouldn't the water run out through the hole too?

TRYGAEUS:
Fellas,
I'm just in pure research. You boys work the bugs out.

LEADER:
That's *ridiculous*! A three thousand dollar *toilet*?

TRYGAEUS:
I
consider *my* ass worth half a million, at a conservative
estimate.

#2:
You mean you'll *buy* it?

TRYGAEUS:
Nope, a little tight
in the crotch here. Sorry.

#3:
What am *I* supposed to do,
Mr. Trygaeus, with one hundred twenty-three Phantoms in my
warehouse packed for shipping?

(Trygaeus is getting bored with all this.)

TRYGAEUS:
I don't know. Sell them
to American Airlines.

They only carry one man.

TRYGAEUS:

Sell them
for private planes then.

#3:

They'd be much too expensive
for any *individual* to operate.

TRYGAEUS:

Look, this is *your* field,
not mine. Think! What are their selling points?

#3:

Well,
they're fine for bombing and strafing and deforestation and . . .

TRYGAEUS:
No, no, what *else*?

#3:

Well . . . Nothing, I guess. I mean,
these are specifically developed and highly specialized
machines, Mr. Trygaeus, they're . . .

TRYGAEUS:

How about paperweights?
I don't *give* a goddamn.

(He turns to go, but #4 buttonholes him.)

#4:

Mr. Trygaeus, our corporation
has spent over thirteen million dollars in the development
of this bacteriological . . . ah . . . product . . .

TRYGAEUS:

Get it out of *here*!

(He claps his hands. Three slaves rush on and bounce #4, still carrying his jerrycan, still protesting. Trygaeus shouts after him:)

You might try Nasser!

(Again he turns to go, #5 gets him.)

#5:

We at Dow Chemical . . .

TRYGAEUS:

No problem.

Lighter fluid.

#5:

But you can't put it *out*!

TRYGAEUS:

Your problem.

LEADER:

Gentlemen, I fear free enterprise is dead. It's impossible
to speak sensibly with a Communist. And it's quite evident
that they have . . .

TRYGAEUS:

Hey. Do any of you make just plain *guns*?

(#6 jumps forward.)

#6:

Do you mean *rifles*?

TRYGAEUS:

Right.

#6:

We have rifles, complete with
bayonets, infrared telescopic sights, stopping-power of . . .

TRYGAEUS:

I was just . . .

#6:

And discounts on orders of over ten thousand!

TRYGAEUS:

Well, what I *want* is to buy me a .22. Been a bunch of
rabbits at the lettuce lately.

#6:

A .22?

(Trygaeus nods.)

Do you mean *one*
rifle?

(He nods.)

for your *own use*?

(He nods.)

for *rabbits*?

(He nods.)

(#6, to Leader:)

He's making *fun*
of us.

LEADER:

It's what we get for trying to talk with a Red. No
possible communication.

*(He signals. As a body, the businessmen wheel and march out. Try-
gaeus yells after them:)*

TRYGAEUS:

You could try them on each *other*!

(And goes into the house. A moment later the five slaves of the Chorus enter, from both sides, to piss; they stand in a row, against the stable wall. And a moment after that Trygaeus emerges for the same purpose now carrying a large bottle; he pisses against the opposite wall. All finish simultaneously. As Trygaeus turns and sees them (now a bit tipsy:)

TRYGAEUS:
Hey! You boys over there!

(The five react violently, desperately attempting to stuff their phalluses back into their pants.)

No, hey. Hey! I just thought,
as long as I was getting hitched to Prosperity and all that,
and as long as Peace had finally arrived all over the world,
you might have some song to sing. For Peace.

PAPA:
Yassuh, boss!

(They arrange themselves as in their Steven Foster chorus and, again, Papa John sings baritone, the others hum:)

CHORUS:
Gwine lay down my swo'd an' shiel',
Down by de ribber side,
Down by de . . .

(Trygaeus breaks in, approaching them:)

TRYGAEUS:
No, that's for when it might be happening *sometime*! How're
you fixed for *now*?

(The Chorus turns and discusses the problem among themselves. Trygaeus passes them the bottle as he waits; it is passed around, then back.)

417

PAPA:
>Thank yo', massa. How dis one?

(All sing, lugubriously:)

>We shall overcome,
>We shall overcome,
>We shall . . .

TRYGAEUS:

NO! You don't get the point! Isn't there some kind of song
you can sing for a real Peace now you can hold on to?

*(Discussion. Bottle. The Chorus turns to Trygaeus again; this time
Sam, with offstage accompaniment, sings lead, à la James Brown:)*

SAM:
>I feel good, I knew that I would now,
>Hoooooooooo,
I feel good, I knew that I would now . . .

(He breaks off and addresses Trygaeus: defiantly:)

How you like *dat*, boss?

TRYGAEUS:
>What oft was thought, but ne'er
so well expressed . . . Seems kind of appropriate. *Do* it.

*(They continue. Trygaeus and the bottle join them; they are harmo-
nizing very well indeed, and Trygaeus takes the last chorus himself, at
least creditably:)*

TRYGAEUS:
>I feel good, so good: I got *you*!

OFFSTAGE:
Bump bump bump bump bump bump bump bump bump:

418

TRYGAEUS:
AHHHHHHHHHHHHHH!

(There is a pause. Physical contact is broken. No one seems to know quite what to do. At last Trygaeus shouts toward the house, fairly drunk now:)

TRYGAEUS:
All you people in there! *Eat up!* More where that came from. *Drink up!* My cellar's crammed full.

SAM:
                                        Does that include us
too?

TRYGAEUS:
        That includes *everybody*!

(The slaves vanish into the house.)

                              Throat's no good unless you
swallow with it, right? Hungry in there, you *eat*!
Anybody thirsty, *drink*!

('Here comes the Bride,' very quietly from backstage on organ. Liza enters with Prosperity, Prosperity fully equipped as a bride; they join Trygaeus at center stage.)

LIZA:
                 Dis here am yo' woman, massa.

TRYGAEUS:
Hello, woman. Are you my woman?

(Very slowly, Prosperity holds out her hand; very slowly, Trygaeus takes it. A pause.)

                             You got yourself a man . . .

(Chinese lanterns come up. Guests pour from the house—all the previous characters in complete disorder, all drunk, all cheering. Sound effect of cheering gradually increasing from now to curtain. The Chorus is now uniformed as a New Orleans band, playing 'Dixie.' Over it Trygaeus shouts:)

I want everybody to have a good time. I want everybody
to do what he *likes*!

(Sam's clarinet, in the band, begins to work with 'Straight No Chaser,' still to the beat of 'Dixie.' The backstage organ continues playing 'Here Comes the Bride,' and the businessmen are off on one side singing, arms about one another's shoulders, 'For he's a jolly good fellow.' It would take Ives to score this. The effect is not total cacaphony; all are somehow related, although it is all very loud and confusing. And over this Trygaeus, almost but not quite inaudible, continues to shout as the curtain slowly descends:)

             And I want everybody to have all they want
to *drink*! And you want to tear off a little Peace
once in a while, it won't *hurt* you! BECAUSE THIS IS MY PARTY!
AND I WANT EVERYBODY TO HAVE THEMSELVES A GOOD
    TIME! AND I
WANT EVERYBODY TO COME TO MY PARTY!

(He begins to point out into the audience:)

                            I WANT YOU!
    AND YOU!
AND YOU! AND . . . .

(Mercifully, the curtain descends.)

The Rope

Plautus

Translated by

W. Thomas MacCary

Introduction

The Rope is a romantic comedy which has much in common with *The Tempest:* exotic setting, storm, manipulation of human beings by supernatural forces, reunion of estranged family members, the triumph of virtue and justice. What is really at issue in both plays, as in all romantic comedies, is the life force itself. We are constantly reminded of the sea's proximity and men and women are washed ashore and forced to rearrange their lives in such a way that these become more meaningful than they were before. The end of romantic comedy is marriage; those who marry inaugurate a new life for themselves and others. Marriage is thus a symbolic action and the sequence of events to which it is culmination should be seen as a ritual of fertility.

In *The Tempest* Shakespeare develops many themes out of this basic pattern: Prospero, in relinquishing his daughter Miranda to marriage with Ferdinand, gives up his magical art, his creative force and life itself:

> If I have too austerely punished you,
> Your compensation makes amends. For I
> Have given you a third of mine own life,
> Or that for which I live, who once again
> I tender to your hand. (IV. i. 1-5)

>   But this rough magic
> I here abjure, and when I have required
> Some heavenly music—which even now I do—
> To work mine end upon their senses, that

This airy charm is for, I'll break my staff,
Bury it certain fathoms in the earth,
And deeper than did ever plummet sound
I'll drown my book. (V. i. 50-57)

> And in the morn
> I'll bring you to your ship, and so to Naples,
> Where I have hope to see the nuptial
> Of these our dear-beloved solemnized,
> And thence retire me to my Milan, where
> Every third thought shall be my grave. (V. i. 306-11)

With all this richness of suggestion we must not lose sight of the plot it-self, in which lies the essential meaning of the play: giving up his beauti-ful, young daughter means, for the old father, giving up his hold on life. The abjuration of poetry and magic is then but a sublimated expression of his real loss: the sexual prerogative he has over her. Shakespeare dou-bles this pattern by making Alonso the father of a recent bride, his daughter Claribel. Age yields to youth the power to rule and to create; the essence and image of this cession is the impotence of age and the marriage of youth. In *The Tempest,* as in so many comedies, the fertile symbol is a young girl who must be released from infertile bondage to her father or an unchosen lover. Only when this is accomplished can the new season, the new life, be inaugurated by her marriage to a lover she has chosen for herself, with her father's approval.

The Tempest is Prospero's play: we see the action from his point of view and his resignation to impotence and death is its most moving as-pect. The other characters are puppets in his control, like the airy spirits he summons up and then dismisses. In *The Rope* we have a strong father figure in Daemones, but we are encouraged to see the action through his daughter's eyes. Palaestra suffers shipwreck and is washed ashore on a desolate coast. This catastrophe is brought on by Arcturus, the constellation, as a means of rescuing her from her evil owner, the pimp Labrax. He had bought her from pirates who stole her from her parents many years before. The contrast between Labrax and Daemones is complete: the pimp is sexually threatening and offensive; Daemones is benevolent and protective. Clearly we have here two images of the father as seen by the young girl. The pimp is the bad father, the false father, who would give the girl to an unchosen lover or keep her for himself; Daemones is the good father, the true father, who ratifies the girl's own choice of lover. That the man to whom Labrax has sold Palaestra, and the man to whom Daemones marries her, after she is recognized as his daughter and thus free-born and Athenian, is the same man, Plesidippus, emphasizes the decomposition that has made of the father two contrasted figures. In romantic comedy it is never enough for the girl to be simply reunited with her lover, who is always weak and ineffective. What is required is acquiescence of the father in the daughter's choice of lover: he must relinquish his sexual prerogative over her. Nor can we ignore in this pattern the daughter's original and continuing acquiescence in that prerogative: by escaping the threatening older man she denies her attraction to her father, but by requiring the benevolent older man to approve her choice of lover, she confirms it. No lover will ever replace the father, but since society will not allow her to have her father as lover, she chooses a lover he would have chosen for her, one who is no challenge to his pre-eminence in her eyes.

This is the fantasy of the young girl, the fulfillment of her dreams, and it is best supported on the stage by rich poetry and enchanting music. These are elements common to *The Tempest* and *The Rope*, though Plautus cannot—nor indeed could any other playwright—soar to Shakespearean heights. I have resorted to a gentle parody of Shakespearean diction and to the hackneyed verse of American musical comedy, a genre which conveys through its formula plots and *cliché* lyrics the realization that its theatrical dream is tarnished and trite, but nevertheless better by far than the life we live in the world outside the theatre.

W. Thomas MacCary

CHARACTERS
in order of appearance:

ARCTÚRUS, the constellation, who speaks the prologue.

SCEPÁRNIO, "little helmet," a slave belonging to Daemones.

PLESIDÍPPUS,"delighting in horses," a young Athenian.

DAÉMONES, "subject to destiny," an old Athenian living in exile.

PALAÉSTRA, "wrestling mat," the daughter of Daemones, stolen by pirates as a child and sold to Labrax.

AMPELÍSCA, "vine shoot," a young girl belonging to Labrax.

PTOLEMOCRATÍA, "strong in battle," a priestess of Venus.

CHORUS OF FISHERMEN

TRACHÁLIO, "stiff-neck," a slave belonging to Plesidippus.

LÁBRAX, "fish of prey," a pimp.

CHÁRMIDES, "child of grace," a friend of Labrax.

SPÁRAX, "the chopper," slave of Daemones.

TURBÁLIO, "the mixer," slave of Daemones.

GRÍPUS, "hawk-face," slave of Daemones.

426

SETTING: The coast of North Africa, near Cyrene; a modest house is perched on a cliff above the sea, which is off-stage right. There is a shrine to the left. All physical features important to the action are described in the dialogue, so the set itself should be minimal.

(Enter Arcturus, lowered from above in a cloud-like contraption.)

ARCTURUS:
Of like lineage and degree
With him who rules the lands and sea
Count me. For contemplate how bright
A star above I shine by night,
By day a star upon this stage,
I come, Arcturus, to engage
Your attention. At times I move
Among you, as other stars above
Are wont to do, at his request,
Jupiter, of gods, men and the rest
Lord, who sends us to report
On men, and good from bad to sort,
That virtue should with wealth e'er be
Rewarded, the vice of perjury
Punishéd. We inscribe the names
Of those seeking evil gains
Through lying, cheating and deception:
Jove exacts just retribution,
Duns them twice the price of profit.
(Good men's names another tablet
Bears.) Some do themselves deceive:
With gifts to him they must believe
Forgiveness can be bought, but he
Ne'er heeds from perjurers a plea.
Only the just and good are heard,
So hearken to this warning word,
And if the narrow path you've trod
Err not; for thus far you please God,
And true joy will await you.

427

But now, my friends, without ado,
I must fulfill my obligation
And introduce this dramatization.

The city in the distance there our poet
Diphilos would call Cyrene. And this
The house of Daemones, close by the sea,
A man noble and good, exiled from Athens
Where he committed no crime more severe
Than too great friendship, but for this he lost
His fortune, making good a bad friend's
Bad debts. Thence he came to live in poverty
Among those who knew not his former wealth:
For the destitute obscurity is best.
But dearer far than gold he lost his daughter,
Snatched by pirates when his ship was boarded,
Her golden hair they knew would fetch for them
High price from those who traffic in the flesh
Of human beings. Thus she came to be
Immured within a pimp's place of business
In this very town, Cyrene, and here
A young Athenian saw her, before she had
Been forced into a life of shame. In love
He signed a contract with the pimp and made
Deposit, to save her, still a virgin,
From the pimp; But he, the vile procurer,
Broke faith, according to the custom of his
Trade, nor honored his agreement with the youth.
Instead he was convinced by a Sicilian,
Despicable, who'd sell his own mother,
To take the girl and others in his house
To Sicily, and start a brothel there.
In Sicily, he said, there were more lechers
To make them rich. A ship was hired
In secret. All he owned the pimp had loaded:
His girls, his gold, his friends, his bags and baggage.

428

Meanwhile he told the young Athenian
To meet him at the temple here of Venus
Where they would sacrifice and close their deal.
He lied, so I then took control of things,
And when I saw the virgin forced aboard,
For her I planned salvation, for the pimp
Destruction. I broke a storm and raised the waves,
For I am of the constellations
Stormiest when I rise, and violent,
More violent yet when I set. Now the pimp,
Ship-wrecked upon a rock, fights his way ashore;
His friend, no friend, laments the day they met.
The virgin and a faithful lone companion,
Frightened but safe, escaped the wreck and now
Are carried by the waves to this forlorn,
This isolated spot, this very house
Where Daemones, the old man whom you'll meet,
Lives. Here comes his servant now, and soon
You'll see the young man here, seeking out
The pimp. I bid you fare well and keep strong
So that your enemies may bow before you.

(Exit Arcturus in contraption.)
(Enter Sceparnio from the house, dressed in rough, simple clothes. He is middle-aged, with a beard.)

SCEPARNIO:

By the gods in heaven I swear the heavens have never seen such a storm as the gods sent last night. The winds, I say, stripped the house of its covering. But why should I say what you can see—how naked it stands, without its tiles. But that was no wind, that was the *Alcumena* of Euripedes, the scene where Zeus announces in thunder and lightning the birth of his son Hercules. We now have more windows than we can look through: the house is but a sieve for light.

(Enter Plesidippus stage left, accompanied by three middle-aged men. He is beardless, finely dressed and slightly affected in manner.)

429

PLESIDIPPUS *(To his companions):*
My friends, I have detained you from your affairs to aid me in my own, which now, it seems, cannot go forward: the man I was to meet—no man, in fact, but a pimp—was not at the port as planned. Nevertheless I beg your indulgence, and a few more minutes of your time; he should be here since we had planned to make sacrifice at this shrine of Venus, she being the patron goddess of his trade.

SCEPARNIO:
If I know what's good for me I'll mix this mortar before my master fills the cracks with my own flesh.

(Enter Daemones from the house, middle-aged, with a beard; he is simply dressed.)

DAEMONES:
Hey there, Sceparnio!

SCEPARNIO:
Who calls me so rudely?

DAEMONES:
Your owner.

SCEPARNIO:
Well, your slave would like you to show a bit more respect.

DAEMONES:
We need all the mortar you can mix: the whole house is a hole.

PLESIDIPPUS:
My greetings to you, father, and to your slave as well.

DAEMONES:
And mine to you, young fellow.

SCEPARNIO:
Is he a man or a woman? I can't tell from his appearance, so you could be his father.

PLESIDIPPUS:
How dare you? Of course I'm a man.

SCEPARNIO:
Then he is not your father.

DAEMONES:
I had a daughter, young man, but I lost her, and I've never had a son.

PLESIDIPPUS:
The gods may yet bless you.

SCEPARNIO:
The gods should curse you for the trouble you cause us. Can't you see we're busy?

PLESIDIPPUS:
Is this your house?

SCEPARNIO:
Why do you ask? So you can come back later to rob us?

PLESIDIPPUS:
This slave of yours must be honored in your house to enjoy such freedom of speech.

SCEPARNIO:
And you must have no sense of what's right and proper, bothering perfect strangers who owe you nothing.

DAEMONES:
Be still, Sceparnio. *(To Plesidippus:)* But what can I do for you?

PLESIDIPPUS:
First, you can punish this surly slave who speaks for his master in his master's presence, and then, unless you are too busy, you might answer a few questions for me.

DAEMONES:
Even though I am busy, I will help you if I can.

431

SCEPARNIO:

Why don't you make yourself useful? Go fetch some reeds from the swamp for patching these holes.

DAEMONES:

Be still. Now, young man, tell me what you want.

PLESIDIPPUS:

Have you seen around here a man with gray, kinky hair, a liar, a cheat and a cur?

DAEMONES:

I've seen many such, and it's due to them I'm no better off than I am.

PLESIDIPPUS:

But I mean here, in this shrine of Venus, a man who had two young girls with him, who was preparing to make sacrifice, yesterday or today.

DAEMONES:

No. No one has been here for the last few days. Believe me I would know if they had. They pester me for fire and water, pots and knives and spits, or a copper-lined number five saucepan with louvered lid for steaming entrails. You know how these people are: they make me an attendant of Venus rather than her neighbor. But for the last few days I've had some relief—there's been no one here.

PLESIDIPPUS:

Then I'm a dead man.

DAEMONES:

Oh, I hope not; I would save you if I could.

SCEPARNIO:

Damn you anyway for coming to a shrine simply for a free lunch.

Cook for yourself at home.

DAEMONES:
Were you invited here and now find no host?

PLESIDIPPUS:
So it seems.

SCEPARNIO:
No reason why you shouldn't go home hungry; you ought to have worshipped Ceres rather than Venus. Men have lived for love and died of love, but bread alone stops hunger.

PLESIDIPPUS:
This man of yours ridicules me in a most unseemly manner.

DAEMONES:
Ye gods, Sceparnio, do you see those men there along the shore?

SCEPARNIO:
They must have been asked out to dine.

DAEMONES:
How so?

SCEPARNIO:
Look how carefully they bathed.

DAEMONES:
Their ship's been wrecked.

SCEPARNIO:
Yes, and we've got work to do.

DAEMONES:
Alas, what pitiful creatures we men are! Look how the wretches swim

for their lives.

PLESIDIPPUS:

Where are they? Show me.

DAEMONES:

There, to the right, along the shore.

PLESIDIPPUS:

I see them now. You men follow me. This must be the man I'm look-ing for; the gods have shipwrecked him for his crimes. Farewell.

(Exit Plesidippus stage right; his friends follow.)

SCEPARNIO:

We'll fare much better without you to bother us. But oh, ye gods of the sea, Palaemon and Neptune and companion to both Hercules, to what wild spectacle am I witness?

DAEMONES:

Where? What is it?

SCEPARNIO:

It is a pitiable sight; two young girls alone in a boat no larger than a cradle, rocked violently by the waves with a watery grave awaiting them. But see, see, how the sea itself rises up to save them, and Nep-tune as helmsman guides them to the shore. But wait, wait, the waves are prodigiously large and I doubt they can escape. Now, now is the crisis—ah, one is cast into the surf, but she swims, she is saved! Ah, how the babe is thrown from the cradle, into the arms of the sea— a miracle! The other is ashore now, too, but falls to her knees in the surf from fear. She moves on to dry land—but wait! She turns wrong, toward the rocks, she'll fall and die.

DAEMONES:

Why such concern?

SCEPARNIO:

But what an end to her struggles!

DAEMONES:

If those girls are going to feed you tonight, then your concern for them is proper. As long as you live with me, though, you must work for your supper.

SCEPARNIO:

You're right. What are they to me or me to them?

DAEMONES:

Then follow along.

SCEPARNIO:

Lead on.

(Exit Daemones and Sceparnio into the house.)

(Enter Palaestra stage right, a beautiful young girl, blonde; she is wet, with clothes torn and seaweed in her hair.)

PALAESTRA:

Am I to live in fact the fate oft told
Of wretched girls in tales who are bereft
Of friends, of succour of all kinds, and cold
Upon a lonely shore lament the theft
Of parents, youth and contentment. For sure
'Tis worse to know the truth than hear the fiction,
And unbearable the pain when hearts are pure
And disaster undeserved without prediction
Strikes. Did they who bore and raised me sin
And do I pay the price for them? 'Tis false.
What warning then is this for impious men
When piety its own to peril calls?
    The gods do thus confound us with their play,
    And mock our expectation of a judgement day.

Associates in the guilt of that perjured bawd,
We are denied, my friend and I, company
In death. Alone, alone, all alone, oh god!
Was it for this my parents bore me?

435

(Enter Ampelisca stage right, wet, with clothes torn; she is brunette, older and plainer than Palaestra. No attempt need be made to stage their meeting realistically. One must simply accept the convention that they do not see each other until they say they see each other.)

AMPELISCA:
Why should I live? What does life hold for me?
Why should the breath remain in my body?
What hope I had is lost, my dear friend dead.
And all the fears that swell within my head
Tell me to end my suffering here, nor extend
My woe to know new sorrow without end.
I've looked and looked but found no trace at all
Of her whose fate was tied to mine, whose fall
Was like my own, though her parentage is known
To be above me. Lost, lost, she died alone
And now I wander these forsaken shores
And cry aloud and listen to the echoes.
No one lives here, nor ever did, and I
Shall die alone. But with the life that's in me
I will seek for her alive or dead and we
Will both live or together in death lie.

PALAESTRA:
Is that a human voice I hear nearby?

AMPELISCA:
Hark! I hear, and fear, but hear a voice clearly.

PALAESTRA:
Is there hope yet for my salvation?

AMPELISCA:
Could someone have heard my lamentation?

PALAESTRA:
I would swear that sound is a woman's cry.

436

AMPELISCA:

    I declare that cry is of a girl nearby.

PALAESTRA:

    Is it Ampelisca then, my lost companion?

AMPELISCA:

    Palaestra is alive, as I was praying.

PALAESTRA:

    Come, my own, my only friend.

AMPELISCA:

    Come to me; my sorrows end.

PALAESTRA:

    Follow my voice; you'll find me.

AMPELISCA:

    Where, oh where? You flee from me.

PALAESTRA:

    Here, in sorrow and despair.

AMPELISCA:

    Both of us that place do share.

PALAESTRA:

    Ampelisca, over here!

AMPELISCA:

    Show yourself, Palaestra, dear.

PALAESTRA:

    Here you are, at last, at last.

AMPELISCA:

    Now all fear and sorrow's past.

PALAESTRA:

    Dearer far than life itself.

AMPELISCA:
Now I know no fear of death.

PALAESTRA:
Never shall we part again.

AMPELISCA:
Not as long as friend needs friend.

PALAESTRA:
What we need now is a guide.

AMPELISCA:
Rocks here, there the rising tide.

PALAESTRA:
Follow me along the shore.

AMPELISCA:
See, these wet clothes make me slow.

PALAESTRA:
Hurry though. See there? A shrine.

AMPELISCA:
What a place for rites divine!

PALAESTRA:
Strange the charm it has over me.

AMPELISCA:
Must be the sea's proximity.

PALAESTRA:
I feel I've seen this shrine before.

AMPELISCA:
What god do men in it adore?

PALAESTRA:
He will have mercy on us.

AMPELISCA:

To him our souls we must entrust.

PALAESTRA:

Give us refuge from the sea.

AMPELISCA:

Help poor, wretched, storm-tossed me.

(Enter Ptolemocratia from the shrine, an older woman, dignified, dressed in dark robes, with a leafy garland on her head and a dove-topped staff in her hand.)

PTOLEMOCRATIA:

My patron goddess sends me forth to see
Who suppliant seeks her beneficence.
Nor will they find her grudging of response,
But bountiful to all who do her homage.

PALAESTRA:

Hail, holy mother.

PTOLEMOCRATIA:

Daughter, hail to you.
Whence comest thou in rags so wretched torn?
And wet, bedraggled, shivering, forlorn?

PALAESTRA:

Short the way by foot but long by sea.

PTOLEMOCRATIA:

                      Borne
By the stately charger of the deep have you
Traversed the wine-dark ways?

PALAESTRA:

                      Yes, holy mother.

PTOLEMOCRATIA:

But you should show respect for this holy shrine

Approaching only when you wear the clothes
Appropriate to a holy place, and then
Bear proper offerings, blood sacrifice.

PALAESTRA:

But, holy mother, there our vessel lies
Wrecked, upon the bottom of the sea,
With all we ever had or hoped to find.
Where would we, Neptune's innocent victims,
Find victims of our own for sacrifice?
I beseech you, holy mother, helpless,
Hopeless as I am, lost and without means
To find myself, have pity on me, pity
On my friend. Receive us to your bosom
As children, your own children, lost, now found,
With nothing, needing all. Pity, dear mother.

PTOLEMOCRATIA:

Give me your hands, my daughters; rise and follow.
No woman lives more motherly than I.
Though I am poor and live my life for her
Whom I serve, yet I shall share what I have
With you, my children, orphans of the storm.
Venus, my mistress, Venus shall protect you.

PALAESTRA:

I beg you, mother, is this then Venus' shrine?

PTOLEMOCRATIA:

Yes, my child, and I her priestess. But come
With me and take what's mine, for all is yours.

PALAESTRA:

We follow you, holy mother, and thank you.

(Exit all three into the shrine.
Enter chorus of fishermen stage right, dancing and singing. They are
various ages, wearing only tunics and carrying nets.)

440

FISHERMEN:

We have a song to sing to you
   Of poverty and woe.
The two live side by side with us;
   From experience we know:
Of poor there are two separate types,
   The difference being skill.
Some sit at home, lament their fate;
   Others hunt or herd or till.
We're proud to practice our trade
   Though it earns us little money.
We live by the fish of the sea,
   You see—perch and bass and tunney.

Each day we venture forth
Although the wind be north
   -erly and the sea
    As high as the eye
    Of a bee.

For us instead of the stuff of
Leisure is the groan and grunt of
   Setting the hooks,
   Searching the nooks
   For sea urchin.

On days when all else fails
We give our lady fifty "Hails!"
   Since she can lead us
   To conches called Venus,
   Whence she came.

(Enter Trachalio stage left, a young slave, clean-shaven and well-dressed.)

TRACHALIO:

I cannot understand my master's plan.
He told me he was off to meet the pimp

441

At the port, thence to come to Venus' shrine,
Where I should meet him. But what have we here?
Some fishermen are come whom I can ask.
All hail, thieves of Neptune's wealth, crooks by hooks,
Despoilers of the conch, if not the couch,
Of Venus, descendants of Starvation,
How goes it? Lean and hungry as always?

FISHERMAN:
Famine and false hope are our companions.

TRACHALIO:
I need your help in finding my young master.
You must have seen him here, a stalwart youth,
Bold and with the glow of health upon him.
With him were three satyr-like companions.

FISHERMAN:
We've seen none such in this vicinity.

TRACHALIO:
I seek another man, no man, but a bag
Of ugliness and decrepitude, half-bald, lame,
With a huge belly and no behind, his face
A mass of twisted brown and wrinkled skin,
A perjurer, cursed by the gods and men,
Who profits from the sale of female flesh.
There were with him two beautiful young girls.

FISHERMEN:
What commerce could a man like this have had
With our lady Venus? Seek him instead
On the gallows; he's not here. Good day.

(Exit Fishermen stage right with music and dance.)

TRACHALIO:
Good day to you. It's true, then, as I knew,

442

That the pimp has fleeced my master to the quick—
Skipped town with the girls in tow—I should hire out
As a soothsayer. I knew no good could come
From that bad seed. But what's there now for me
To do but wait my master's coming hither?
I'll ask the priestess if perchance she's seen him.

(Enter Ampelisca from the shrine, carrying a water-pot.)

AMPELISCA *(To someone in the shrine):*
Yes, I understand; I'm to ask for water at the house next door.

TRACHALIO:
I seem to recognize that voice.

AMPELISCA:
Whose voice is that I hear

TRACHALIO:
Can it be? Is that Ampelisca coming out of the shrine?

AMPELISCA:
Can this be Trachalio, Plesidippus' slave?

TRACHALIO:
It is Ampelisca. Hello!

AMPELISCA:
It is Trachalio. Hello!

TRACHALIO:
How are you?

AMPELISCA:
Not as well as I could be.

TRACHALIO:
Don't tell me that.

AMPELISCA:
You asked me, didn't you? Anyone with sense can tell when things are

443

going all wrong for them. But where's your master Plesidippus?

TRACHALIO:

Now don't fool with me. You know he's inside.

AMPELISCA:

He certainly is not and never has been.

TRACHALIO:

Not at all?

AMPELISCA:

That's what I said.

TRACHALIO:

That's what I thought you said. But when will dinner be ready?

AMPELISCA:

What dinner?

TRACHALIO:

The dinner you're preparing for the sacrifice.

AMPELISCA:

What are you talking about?

TRACHALIO:

I know that your master invited my master here for dinner.

AMPELISCA:

Well, what you say is not surprising. If Labrax cheated the gods of their sacrifice and your master of his dinner, then he was only behaving as pimps usually do.

TRACHALIO:

Then you are not going to sacrifice here today?

AMPELISCA:

Now you've got it; you should hire out as a soothsayer.

TRACHALIO:

Funny you should say that. But what are you doing here?

AMPELISCA:

Palaestra and I were in great danger; we had no one to turn to for help until this priestess of Venus took us in.

TRACHALIO:

So Palaestra's here too, my master's mistress?

AMPELISCA:

Indeed she is.

TRACHALIO:

Nothing could give me greater pleasure. But tell me what danger you were in.

AMPELISCA:

Our ship wrecked last night, Trachalio.

TRACHALIO:

What ship? What are you talking about?

AMPELISCA:

Didn't you know the pimp's plan was to move us all to Sicily. He packed up and stole aboard a ship last night. Well, all is lost now.

TRACHALIO:

Thank you, Neptune: how clever to catch that perjured pimp in your trap and skin him alive. But where is he now?

AMPELISCA:

Dead of drink, I think. Neptune drank him under the table last night.

TRACHALIO:

How grateful I am to you, Ampelisca, for telling me this; how I delight in his discomfiture! But tell me, how did you and Palaestra escape?

AMPELISCA:

With pleasure. When we saw our ship was headed for the rocks, we jumped in the little life-boat. Fear gave us courage. I loosed the rope; we slipped away while the others just sat there panic-stricken; the storm drove us away from them. Tossed all night long by wind and wave, we finally made shore at daybreak.

TRACHALIO:

I should have known: old Neptune returned the bad merchandise.

AMPELISCA:

Damn you.

TRACHALIO:

And you. But I knew all along the pimp would break faith. I swear I should hire out as a soothsayer, though I'd have to let my hair grow long.

AMPELISCA:

And since you knew, what precautions did you and your master take to prevent the pimp's getting away?

TRACHALIO:

What could we do?

AMPELISCA:

Well, one can tell how much he loves her by the care he took of her.

TRACHALIO:

You have no right to say that. It's much easier to steal something than prevent its being stolen. You can go to the baths and watch out for your clothes ever so carefully, and still lose them, since you won't know who the thief is, while he can easily see who you are and get away. So it was with Palaestra. But tell me where she is now.

AMPELISCA:

In the shrine there, lamenting her fate.

TRACHALIO:

Anything in particular?

AMPELISCA:

She had a little basket of tokens which the pimp took from her and these were the only means she had of finding her parents. Now they're lost.

TRACHALIO:

What do you mean?

AMPELISCA:

They were in the ship when it sank. The pimp had them in his trunk, keeping them from her so she could never establish her identity.

TRACHALIO:

There's no worse crime: he knew she was free and still he kept her for his slave.

AMPELISCA:

Now the tokens are lost along with the pimp's gold.

TRACHALIO:

Well, I expect someone has already gone and fished them out.

AMPELISCA:

It's their loss she most laments.

TRACHALIO:

I can see I had best go in and comfort her so she won't upset herself too much about them. So many things happen in this world against expectation; so many times we think the worst has happened and we find the gods have treated us better than we could have hoped.

AMPELISCA:

Just as often the gods deceive us of our hopes.

TRACHALIO:

Still, it's best not to despair, even in time of trouble. I'll go speak to her now, unless you need me for something.

(Exit Trachalio into the shrine.)

AMPELISCA:

Go ahead. I'll go after the water as the priestess bade me. She said the people next door would give it willingly when I asked in her name. I don't think I've ever seen a nobler woman, more deserving of the best from gods and men: so freely and without hesitation did she take us in, wretched as we were, wet, cold and lost. It was just as if we were her daughters. But I mustn't keep her waiting. Hello there! Is anyone home?

(Ampelisca knocks at the door of the house.)
(Enter Sceparnio from the house.)

SCEPARNIO:

Who is that doing such damage to my door?

AMPELISCA:

It's only me.

SCEPARNIO:

(Aside: Ah, ha! Just look what's landed on my doorstep: a beautiful girl. I can't believe it.)

AMPELISCA:

Good day, young man.

SCEPARNIO:

(Aside: Young man, she calls me!) Good day to you, my dear young lady.

AMPELISCA:

I was hoping to find you at home.

SCEPARNIO:

(*Aside:* She must be kidding.) And it would give me great pleasure to receive you, if you could only come back this evening. At the moment I am engaged elsewhere. In the meantime, though, smiley, give me a sweet—I mean, give me a smile sweetie.

AMPELISCA:

Young man, how dare you treat me in so familiar a fashion!

SCEPARNIO:

(*Aside:* Ye gods, how beautiful! Like a statue of Venus, but she's alive and she's got arms. Just look at the sparkle in her eyes, and what a body she's got and that dark complexion, like a precious jip—I mean a gypsy princess. And what lips! Just imagine what she could do with those lips! And my god, those breasts!)

AMPELISCA:

Look here, fellah, ya think I'm a public playground or somethin'? Keep yer hands to yerself.

SCEPARNIO:

Oh, ho! The beastie is a brute—I mean, the beauty is a beast, when roused.

AMPELISCA:

Look, I'll give you a rouse when I'm good and ready. But now I want what I came for.

SCEPARNIO:

Well, what's that?

AMPELISCA:

What's that, he says. You think I'm carrying this pail to catch pennies in?

SCEPARNIO:

Well, you think I'm carrying this flag for a parade?

449

AMPELISCA:

All right, all right. You fill my pail and I'll lower your flag.

SCEPARNIO:

Right! (*Aside:* I've got her! I've got her! I've got her good!) Now give me the pail and paint right here—I mean, give me the pail and wait right here.

(Exit Sceparnio into the house.)

AMPELISCA:

I'm waiting. I'm waiting. But what will I tell the priestess? It's taken so long. Yecch! those waves: I get sick every time I see them. But what is that moving along the shore? Oh, no! The pimp and his Sicilian friend, and I thought they drowned. Now what can I do? I hadn't expected this. I better tell Palaestra so we can seek sanctuary before that pirate tries to recapture us. And fast!

(Exit Ampelisca into the shrine.
Enter Sceparnio from the house with the water-pot.)

SCEPARNIO:

God damn! I never thought drawing water could be such a pleasure, but believe me it was. The well seemed only a few feet deep. I've been enchanted, I can feel it. That girl's got a spell on me, and everything is different. She came from Venus' shrine; she could be a votary or a priestess or the goddess herself. Here's your water, sweetie; now I'll bet part of my carcass, you bet yours—I mean, I kept my part of the bargain, you keep yours. But where are you, delight of my life? Come take your urn. (*Aside:* And I'll take my turn. She must be teasing me, making me look for her like this.) Where are you, honey lips? There's a big bee buzzing about. (*Aside:* I know she loves me; this is her way of showing it.) Come get your water, little nymph. But where are you, really? I can't stand it any longer. I don't see her anywhere. She's gone. She's made a fool of me. But maybe she wasn't real; maybe Venus sent a phantom to enchant me and drive me mad. And what should I do with this urn now? It belongs to Venus and they'll say I stole it. That's what she was up to; I've heard stories about how gods

450

trick men, make them fall in love and then punish them for it. I can't keep the thing. It's all written on and calls out its owner's name. I'd better give it to the priestess. Hey there, Ptolemocratia, come take your urn back. Some girl I've never seen before gave it to me. (*Aside:* This is my penance now, having to haul water for the goddess.)

(Exit Sceparnio into the shrine.)

(Enter Labrax stage right, with Charmides following. The pimp is middle-aged, potbellied and bald; his friend equally unattractive, and effeminate.)

LABRAX:
> The man who has no care
> > For life and property
> Should put his faith in Neptune
> > And suffer accordingly.
> Just look at me! Now I know
> > The meaning of the term
> Sea-changed: deranged and short-changed—
> > The gods confuse their victim
> To abuse their victim, me.
> > I've been robbed by the god of the sea.
> Now where is my travelling companion,
> The witting instrument of my destruction—
> Charmides, where are you?

CHARMIDES:
> > > > > > > Labrax, I'm here,
> But I can't keep up this frantic pace, my dear.

LABRAX:
> Would that you had died back there in Sicily
> Some horrible death, before you touched me,
> Innocent as I am, with your disaster.

CHARMIDES:
> Would that I had slept elsewhere, whoremaster,

Than with you, since it was you, unworthy friend,
Who was the first beginning of my end.
I pray the gods to give you in the future
Guests sharing in your impious nature.

LABRAX:
When I took you into my house, you louse,
I took the devil himself into my house.
It was your idea and my misfortune
To undertake this voyage inopportune.
Why did I listen, why was I convinced,
To trust all I owned to the elements?

CHARMIDES:
You wonder why the ship wrecked? I do not,
When you and all that's yours was evilly got.

LABRAX:
You're the evil; I see your cloven hoof.
I brought destruction under my own roof.

CHARMIDES:
You are your own destruction; like Satan
You make of heaven hell, of hell heaven.

LABRAX:
Support me, please, my stomach is churning.

CHARMIDES:
Throw up your toenails, it's none of my concern.

LABRAX:
Safety for my girls is all I wish for.

CHARMIDES:
But they've long since been turned into fish food.

LABRAX:
Then I owe to you my beggarly status.

452

CHARMIDES:

Don't mention it, friend, I give it you gratis.

LABRAX:

No one could live more miserably than me.

CHARMIDES:

I do since I don't deserve my misery.

LABRAX:

I wish I were a bullrush, head held high,
Standing in the water, but always dry.

CHARMIDES:

I wish I weren't so like a man in battle:
Brandishing my words, I make them rattle.

LABRAX:

Neptune should install a heater in his baths;
Even with my clothes on the chill still lasts.

CHARMIDES:

He should revive his guests with a hot toddy;
Instead he serves iced brine to freeze the body.

LABRAX:

I envy smithies at their furnaces;
They'll never know how cold this goddamned place is.

CHARMIDES:

If I were a duck, I'd take to water.
If I were a duck, the wet wouldn't matter.

LABRAX:

If I were the madman at the circus,
My gnashing teeth would cause a fracas.

CHARMIDES:

The sea shows a certain fastidiousness,

To vomit you up and keep your largesse.

LABRAX:

The gods so confused me that you were able
To entice me on board with the fable
Of riches in Sicily to be had
By a pimp with girls to drive men mad.

CHARMIDES:

You expected to swallow the island whole,
A voracious monster who eats only gold.

LABRAX:

But now some whale has swallowed my gold;
I'm left with nothing but you, Ass-hole.

CHARMIDES:

Your gold, fine, but mine as well, which was stowed
In the hold and, along with yours, swallowed.

LABRAX:

I'm reduced to these rags upon my back,
And this pitiful cloak, barely intact.

CHARMIDES:

I've been thinking you should give me that cloak.
Because mine was lost and my shirt is soaked.

LABRAX:

If only my girls had survived I might
Have hope for an end to this financial blight.
As it is, as a pimp I've lost all that counts:
My girls, my gold, my girls, my fillies, my mounts.
Palaestra was sold and the earnest money
Is lost now and I'll be sued by her honey.

CHARMIDES:

You forget yourself and your pimply talents;

454

You'll manage somehow to tip Justice's balance.

(Enter Sceparnio from the shrine.)

SCEPARNIO:
I wonder why those two girls are clinging to the goddess' statue. Wonder what they're afraid of, poor, pitiful things. They say they were shipwrecked last night and washed ashore this morning.

LABRAX:
I beg your pardon, young man, but did I hear you mention girls?

SCEPARNIO:
Indeed you did; they are there, in Venus' shrine.

LABRAX:
How many?

SCEPARNIO:
As many as we are.

LABRAX:
I'm sure they belong to me.

SCEPARNIO:
I'm sure I don't know.

LABRAX:
And are they attractive?

SCEPARNIO:
You can be sure of that. I'm sure I could make love to both of them— if I were too drunk to tell them apart.

LABRAX:
They're mine.

SCEPARNIO:
You surely are a nuisance. Go see for yourself.

LABRAX:

Charmides, did you hear? My girls are found.

CHARMIDES:

Damn you and your girls.

LABRAX:

Now I'll break into the shrine and drag them away.

(Exit Labrax into shrine.)

CHARMIDES:

(After Labrax:) I hope you break your neck. *(To Sceparnio:)* But look, friend, provide me a place to rest.

SCEPARNIO:

Provide yourself; this is public property.

CHARMIDES:

But can't you see I'm soaked to the skin? Take me in and give me dry clothes until I can dry my own. I'll repay you somehow.

SCEPARNIO:

Here, take the shirt off my back; it's the only one I've got, but you're welcome to it.

CHARMIDES:

That's hardly a fair trade. Must I be bilked by you as well as the sea?

SCEPARNIO:

I don't care whether you're bilked or bilged. I'm not about to trust a stranger. Sit and shiver and shake, sweat and ache. I've wasted time on you.

(Exit Sceparnio into the house.)

CHARMIDES:

Don't leave me here. He's gone. What a mean spirit! Just like a slave —no pity at all. But why should I suffer out here when I can seek refuge inside. I'll sleep off this hangover from Neptune's party in Venus' shrine. I was his unwilling guest at any rate. He forced me to drink and that last round almost killed me. Now I'll see what the pimp is up to.

(Exit Charmides into shrine.)

(Enter Daemones from the house.)

DAEMONES:
    The gods play games upon us when we sleep:
    They send us dreams whose meaning we can't see
    Then or when we wake. Last night I had a dream
    And it remains to me a mystery.
    I dreamed I saw an ape attempt to climb
    The tree in which a swallow had her nest.
    There were two fledgelings without their mother,
    But they were out of reach. The monkey came to me
    And asked me for a ladder, but I replied
    That these birds were descendants of Procne
    And Philomela, daughters of King Pandion
    Of Athens, and I, an Athenian,
    Considered them my fellow countrymen.
    He would not listen to my argument,
    But threatened me with violence. To court
    He took me, where I found the strength to seize
    Him, cast him into chains, vile, hairy beast.
    Now I have no way of knowing what this dream
    Could mean, nor how I should construe it
    In the context of my life. But what is this
    I hear? Some commotion in the shrine of Venus.

(Sounds from the shrine of feet scuffling, pottery breaking and women screaming. Enter Trachalio from the shrine.)

TRACHALIO:
    Oh, you citizens of Cyrene, hear me,
    I beseech you. Help the helpless, punish
    The guilty—Justice! Justice! If you take pride
    In the reputation of your city

You must not let brute force o'erwhelm unarmed
Innocence, but make a sign to all
That violence shall not with you prevail,
The meek shall find protection under law
Which here established is omnipotent.
Come, ye citizens, gather at the shrine
Of Venus. By your good faith, I beseech you,
Whoever hears my voice, my call to arms,
Defend the suppliants who by ancient rite
Have claimed protection at the goddess' altar,
And been received there by her appointed priestess.
Destroy this evil lest it get you first.

DAEMONES:

Young man, what mischief is it you describe?

TRACHALIO:

Although, dear sir, I do not know your name,
I beg your intercession, I beseech—

DAEMONES:

Come to it, fellow. Tell me what you want.

TRACHALIO:

I beg and plead that you, sir, if you care, sir,
For your crops, your wheat and barley; if you
Have a thought, sir, for the safe arrival
Of your goods at Capua; if you seek
A cure for rheumy eyes and runny nose—

DAEMONES:

You've lost your mind.

TRACHALIO:

If you depend upon
A bumper crop of rye, do not deny, sir,
My request, but give me aid as I require.

DAEMONES:

If you are accustomed, as I expect,
To a beating twice a day, and if you want,
As I intend, to receive of those two one
From me today, then I can promise you
A crop of rods, a crop of whips, a bumper
Crop of bruises, unless you tell me now
What is going on and what you want, sir.

TRACHALIO:

Well, sir, you have no call to threaten me.
After all, I only wished the best for you.

DAEMONES:

And I for you: the best that you deserve.

TRACHALIO:

But, I beg you, listen.

DAEMONES:

Speak, then, to the point.

TRACHALIO:

In primis, now, in the shrine of Venus,
Two women have been feloniously
Assaulted; nor do they have protection
From kin or friend, but must rely upon
The honest people of this land; then, too,
The priestess has herself been outraged and this
No man who gives the gods their due can bear.

DAEMONES:

Lives there a man who dares so dire a deed?
Who are these women and what exactly
Is the purpose of him who would them harm.

TRACHALIO:

If you will come to their assistance, I

Will tell you all: there is a man, no man,
In truth, but a most impious beast intent
To drag them from the altar where they cling,
Though free-born and deserving better treatment.

DAEMONES:
Describe the one who thus offends the gods.

TRACHALIO:
I shall tell you: he is the most obnoxious
Creature ever born, not content with crimes
Of common usage, but determined his
Will make him famous for scurrility:
Parricide, perjury, impiety,
Bastardy, buggery, blasphemy—
A litany of evils all contained
In the title of his profession: pimp.

DAEMONES:
No doubt but that this beast should pay for all
He's done.

TRACHALIO:
                      Did I mention that he did in fact
Lay hands upon the priestess of the goddess?

DAEMONES:
For that he shall pay dearly. You, there, Sparax,
Turbalio, come here; I have need of you.

TRACHALIO:
Do, I beg you, go within the shrine.
Help them! Save them!

DAEMONES:
                              Come out, I say, you slugs!

(Enter Sparax and Turbalio from the house, two huge slaves, slack-jawed, wearing only tunics.)

460

DAEMONES *(To Sparax and Turbalio):*
Follow me.

(Exit Daemones, Sparax and Turbalio into the shrine.)

TRACHALIO:
        Yes, go in and seize the villain.
Have his eyes gouged out; that would serve him right.
Then, if he lived, he'd go through life a blind bawd,
Unable to appraise his own merchandise.

DAEMONES *(From within the shrine):*
Hang him up by the feet like a butchered hog.

TRACHALIO:
Just listen to the tumult raised inside.
I do believe the pimp has been pumped,
And here the girls come now, frightened but safe.

(Enter Palaestra and Ampelisca from the shrine.)

PALAESTRA:
Now I see our situation
In a clear and certain light.
There's no hope for our salvation
No possibility for flight.
Where can we turn for succour,
Who can defend us from attack?
Two women, no protector:
How dare prepare we to fight back?

For a while there was some reason
To believe the pimp was drowned.
That hope we must abandon:
The beast his prey has found.

Not even Venus could screen us
From his violence, our disgrace.
Her priestess called down curses;

461

He hurled them back in her face.

He tore us from the goddess' feet,
Then threw us from her shrine.
But his conquest won't be complete:
The choice of death's still mine.

TRACHALIO:
But what is this? What do I hear?
A girl, two girls, crying near.

PALAESTRA:
He's come for us. 'Tis time we die.

TRACHALIO:
Palaestra, I heard your cry.

AMPELISCA:
Don't answer him; this is a trick.

PALAESTRA:
Who calls me? Tell me and be quick!

TRACHALIO:
It's only me, Trachalio.

PALAESTRA:
My saviour, lord and hero.

TRACHALIO:
Have courage both; you must not yield.

PALAESTRA:
Death's all that's left; our fate is sealed.

TRACHALIO:
That's foolish; I've come to help you.

PALAESTRA:
What good can words of comfort do?

AMPELISCA:

    I've sworn to die if he attacks,
    But unlike her, my timorous heart lacks
    Courage to face a painful death,
    To be this day of life bereft.

TRACHALIO:

    Assume a suppliant posture
    Here at Venus' altar, and I
    Will stand by as your defender,
    And if attacked 'tis I shall die.

AMPELISCA:

    What hope is there for your success
    When ev'ry other plan has failed?
    He overcame Venus' own priestess;
    Not even divine strength prevailed.

    The pimp will now force this refuge
    Just as violently as before
    He drove us from the shrine, abused,
    Imploring not to suffer more.

TRACHALIO:

    Consider this to be your fort
    And me its chief commander.
    With Venus' help we shall cut short
    The siege laid now by the pander.

PALAESTRA:

    In you we trust, and in Venus,
    Prostrate upon her altar, suppliants
    As the ancient custom is,
    Depending on her for deliverance.

    Venus, listen to our prayer:
    Protect us now in our distress.
    Lead us out of the beast's lair;

We are pious, he shameless.

Cast not a disapproving eye
On our dishevelled state, but mark
How Neptune did us purify
By storm, by sea, in the dark.

(The girls remain at the altar for the rest of the scene.)

TRACHALIO:
And, Venus, I pray, since you
Arose from the foam of the sea
And these girls have done that too,
Deliver them from evil—deliver me.

(Enter Daemones from the Shrine, followed by Sparax and Turbalio, who drag Labrax between them.)

DAEMONES *(to Labrax):*
You, who break the laws of gods and men, get out of Venus' shrine. And you young girls, stay there at the altar.

TRACHALIO:
They're there, right where you want them.

DAEMONES:
Good. Now tell the pimp to come over here. Did you really think we would stand by and allow you to defy the gods? *(To Sparax and Turbalio, who hold Labrax by either arm):* Hit him in the face for that.

LABRAX:
I don't deserve this treatment and it's you will pay for it.

DAEMONES:
Dare you threaten me?

LABRAX:
I know my rights and you have deprived me of them when you take away my slaves against my will.

TRACHALIO:

Your rights, you say? Choose any man of Cyrene, any leading citizen, to arbitrate. Ask him whether or not these girls should be allowed to go free, whether or not you should be forced to rot in prison.

LABRAX:

I have no intention of disputing this matter with a scurrilous slave. It is you, sir, I mean to address.

DAEMONES:

But this man knows you and the situation. You must deal with him.

LABRAX:

No, I will speak only to you.

TRACHALIO:

You'll speak to me whether you like it or not. Now tell me, are these girls yours?

LABRAX:

Of course.

TRACHALIO:

Well, just you touch them; just lay your littlest finger on them.

LABRAX:

And what if I do?

TRACHALIO:

Then I'll turn you into a punching bag and knock the stuffing out of you. So should all perjurers perish.

LABRAX:

You mean I can't remove my slaves?

DAEMONES:

No. Our laws forbid it.

LABRAX:

Your laws mean nothing to me. I intend to take my girls away with me now. But, old man, if you have taken a fancy to them, they're available on a cash-and-carry basis. I'd make a deal with Venus herself, if she could pay the price.

DAEMONES:

You'd ask payment from the gods? But so you understand me, if you so much as make a move in jest to threaten these young girls, I'll alter your anatomy so you won't recognize yourself. And you who guard him, if, when I give the signal, you hesitate to knock the eyes right out of his head, I'll wrap so many rods around your legs you'll look like vine-covered trees.

LABRAX:

You threaten me with violence?

TRACHALIO:

Violent punishment for the violent crimes; you can't claim we are not fair.

LABRAX:

But you, you thrice-whipped slave, how dare you speak to me like that?

TRACHALIO:

Have it your way then: I'm a slave fit for beating and you're an upright citizen. But answer me this: does that make these girls any the less free?

LABRAX:

Free? Who said they were free?

TRACHALIO:

Not only are they free, but Greek and of a rank far above yours; one is even Athenian by birth.

DAEMONES:

What is that you say?

TRACHALIO:

I say that this girl here is a free-born Athenian citizen.

DAEMONES:

That means that she and I are related—by national origin, that is.

TRACHALIO:

How so? I thought you were a native of Cyrene.

DAEMONES:

No, but born and raised in Athens.

TRACHALIO:

Then, sir, defend your own, native of your native land.

DAEMONES:

Oh gods, this girl reminds me of my daughter, and makes me miserable since here she stands and my daughter I shall never see again. She was only three years old when stolen from me and would be the same age as this girl, if she's still alive.

LABRAX:

What difference does it make to me whether these girls come from Athens or Thebes or Dryopian Argos? They're mine. I paid for them. They must do as I tell them.

TRACHALIO:

And so, pimp, you think that like some tom-cat you can prowl about and pick up all the kittens in the neighborhood and force them to comply with your vile wishes? Aren't you ashamed to people your brothels with free-born girls? I don't know where the other girl came from, but certainly this one is nobler born than you—though that's not saying much.

LABRAX:

Are they yours?

TRACHALIO:

I'll make a bet with you if you put them up as surety. You called me a whipping post; I'll bet my back is less familiar with the rod than yours. Just make the wager. Your hide, I know, is so scarred it could be used for alligator shoes, while mine is soft and smooth as any glove-maker would be proud to use. And, into the bargain, when I win, I'll pry your eyeballs out and play marbles with them.

LABRAX:
Since it means so much to you, I'll go and take them.

DAEMONES:
How?

LABRAX:
I'll burn them off the altar, that's how. Venus and Vulcan don't get along, you know.

TRACHALIO:
Where is he going?

LABRAX *(Knocking on door of house):*
Is anyone here? Open up!

DAEMONES:
If you so much as touch that door, I'll use my fists on your face like pitchforks in hay.

SPARAX:
There's no fire here; we only eat dried figs.

DAEMONES:
Is it fire you want? I'll give you fire enough to burn your beard.

LABRAX:
I'll try somewhere else, thank you.

DAEMONES:
And what will you do when you find it?

LABRAX:

I'll make a huge bonfire here at the altar.

DAEMONES:

And burn yourself alive?

LABRAX:

And force these girls from their sanctuary.

DAEMONES:

Rather I'll cook your goose and serve you up to the vultures as a snack. Now that I think of it, I do believe this pimp is the monkey in my dream, and these girls that he would capture are the swallows nesting out of reach.

TRACHALIO:

I beg you, sir, watch him until I can return with my master.

DAEMONES:

So I shall; be off.

TRACHALIO:

But take care.

DAEMONES:

Yes, yes; be off.

TRACHALIO:

Remember, though, this pimp has a date at the gallows; let's be sure he keeps it.

DAEMONES:

I'll tend to that; you find your master.

TRACHALIO:

I shall return.

(Exit Trachalio stage left.)

DAEMONES:

Now, pimp, it's up to you. Choose whether you want to remain here quietly with or without a beating.

LABRAX:

I'm not paying any attention to you, old man. I intend to take my girls whether you like it or not. Whether Venus likes it or not. Whether Jupiter himself likes it or not. I'll take them by the hair and drag them off the altar.

DAEMONES:

Just you try.

LABRAX:

I certainly will.

DAEMONES:

Attack, men.

LABRAX:

Tell them to retreat.

DAEMONES:

No, indeed, they will attack.

LABRAX:

I don't believe you.

DAEMONES:

And if they do?

LABRAX:

Then I'll retreat. But listen, old man, if I ever meet up with you again, I'll get even or I'm no pimp.

DAEMONES:

Do what you like in the future, but for now, if you so much as touch them, I'll beat the hell out of you.

LABRAX:

Why such a violent threat?

DAEMONES:

Because I'm dealing with a worthless pimp.

LABRAX:

You may threaten me all you want. I'm taking my girls with me.

DAEMONES:

Go ahead and try.

LABRAX:

I will.

DAEMONES:

Do, but do you know what will happen? Turbalio, fetch me two clubs from the house.

(Exit Turbalio into the house.)

LABRAX:

Clubs did you say?

DAEMONES:

Yes, big ones, so I can give you the beating you deserve.

LABRAX:

Oh, damn! I left my helmet on board ship. If I could arm myself I might survive. But am I allowed at least to speak to them?

DAEMONES:

Certainly not. Ha! Here comes the club-bearer now.

LABRAX:

My ears are ringing in anticipation.

(Enter Turbalio from the house with two Herculean clubs.)

DAEMONES:

Sparax, you take one of the clubs and stand on this side; Turbalio, you on the other. Now listen to my orders: if he so much as points at these girls, I'll knock *you* senseless unless you knock *him* senseless. If he calls to them, you answer. If he tries to run away, cripple him with blows.

LABRAX:

You mean you won't even let me leave?

DAEMONES:

Right. And when that slave returns with his master, send them to me at once.

(Exit Daemones into the house.)

LABRAX:

Ye gods, this temple has changed hands. It used to belong to Venus, but now Hercules has taken over, and there are two of him. Now I have no place to run. By sea, by land, the spirits of this place have risen up against me. Palaestra!

SPARAX:

Yes, what is it?

LABRAX:

What confusion! This is not my Palaestra. You, Ampelisca.

TURBALIO:

You'd better watch yourself.

LABRAX:

For no-good slaves, they give good advice. But, listen, it does no harm for me to approach them, does it?

SPARAX:

No harm to us, but a great deal to you.

LABRAX:

You mean you'd beat me just for moving?

TURBALIO:
Try us and see.

LABRAX:
I'll take just one little step.

SPARAX:
Then you'll get just one little beating.

LABRAX:
On second thought, I'll stay where I am. (*Aside:* Somehow I must plunder this citadel in spite of these sentinels.)

(Enter Plesidippus and Trachalio stage left.)

PLESIDIPPUS:
You say the pimp attempted to force my girl from Venus' altar, to use violence upon her?

TRACHALIO:
That's what I said.

PLESIDIPPUS:
Why didn't you kill him on the spot?

TRACHALIO:
Well . . . I didn't have a sword.

PLESIDIPPUS:
You could have used a rock.

TRACHALIO:
Am I to go chasing mad dogs, pelting them with rocks?

LABRAX:
Oh, god! Now I'm done for; here comes Plesidippus. He'll beat the stuffing out of me and sweep it all away.

PLESIDIPPUS:
Were the girls still at the altar when you left?

473

TRACHALIO:

There they sit.

PLESIDIPPUS:

But who's protecting them?

TRACHALIO:

Some old man who lives next door to Venus. He's been most helpful, told his servants to stand guard, did everything I told him to, since I, of course, took charge.

PLESIDIPPUS:

Just let me get my hands on that pimp. Where is the beast?

LABRAX:

Greetings, friend.

PLESIDIPPUS:

Don't greet me, you villain, just decide whether you want to be throttled here or dragged off to jail.

LABRAX:

That's hardly a choice.

PLESIDIPPUS:

Run to the shore, Trachalio, and tell those men I had with me to meet me back in town. I need them to bear witness when I turn him over to the hangman. Then come back here. I'm going to take him to court. *(To Labrax):* Move on, you. Move on!

LABRAX:

But what have I done wrong?

PLESIDIPPUS:

Need you ask? What about that money I paid you for this girl? You ran off with her and it.

LABRAX:

I did no such thing.

PLESIDIPPUS:
How dare you deny it?

LABRAX:
I put her on board ship but, as you can see, we didn't get far. Just as I said yesterday, "Meet me at the shrine of Venus," and here we are.

PLESIDIPPUS:
You can make that plea in court. I've heard enough. Now, follow me.

LABRAX:
Charmides, help me, I beg you. I'm being led off in chains.

CHARMIDES:
Did I hear someone call me?

LABRAX:
Don't you see what's happening? He's taking me to jail.

CHARMIDES:
Yes, I see. Have a good trip.

LABRAX:
And you'll do nothing to help?

CHARMIDES:
Who's finally caught up with you?

LABRAX:
Plesidippus, the boy who paid me for Palaestra.

CHARMIDES:
Well, you must take things as they come, and tip the hangman generously. Plesidippus only takes the vengeance on you which many others would like.

LABRAX:
But help me, please.

CHARMIDES:

If you were a better man, I'd be a better friend. As it is, you go your way to the gallows and I'll mind my own business here.

LABRAX:

Done for!

PLESIDIPPUS:

I hope so! But Palaestra, you and Ampelisca stay here 'til I return.

SPARAX:

I think they'd be better off in our house.

PLESIDIPPUS:

That's true. Thank you.

LABRAX:

You're robbing me.

TURBALIO:

How so? Get on with you.

LABRAX:

Please, Palaestra, I've always been good to you.

PLESIDIPPUS:

Come on, the hangman's waiting.

LABRAX:

Friend, Charmides, please.

CHARMIDES:

I'm no friend of yours. Your friendship has been my undoing.

LABRAX:

And so you turn on me in my hour of need?

CHARMIDES:

I do indeed.

LABRAX:
Damn you, then! Damn you all!

CHARMIDES:
And you. Now I expect a metamorphosis: the pimp will be turned into a gallows bird and flutter in the noose. I'll go along and applaud his swan song.

(Exit Plesidippus, Trachalio and Labrax stage left, with Charmides following.
Exit Sparax and Turbalio, with Palaestra and Ampelisca, into the house.
Enter Daemones from the house.)

DAEMONES:
It gives me the greatest pleasure to have done
Some service to these girls, obliged them to me.
The one they call Palaestra turns my thoughts
To youthful days when I did woo my wife.
That wife pours woe now on my hoary head;
She sees what change the girl has wrought in me.
I come outside to 'scape her constant tongue
And look for Gripus, who's been gone since dawn.
A foul day for fishing, after such a storm.
I doubt he's caught more than cold in's head.
Well, that's for him to worry. I have my wife.

(Exit Daemones into the house.
Enter Gripus stage right, dragging a large trunk behind him at the end of a long rope. He looks just like Sceparnio and could be played by the same actor.)

GRIPUS:
To Neptune I give thanks,
Who guards these fishy banks,
And rules his salty kingdom undersea.

477

To him I owe it all,
This super-abundant haul,
Plunder taken by me in victory.

Neither men nor equipment
Did I lose where I went
In pursuit of lasting glory and riches.

Here I hold in my trusty net,
From the stormy sea still wet,
The most marvelous of all the fishes.

This is just reward for my industry,
Which I inherit from my ancestors.
We are a long line of energetic slaves
And never have been slack in our profession.
There are some slaves who must be told to do
What must be done; with me, I see the task
And set me to it, before my master
Has to command. Today is an example.
While the storm raged and the waves rose higher
And all the sluggish members of my race
Used this excuse to linger in their beds,
Then it was, before dawn, I roused myself
And undertook this unattractive task,
To fish the seas to feed me and my master.
The fish I caught is an uncommon kind,
Which, though almost starved, I shan't attempt to eat.
Inside I know there is vast treasure stored
And this I'll use to buy my liberty.

And when I'm free
I'll buy me a farm
With fields and a house and a lot of slaves.
I'll buy me a fleet
Of merchant ships
And be known as an equal of kings.

I'll have my own yacht
And cruise a lot
Like Ari Onassis and friends.

And at my apogee
A pleasure dome I'll decree
And call it after me:
Villa Gripe, Gripton, Gripolia.
It'll be a monument to my name,
A repository of my fame,
With all my great deeds recorded.

(Enter Trachalio stage left. They engage in a tug-of-war.)

TRACHALIO:
You, there! Wait a minute!

GRIPUS:
Who, me? Why should I?

TRACHALIO:
I'll give you a hand with this rope so you won't get hung up.

GRIPUS:
Just you leave my rope alone.

TRACHALIO:
But, as the saying goes, *bonis quod bene fit, hau perit,* which means, roughly, *manus lavat manum.*

GRIPUS:
I don't want my hands washed, and if you think I've got fish to give you, you're mistaken. There was a storm last night and I've come home without so much as a minnow.

TRACHALIO:
It's not your fish I want, but a minute of your time. I have a question for you.

479

GRIPUS:

I don't know who you are, but you're making a nuisance of yourself.

TRACHALIO:

Well, you might as well answer my question, since I won't let you go 'til you do.

GRIPUS:

Don't threaten me, fellow. What the hell you think you're doing, anyway, pulling on my rope like that?

TRACHALIO:

Just listen to what I have to say.

GRIPUS:

No.

TRACHALIO:

Oh, but you will!

GRIPUS:

Then tell me what you want—quick!

TRACHALIO:

There's some advantage in what I have to say.

GRIPUS:

Then say it.

TRACHALIO:

First, let's be sure we're not overheard.

GRIPUS:

Now what is it?

TRACHALIO:

Okay, the coast is clear. But swear you won't tell anyone.

GRIPUS:

Tell anyone what?

TRACHALIO:

Sh! First swear you won't breathe a word of what I have to tell you.

GRIPUS:

I swear. I swear.

TRACHALIO:

Then, listen: I just saw somebody steal something. I know the man he stole it from, so I went to the thief and said, "Listen, fellow, I'll make a deal. I know what you did and who you did it to and if you'll give me half, I won't tell." He wouldn't agree. Now give me your opinion: How much should he give me. Say, "Half."

GRIPUS:

Oh, I'd say more than half, and if he didn't pay up, you ought to tell.

TRACHALIO:

Right! I think I'll follow your advice. Now listen carefully: the thief I've been talking about is you.

GRIPUS:

What do you mean?

TRACHALIO:

I know whose trunk this is.

GRIPUS:

You what?

TRACHALIO:

And I know how he lost it.

GRIPUS:

Well, listen, Mr. Know-it-all, I know who found it and how he found it and what he's going to do with it: he's going to keep it. My information's more valuable than yours since you only know what's already happened and I know what's going to happen: nobody's going to take this from me, so don't even think about trying.

TRACHALIO:

You mean even if the owner himself comes along?

GRIPUS:

Look, I'm the owner now; I caught it; I'm going to keep it.

TRACHALIO:

You caught it?

GRIPUS:

Yes. Don't you think the fish I catch are mine? I treat them as my own. No one claims them or any part of them. I sell them in the market like I would anything else that belongs to me. Nobody owns the sea; It's common property.

TRACHALIO:

I agree with you there. So how come, if the sea is held in common, this trunk, which was found in the sea, doesn't belong to me as much as it does to you?

GRIPUS:

You stop at nothing, do you? If what you say were true, how could fishermen make a living? They'd take their catch to the market, but no one would buy, since everyone would say, "Hey, that fish is mine; you caught it in the sea, and the sea belongs to me."

TRACHALIO:

Don't be ridiculous. How can you compare a trunk with a fish. They're not the same thing at all.

GRIPUS:

I can't help that. Look, I'm a fisherman. I put out my nets and draw them in. Whatever's there is mine. It's that simple.

TRACHALIO:

Simple? Simple-minded, you mean. How can that apply to a trunk?

GRIPUS:

Oh, well, if you want to split hairs . . .

TRACHALIO:

Look, you charlatan, you can't turn a trunk into a fish. Have you ever seen a fisherman catch a trunk-fish and take it to market? You can't have it both ways. You can't be a luggage-merchant and a fisherman at the same time. You've got to prove to me that a trunk is a fish or stop laying claim to something that has no scales and doesn't even belong in the sea.

GRIPUS:

You mean you've never heard of a trunk-fish before?

TRACHALIO:

Of course not, you crook.

GRIPUS:

Well, I should know; I'm a fisherman. They're very rare, understand; the larger ones are blue, and some are even black.

TRACHALIO:

Is that so? Well, I expect to see you turned first into one and then the other: first black and then blue.

GRIPUS:

(Aside: What bad luck to run into such a clever bastard!)

TRACHALIO:

But, look, we're wasting time. Let's take this case to someone else to decide.

GRIPUS:

You mean to make a federal case out of a suitcase?

TRACHALIO:

What a fool you are!

GRIPUS:

Excuse me, please, Socrates.

TRACHALIO:

I can guarantee you one thing: you won't get away from me unless you agree to settle it my way.

GRIPUS:

You must be sick in the head.

TRACHALIO:

Now that you mention it, I have been bothered by a headache.

GRIPUS:

Really? I often have a pain right here, above my left ear.

TRACHALIO:

Then if I box your right ear, the pain will balance out.

GRIPUS:

If you so much as touch me, I'll flatten you like a jelly-fish.

TRACHALIO:

Then I'll attach myself to you like a sponge and soak up your vital fluids.

GRIPUS:

If you want a fight, I'm ready.

TRACHALIO:

But what's the use? Why not just divide the spoils?

GRIPUS:

Why don't you give up? You're not going to get anything out of this but trouble. I'm leaving.

TRACHALIO:

You're not going to get out of this port with that cargo. I'll ram you broadsides.

GRIPUS:

You think you can stop me? You're just a tugboat and I'm an ocean liner. Now cast off my starboard line.

TRACHALIO:

I'll cast you off, alright, off the cliff there, if you don't let go of that trunk.

GRIPUS:

You're not going to get one cent out of this, so give it up.

TRACHALIO:

You'll never get rid of me that way. Either divvy up or agree to arbitrate.

GRIPUS:

Divvy up what I caught in the sea?

TRACHALIO:

What I saw you steal from the shore.

GRIPUS:

I caught it; it was my luck, my nets, my boat.

TRACHALIO:

That doesn't matter. I'm just as guilty of the theft as you are, if the owner comes along and I don't admit I saw you take it.

GRIPUS:

That's not true.

TRACHALIO:

Hold on, I say, you fugitive from a chain gang. I'm not through talking to you. Now tell me how you can say I'm not as guilty as you.

GRIPUS:

Look, I don't know how to quibble over laws like you city boys. All I know is, this is mine.

TRACHALIO:

And I say it's mine.

GRIPUS:

Wait a minute. I know what you can do so as not to be guilty of any crime.

TRACHALIO:
 What?

GRIPUS:

Just let me go off this way and you go off that way and I won't say anything about you and you don't say anything about me. I keep my mouth shut; you do the same. Now how's that for a deal, fair and square?

TRACHALIO:

You think that's a good deal, do you?

GRIPUS:

I sure do. You go on about your business; let go of my rope and leave me alone.

TRACHALIO: .

Just wait a minute; I've got a proposition.

GRIPUS:

The only offer I'd accept is for you to get the hell out of here.

TRACHALIO:

Do you know anybody around here?

GRIPUS:

I know my neighbors.

TRACHALIO:

Where do you live?

GRIPUS:

Way over there beyond that last field.

TRACHALIO:

How would it be if we were to ask whoever lives in this house to arbitrate for us?

GRIPUS:

Just let go of my rope a minute and let me think about it.

TRACHALIO:

Sure, there you are.

GRIPUS:

(Aside: Great! My troubles are over and the treasure is mine. He's taking me to my own master for arbitration. He won't give him a cent. This jerk doesn't know what he's getting into.) Okay, I'll arbitrate. It's easier than fighting with you.

TRACHALIO:

Now, you're talking.

GRIPUS:

Even though I don't know the man who's going to judge, if he's just, he's the best man for the job; if he's not just, I wouldn't want him to judge even if he were my dearest friend.

(Trachalio is about to knock on the door of the house when it opens and Daemones comes out, leading Palaestra and Ampelisca. Sparax and Turbalio follow.)

DAEMONES:

Believe me, girls, I am concerned for your welfare, but what can I do? My wife threatens to lock me out of the house. She says I'm hiring whores and bringing them home. You'll have to go back to the altar or I'll have to take refuge there myself.

PALAESTRA:

Now all is lost; there's no hope for us now.

DAEMONES:

Please don't start that again; I'll protect you, I promise. *(To Sparax and Turbalio:)* You two can go back inside now. As long as I'm here no one will bother them. I relieve you of your sentry duty.

*(Exit Sparax and Turbalio into the house.
Palaestra and Ampelisca take up their former positions at the altar.)*

GRIPUS:

Greetings, master.

DAEMONES:

Gripus, how are you? What have you been up to?

TRACHALIO:

What is this? Is he your slave?

GRIPUS:

Yes, and he has no cause to be ashamed of me.

TRACHALIO:

I've got nothing to say to you.

GRIPUS:

Then stop bothering me. Get lost.

TRACHALIO:

Please, sir, answer me this: is he your slave?

DAEMONES:

Yes, he is.

TRACHALIO:

So much the better. But we've met before; I'm glad to see you again.

DAEMONES:

And I you. You left here earlier to find your master.

TRACHALIO:

That's right.

DAEMONES:

Now what is it you want?

TRACHALIO:

Well, tell me, is this man really your slave?

DAEMONES:

Yes, he's really mine.

TRACHALIO:

Well, I'm glad.

DAEMONES:
I'm glad you're glad; but what can I do for you?

TRACHALIO:
Do something about him; he's a crook.

DAEMONES:
And what did this crook do to you?

TRACHALIO:
I think you ought to punish him; crucify him or beat him to death or something like that.

DAEMONES:
Why should I? What's he done to you?

TRACHALIO:
I'll tell you all about it.

GRIPUS:
No, I'll tell him.

TRACHALIO:
It's my place to state the case, if you don't mind. I'm the plaintiff.

GRIPUS:
You're plain trouble is what you are; otherwise you'd get the hell out of here and leave me alone.

DAEMONES:
Wait a minute, Gripus.

GRIPUS:
Are you going to let him speak first?

DAEMONES:
Yes. Now listen to what he has to say. Go ahead.

GRIPUS:
You mean you'll give preference to a stranger?

TRACHALIO:

Can't you force him to be quiet? Now, as I was about to say, that pimp you threw out of the shrine here? Well, your slave has his trunk.

GRIPUS:

Trunk? Who, me?

TRACHALIO:

You can't deny what we can see.

GRIPUS:

I can try, can't I? What if I do have it? What business is it of yours what I do?

TRACHALIO:

What matters is whether you got that trunk legally or illegally.

GRIPUS:

I caught it in the sea, I tell you, and if I didn't, may I hang for it! What I catch is mine, not yours.

TRACHALIO:

That silly game again! Pay no attention to him; the situation is as I describe it.

GRIPUS:

What do you mean? Why should you describe it?

TRACHALIO:

Because I'm the plaintiff and I have the right to speak first. Now, sir, can't you force him to be quiet?

GRIPUS:

Force me? You think he treats me like your master treats you? I'm nobody's pretty boy. That's all you city boys are good for, but not me.

DAEMONES:

He got you there. But go on with your story.

TRACHALIO:

First I want you to understand that I'm not claiming this trunk for myself, nor any part of its contents. I have never said that it belongs to me. All I am saying is that there's a little box inside which belongs to this young lady, and I've already told you that she is free-born.

DAEMONES:

You mean the girl you said was Athenian?

TRACHALIO:

Exactly. And the toys she played with as a child are in the box, which is in the trunk. They are of no use to the pimp or to this slave of yours, but they may help the poor girl identify her parents.

DAEMONES:

I'll see to it that she gets them, and you keep quiet, Gripus.

GRIPUS:

I won't keep quiet and I won't give her anything.

TRACHALIO:

All I ask is the little box and the toys.

GRIPUS:

But what if they're made out of gold or something?

TRACHALIO:

What difference does it make to you? I'll pay for them; whether they're gold or silver, you won't lose a penny.

GRIPUS:

Let me see your money; then I'll let you see the box.

DAEMONES:

Stop bickering before I hit you. Now, say what you have to say.

TRACHALIO:

All I ask is that you have pity on this young girl and give her what is hers—if this is in fact the pimp's trunk and her things are in it. You see I base my whole case on this assumption. I might be wrong.

GRIPUS:
Don't you see, he's trying to trick us?

TRACHALIO:
Just let me finish. If this is the pimp's trunk, these girls can identify it. Tell your slave to show it to them.

GRIPUS:
I'm to show it to them, am I?

DAEMONES:
Show it to them, Gripus. It's the least you can do.

GRIPUS:
The least, you say. It's more than enough for him to trick me with.

DAEMONES:
How?

GRIPUS:
As soon as I show them the trunk, they'll say it's theirs.

TRACHALIO:
Oh, you crook, you! Do you think that everyone is like you?

GRIPUS:
You can say what you like; I don't care. As long as my master sides with me.

TRACHALIO:
He might be on your side now, but the case hasn't been tried yet.

DAEMONES:
Gripus, you pay attention. Now, get on with what you were saying.

TRACHALIO:
I've already finished, but I'll go over it again if you missed the point.

These girls, both of them, are free-born; one of them was born in Athens and stolen from there by pirates as a child.

GRIPUS:

But what does this have to do with the trunk?

TRACHALIO:

You're just trying to put off the verdict with your stupid questions.

DAEMONES:

Don't argue; just get it over with.

TRACHALIO:

There is a little box in this trunk made out of wicker. In it are toys which this girl had when she was stolen from Athens. I've said it all before.

GRIPUS:

God damn you, you cheat. Why should you be pleading their case anyway? Why can't they speak for themselves?

TRACHALIO:

Because they're modest in front of men, as women should be. They need a man to speak for them.

GRIPUS:

Well, why didn't they get one then? But what about my turn? Can I speak now?

DAEMONES:

If you say one more word I'll beat your brains out.

TRACHALIO:

As I said, sir, all I ask is the trinkets. If he insists on being paid for them, then I promise he shall be. Everything else in the trunk is his.

GRIPUS:

You've changed your tune now that you see I've won the case; a while ago you were asking for half.

TRACHALIO:
I still do.

GRIPUS:
Well, cats don't always catch the mouse.

DAEMONES:
Can't you be told anything without a beating? Now, shut up!

GRIPUS:
Shut him up first; if he can speak, I can too.

DAEMONES:
Put the trunk over here.

GRIPUS:
On condition you'll give it back if what he says is in it, isn't.

DAEMONES:
Agreed.

(Gripus pulls the trunk by the rope across the stage to where Daemones is standing with Trachalio and Daemones.)

GRIPUS:
There.

DAEMONES:
Now, Palaestra and Ampelisca, listen to me. Is this the trunk you think contains your box of tokens?

PALAESTRA:
Yes.

GRIPUS:
Damn! She didn't even look at it.

PALAESTRA:
I'll describe everything in detail. There's a little wicker box inside and I can tell you all that's in it without looking. If I'm wrong, keep every-

thing for yourself, but if I'm right, please, I beg you, return the things to me.

DAEMONES:

Agreed. Your request seems just to me.

GRIPUS:

But not to me. What if she's a mind-reader or a spiritualist or something, and can describe everything like she says without them being hers. Will you still give the stuff to her if she cheats like that?

DAEMONES:

She's not going to cheat, and she'll only get the things if she describes them correctly. Now open the trunk so I can see what's in there.

GRIPUS:

It's open.

DAEMONES:

Here's the box. Do you recognize it?

PALAESTRA:

Oh, yes! My parents, I hold you here in my hands. What hope I have of finding you is here in this little box.

GRIPUS:

The gods will punish you for confining your parents in such a tight place.

DAEMONES:

Gripus, come here. This concerns you. Now, young lady, stand over there and describe the contents. If you are wrong the first time, you won't get a second chance, so don't even try to guess.

GRIPUS:

Now you're talking. That'll keep her from cheating.

TRACHALIO:

If only he could keep you from being such a pest.

495

DAEMONES:
Proceed, young lady. Gripus, you keep quiet.

PALAESTRA:
Inside are some trinkets.

DAEMONES:
Yes, I see them.

GRIPUS:
Damn! Felled by the first shot. Don't show them to her!

DAEMONES:
Describe each one in order.

PALAESTRA:
There's a little sword made of gold with an inscription.

DAEMONES:
And what does it say?

PALAESTRA:
It's my father's name. There's a little golden axe, two-bladed, and it has an inscription, too.

DAEMONES:
Hold on. Tell me your father's name.

PALAESTRA:
Daemones.

DAEMONES:
Ye gods, dare I hope?

GRIPUS:
You mean, dare I?

TRACHALIO:
Go on, continue.

GRIPUS:

You shut up.

DAEMONES:

And the mother's name? What is written on the axe?

PALAESTRA:

Daedalis.

DAEMONES:

The gods have sent me salvation.

GRIPUS:

And destroyed me.

DAEMONES:

Gripus, this is my daughter.

GRIPUS:

I don't care about that. All I care about is what I've lost. Damn you for being there when I pulled this trunk out with my net, and damn me for not checking a hundred times to make sure no one was there.

PALAESTRA:

Then there's a little silver sickle and two little clasped hands and a wee little piggy . . .

GRIPUS:

Damn you and your wee little piggy and your wee little pussy.

PALAESTRA:

And there's a little bitty bull my daddy gave me for my birthday.

DAEMONES:

Yes, I recognize it. I can't restrain myself any longer. Daughter, dear, let me embrace you. I am your father, Daemones. Daedalis, your mother, is just inside the house.

PALAESTRA:

I can hardly believe it. But, Daddy . . .

DAEMONES:

Yes, it's true. How happy I am to hold you!

TRACHALIO:

I'm delighted to witness this spectacle: virtue rewarded.

DAEMONES:

Trachalio, you bring the trunk inside.

TRACHALIO:

And Gripus, I'm delighted that things have turned out badly for you. You deserve it.

DAEMONES:

Come, child, let's go in to your mother. She will remember these things better than I.

PALAESTRA:

Let's all go in so we can share this happiness. Come, Ampelisca.

AMPELISCA *(Weeping)*:

I've never been so happy.

(Exit all into the house except Gripus.)

GRIPUS:

I've never been so stupid. When I found that trunk, why didn't I hide it? I thought the winds had blown me something good for a change, but it was nothing but trouble. I know there's gold and silver in that trunk and now I've lost it. I might as well go hang myself; later on, when I'm feeling better, I'll think of some way to get it back.

(Exit Gripus stage right.)

(Enter Daemones from the house.)

DAEMONES:

The gods have never blessed another man
As they have just blessed me. For see now how
My daughter is restored unexpectedly,

She whom I never hoped to see again,
Whose life I had despaired of being saved.
The gods can work such miracles as this
To give to men a sign that they still care
How laws are made and how men live by them.
A pious man can hope for help and know
The gods will make all possible for him.
Who would have thought a helpless female child
Could survive ordeals like pirates, pimps and storms?
Yet here she is and still untouched, a virgin,
And I shall marry her to Plesidippus,
Whom I discover is my noble kinsman.
I want this match arranged this very day
And shall Trachalio dispatch to town
To fetch his master hither. What keeps him?

(He calls through the open door of the house.)

Trachalio, I've need of you, right now.
Leave tears of joy and excess of emotion
To women. Come and take my message to town.
And you, my wife, show some moderation.
A time will come for more rejoicing later,
But now there's need of sacrifice for the gods,
Thanksgiving for the care they've shown of us.
Fresh garlands for the altars in our house
And blood offering for Venus at her shrine.

(Enter Trachalio from the house.)

TRACHALIO:
I'll find my master and return with him,
Wherever he might be. What other orders?

DAEMONES:
Tell him all business else must wait.

499

TRACHALIO:

                              Right.

DAEMONES:
That I intend my daughter for him.

TRACHALIO:

                              Right.

DAEMONES:
That I was known to his father.

TRACHALIO:

                              Right.

DAEMONES:
That he and I are blood relations.

TRACHALIO:

                              Right.

DAEMONES:
Can you remember all I've told you?

TRACHALIO:

                              Right.

DAEMONES:
And you'll waste no time, spare no effort.

TRACHALIO:

                              Right.

DAEMONES:
When you return, dinner will be served.

TRACHALIO:

                              Right.

DAEMONES:
Go on then, if you've got it straight now.

500

TRACHALIO:

Right.

But one thing which I wish you would recall
Is that you promised me I could be free.
You do recall that promise, don't you?

DAEMONES:

Right.

TRACHALIO:
You'll see that Plesidippus frees me?

DAEMONES:

Right.

TRACHALIO:
You'll tell your daughter to entreat him?

DAEMONES:

Right.

TRACHALIO:
And I can marry Ampelisca?

DAEMONES:

Right.

TRACHALIO:
You'll be generous with wedding gifts?

DAEMONES:

Right.

TRACHALIO:
And you'll remember all you've promised?

DAEMONES:

Right.

I am indebted to you for all you've done.

501

Now hurry back from town with Plesidippus.

TRACHALIO:

                          Right.

DAEMONES:

Meantime I'll see that all is ready.

TRACHALIO:

                          Right.

(Exit Trachalio stage left.)

DAEMONES:

Thank god that righteous slave has finally left.

(Enter Gripus from stage right.)

GRIPUS:

Daemones, I need to speak with you right now.

DAEMONES:

What is it, Gripus? What's on your mind?

GRIPUS:

That trunk. You mean to keep it, don't you?
It would be foolish to refuse a god's gift.

DAEMONES:

And foolish to refuse to lie and say
This trunk is mine?

GRIPUS:

                 I found it in the sea.

DAEMONES:

And this good luck will make the owner glad,
But it can never make the trunk be yours.

GRIPUS:

　　No wonder that you live in poverty;
　　You follow rules which only fools approve.

DAEMONES:

　　Oh Gripus, Gripus, can't you realize,
　　That life is full of snares wherein men blind
　　To trickery and deception often fall?
　　The bait is instant and unearned gain,
　　Which lures the victims to destruction sure.
　　Thus men become the authors of their fates
　　And carry in their souls the seeds of doom.
　　But he who seeks no more than he deserves
　　And lives by laws which force men to treat others
　　With due respect and kindest sympathy,
　　The gods will favor him and he will prosper.
　　But Gripus, listen to this warning clear
　　And realize that stolen money steals
　　The very essence of a man, and leaves him
　　A hollow remnant of his former self.
　　Do not expect me therefore to give aid
　　In this deception. Certain of the virtues
　　Are negative, and this I claim is one:
　　Thou must not tainted be by ill-got gain.

GRIPUS:

　　Such noble sentiments are often voiced
　　Upon the comic stage and applauded there,
　　But when the play is over and real life
　　Begins again, I doubt that many men
　　Do then recall the wisdom they have heard.

DAEMONES:

　　Enough of this, now get you in the house
　　And bother me no more with larceny.

GRIPUS:
Whatever's in that trunk I would were dust,
So no one will get gold from my efforts
If I cannot.

(Exit Gripus stage right.)

DAEMONES:
                Such is the slavish mind,
Corrupting all it touches. Another slave,
Approached as I have been, would have helped him
In his scurrilous attempt, and both been ruined.
In search of plunder they'd have plundered been.
Now I must see preparations are made
For sacrifice and the wedding banquet.

(Exit Daemones into house.)

(Enter Plesidippus and Trachalio stage left.)

PLESIDIPPUS:
Trachalio, you must go over all
This news again; I cannot take it in.
Tell me, my own, dear, sweet Trachalio,
Palaestra recognized her parents here
In this deserted place? Is it so?

TRACHALIO:
                       Right.

PLESIDIPPUS:
And she was born like me in Athens?

TRACHALIO:
                       Right.

PLESIDIPPUS:
Her father will marry her to me?

TRACHALIO:

Right.

PLESIDIPPUS:

The wedding will take place today?

TRACHALIO:

That's right.

PLESIDIPPUS:

And when I see him, how should I greet him?
Congratulations are in order.

TRACHALIO:

Right.

PLESIDIPPUS:

And for the mother of Palaestra.

TRACHALIO:

Right.

PLESIDIPPUS:

Perhaps I should run up to them, like this,
And kiss each one, but first Palaestra.

TRACHALIO:

Wrong.

PLESIDIPPUS:

What's wrong with that? You're wrong to say it's wrong.
But come, my patron, father, saviour, lead on.

(Exit Plesidippus and Trachalio into house.)

(Enter Labrax stage left.)

LABRAX:

No man alive is more miserable than me—to lose my possessions twice in one day, first by storm and shipwreck, then by law. The gods and the courts have conspired to rob me of Palaestra, my greatest asset, and men laugh at me in my despair. Pimpery is not a favored profession. I must have been born under an evil star. But one girl at least is left to me; if I can just manage to snatch her from Venus' shrine, there's still some hope.

(Enter Gripus stage right.)

GRIPUS:

I swear I'll not live to see the end of this day unless I get that trunk back.

LABRAX:

Trunk? Trunk? The word rings in my ears and drives a stake through my heart.

GRIPUS:

That little fop Trachalio is free now, for cheating me out of my catch, and here am I empty-handed.

LABRAX:

Do my ears deceive me? Can what this man says concern me?

GRIPUS:

I've learned my lesson now, though: never trust a soul. I just hope someone comes along to claim the trunk. I'll trick him just as surely as I've been tricked.

LABRAX:

There can't be any doubt. He knows who has my trunk. I'll speak to him and, please, god, be on my side this time.

GRIPUS *(To someone in the house):*

What do you want in there? Can't you see I'm out here cleaning the spit? It's made of rust rather than iron. The more I scrub the less there is of it. Like everything else around here today, it's been enchanted: it disappears in front of my eyes.

LABRAX:
Greetings, young man.

GRIPUS:
Greetings to you, and to your bald head.

LABRAX:
What are you doing?

GRIPUS:
Standing on my head spitting pennies.

LABRAX:
Do you feel alright?

GRIPUS:
If I didn't I'd consult a doctor, not a beggar. What do you want?

LABRAX:
As you see, I'm a bit down on my luck.

GRIPUS:
Down and out, I'd say. What happened to you?

LABRAX:
Last night I lost all I owned in a shipwreck.

GRIPUS:
What exactly did you lose?

LABRAX:
A trunk full of gold and silver.

GRIPUS:
Give me a precise inventory of its contents.

LABRAX:
Whatever for? It's gone now.

GRIPUS:
Tell me just the same.

LABRAX:

No, I don't want to talk about it.

GRIPUS:

But if I know who found it? You'll have to describe it so I can be sure.

LABRAX:

Well, let's see, there were eight hundred gold pieces in a sack, and a hundred more vintage-minted Philip's head pieces in a leather pouch.

GRIPUS:

(Aside: What bountiful booty! What generous largesse! Now the gods have given me another chance to get my share. The trunk I found is surely his.) But tell me all the rest.

LABRAX:

Let's see—a talent of silver in a bag; a large silver punch bowl; a tankard; a water pitcher; a wine decanter and a ladle.

GRIPUS:

Ye gods, what a treasure you had.

LABRAX:

That past tense kills me.

GRIPUS:

And what would you give to get it all back? How much of a reward if I could lead you to it?

LABRAX:

Three hundred drachmas.

GRIPUS:

You must be kidding.

LABRAX:

Four hundred.

GRIPUS:

I can't even hear you.

LABRAX:
Five hundred.

GRIPUS:
Peanuts!

LABRAX:
Six hundred.

GRIPUS:
Don't talk to me of trifles.

LABRAX:
Seven hundred.

GRIPUS:
You're wasting my time.

LABRAX:
One thousand is my final offer.

GRIPUS:
You must be dreaming.

LABRAX:
I won't offer a penny more.

GRIPUS:
Then be on your way; we can't do business.

LABRAX:
Look, once I leave, that's it. You'd better reconsider. Eleven hundred.

GRIPUS:
Not a chance.

LABRAX:
All right, you name the price.

GRIPUS:
At an absolute minimum—though I would take more if you insisted—

but for you, a special deal, one talent, that is, sixty minae, a mere six thousand drachmas. Not a penny less! Take it or leave it.

LABRAX:

What can I do? I have no choice, that's clear. Agreed, then, one talent.

GRIPUS:

Just step this way, please. I want Venus to witness the closing of this deal.

LABRAX:

Anything you say.

GRIPUS:

Now, with your hand on the altar, repeat after me.

LABRAX:

Go ahead, then. (*Aside*: Though you could save yourself the trouble. I make and break more oaths in a day than you could count.)

GRIPUS:

Keep your hand on the altar.

LABRAX:

Right. (*Aside*: As if that mattered.)

GRIPUS:

Now, swear.

LABRAX:

(*Aside*: To anything.)

GRIPUS:

Swear you'll pay me a talent as soon as you get your trunk back.

LABRAX:

I swear.

GRIPUS:

Repeat after me: "Venus of Cyrene, I call on you as witness to my oath . . .

LABRAX:

Venus of Cyrene, I call on you as witness to my oath . . .

GRIPUS:

. . . that I shall pay this man Gripus—point to me so she'll know who you're talking about . . .

LABRAX:

That I shall pay this man Gripus . . .

GRIPUS:

. . . one talent on receipt of my trunk, full of gold and silver, which I lost at sea.

LABRAX:

. . . one talent on receipt of my trunk, full of gold and silver, which I lost at sea.

GRIPUS:

And if I break my oath, or in any way attempt to cheat this man"— point to me so she'll know who you're talking about—"of what I owe him, may your wrath fall upon me and destroy me and all members of my profession."

LABRAX:

Venus, destroy me and all other pimps if I don't do as I have sworn to do, on my honor as a pimp.

GRIPUS:

Done. Now that you've sworn I'll bring out my master. He's got the trunk and all you have to do is ask for it. Wait here.

(Exit Gripus into the house.)

LABRAX:

Fool, to think a pimp would keep his word. "It was my tongue that swore; my heart remains unsworn." But I'd better be quiet; here comes the old man.

(Enter Gripus and Daemones from the house.)

GRIPUS:

Just follow me.

DAEMONES:

But where's the pimp?

GRIPUS:

Hey, pimp! Here's the man that has your trunk.

DAEMONES:

I have it and I don't hesitate to admit I have it, and, if it's yours, you're welcome to it. You won't find anything missing. Take it.

LABRAX:

Oh, you gods in heaven, I give thanks for the return of my trunk, dearest thing in all the world to me. Come to daddy, precious.

DAEMONES:

So it's yours?

LABRAX:

Need you ask? *(Aside:* If it belonged to Jupiter himself I'd still claim it.*)*

DAEMONES:

Everything is inside, just as we found it, except for a little box of toys, which belongs to my daughter, whom the gods have just restored to me.

LABRAX:

Your daughter?

DAEMONES:

The girl you called Palaestra is my daughter.

LABRAX:

Good! I'm glad things have turned out well for you.

DAEMONES:

I can't believe that coming from you.

LABRAX:

No, I mean it, and just to prove I'm sincere, I won't charge you a penny for her. I give her to you gratis.

DAEMONES:

My, you are generous.

GRIPUS:

Well, pimp, now you've got your trunk.

LABRAX:

Yes, now I have my trunk.

GRIPUS:

So, get on with it.

LABRAX:

Get on with what?

GRIPUS:

Give me my money.

LABRAX:

Don't be silly. Why should I give you money?

GRIPUS:

You refuse to pay?

LABRAX:

Of course, I refuse.

GRIPUS:

You deny that you swore you'd pay?

LABRAX:

Of course not. I swore and I'll swear again. I'll swear as often as I like, but I'll never let an oath cost me anything. It's easier to break it and swear a new one.

GRIPUS:

You pimply perjurer, give me my money.

DAEMONES:

What money are you talking about, Gripus?

GRIPUS:

The money he swore he'd give me.

LABRAX:

So I swore. Are you the gods' avenger or something, that I should fear to break my oath to you?

DAEMONES:

Why did he promise you money, Gripus?

GRIPUS:

For helping him find his trunk.

LABRAX:

Take me to court and I'll sign an affidavit saying I was tricked . . . . and besides I'm still a minor.

GRIPUS:

Let him be the judge.

LABRAX:

No, I'd prefer someone else.

DAEMONES:

Why? I don't stand to gain from it. Now, did you promise him money?

LABRAX:

Yes, I did.

DAEMONES:

What you promised to my slave, pimp, you owe to me, and don't think you can pimple out of it.

GRIPUS:

Ha! You thought you had found someone you could cheat and get away with it, didn't you? Now hand over the money. I'll use it to buy my freedom.

DAEMONES:

Since you've benefitted from my kindness and recovered your possessions through my good offices . . .

GRIPUS:

Mine, you mean; don't say yours.

DAEMONES:

(*To Gripus*:) If you know what's good for you, you'll keep your mouth shut.
(*To Labrax*:) Now, since you are obliged to me, I suggest you do as I say.

LABRAX:

As long as you recognize my right to refuse.

DAEMONES:

It's unlikely I could succeed in tricking a pimp.

GRIPUS:

Now I've got my freedom. The pimp's about to pop.

DAEMONES:

This man found your trunk and he is my slave; I kept that trunk for you and saved you all that money.

LABRAX:

I'm grateful and I'm willing to give you the money I promised him.

GRIPUS:

Give him the money? Give it to me.

DAEMONES:
Shut up, Gripus.

GRIPUS:
You're not fooling me. I see what you're up to. You act like you're pleading my case and you're really lining your own pockets. I'm not going to let you trick me out of my treasure twice.

DAEMONES:
One more word and I'll beat you.

GRIPUS:
Go ahead, crucify me; I won't shut up until I get my money.

LABRAX:
Don't be an ass; he's looking out for your interests.

DAEMONES:
Come over here a minute, pimp.

LABRAX:
Right.

GRIPUS:
Hey, conduct this business out in the open; I don't like you two whispering behind my back.

DAEMONES:
Tell me how much you paid for the other girl, Ampelisca.

LABRAX:
A thousand drachmas.

DAEMONES:
And would you like to turn a nice profit on her?

LABRAX:
Sure.

DAEMONES:

I'll divide that talent with you.

LABRAX:

Great.

DAEMONES:

I'll give you three thousand for the girl, so you keep that half for yourself; give me the rest to buy this fellow's freedom, since he found your trunk for you and my daughter for me.

LABRAX:

That's a good deal. Thanks.

GRIPUS:

Now when do I get my money?

DAEMONES:

It's all settled, Gripus. I have it.

GRIPUS:

But I want it.

DAEMONES:

That's too bad, because it's already been spent. We're even now and nobody owes anybody anything.

GRIPUS:

I owe it to myself to find a noose for my neck. That's the only way I'll keep you from tricking me a third time today.

DAEMONES:

Now, pimp, join me for dinner, won't you?

LABRAX:

I'd be delighted.

DAEMONES:

Then let's all go in and start the celebration.

(Exit Gripus and Labrax into house.)

DAEMONES:

You out there are not forgot;
There's something for you in the pot,
Though it's not fully cooked as yet;
Come back next year for your fête.
Meanwhile give us your applause;
Overlook our play's few flaws.
All has ended happily,
As we know you'd have it be.

(Exit Daemones into house.)

Thyestes

Seneca

translated by

Douglass Parker

Introduction

Lucius Annaeus Seneca the Younger died in the year 65 A.D., aged not quite seventy. His tragedies, then, must have been written before that date. We can hardly be any more specific, save to remark that the plays themselves embody obvious responses to the absolute and absolutist rule of such emperors as Caligula and Nero—and even that is mere inference. Nor may we necessarily trust inference in this case: if the tradition were not absolutely certain, we might hesitate to assign the authorship of *Thyestes*—a play marked by no sustained moral vision—to one of antiquity's most vocal moralists, a certified sage, a successful Stoic. But write *Thyestes* Seneca did, and left posterity to grapple with the paradoxes of his life and work. Thyestes, the title role, is the play's resident hero-sage for less than ninety lines; his will then collapses, and we helplessly watch his helpless progress toward a ruin which, deserved or not, is monstrous. We hear a playwright, one who on other days in other roles (in his letters and essays) can be Reason Embodied, brutalize his characters and his audience with clots of raw language rarely approached by any other writer, epigrammatic missiles which strike with the shock of cast-iron heated cherry-red. And in this play alone, we see a master of logical structure allow his statement on Behavior in Extreme Situations trail off in a badminton-match of querulous name-calling between the archetypal Wicked Uncle and his nauseated brother-victim. This is a horror-play with little visual horror, a morality with no discernable moral, a character-study of vicious automata, an ultimate work of mannerism in a world where manners are unknown, a mighty piece of theatre written, most likely, for no stage and no actors.

Seneca here took the troubles of the house of Argos/Mycenae, so familiar to generations of rational enthusiasts who have watched Justice hammered out on Aeschylus's anvil, but cut into the legend at an earlier stage: Agamemnon, the swollen bladder of a hero *manqué* in the play that bears his name, is underage and not heard from; his wife Clytaemnestra is not heard *of*. Instead we have his father Atreus and his uncle Thyestes pacing through the choreography of the earlier troubles of the House of Argos, now doggedly, now with verve. Their grandfather Tantalus had fed his son Pelops to the gods, an excess of hospitality that, happily for Pelops, proved reversible. But it was not happy for Tantalus, who was condemned to be a Sad Example in the underworld, snapping at fugitive fruit and sucking at evanescent water through all eternity to demonstrate the futility, not to say the danger, of trifling with basic taboos. And it is Tantalus' ghost, unsettled at a sudden half-holiday from hell, that starts Seneca's play. Whipped into action by a Fury, ex-Tantalus will compel his grandsons to perform a ghastly variation on his original crime: Atreus will butcher his nephews and serve them up at dinner to their all-unknowing father, to Thyestes. Which is precisely what happens, perceived by a Chorus whose determined optimism hasn't a chance, changing to a thoroughgoing nihilism when they hear the boys' death and dissection described by a Messenger whose gift for the vivid phrase wipes out their world: No god (they claim) is minding the store, and the stars, for so long the embodiment of divine order, are sliding crazily down, constellation by constellation, into the sea. Darkness rules all, except for one tiny corner lit by a dinner-candle, where the two brothers who tried to share the rule of Argos now alternate in a whiny slanging match that, blessedly, ends. Or, rather, does not end, but fades quickly to black. All gone.

This is not a happy vision of the world; it is not even a Stoic vision of the world, save for the fact that the inhabitants are locked inside and in place, compelled to play out their assigned traumata. But surviving, or even acquiescing, is no triumph. In this world, there are no triumphs.

But there is shock. And generations of critics, some of them quite recent, have been unable to deal with those shocks, preferring to pigeon-hole this play and its comrades and so forget them. "Theatre of Blood" marks one such ploy: not only is Seneca blamed for his own horrors, he is brought to book for those committed by his successors: the non-manual dexterity of Shakespeare's Lavinia, for example. And if that were not enough, there is one other, even more damning rubric: "Rhetorical Tragedy." This shrinks the magnificence of Seneca's style to the piled-up frigidities of drama's worst practitioners: he might as well have written *Mustafa*. Even classicists, a not overly moral or anti-rhetorical breed as academics go, have been known to throw up their hands.

But now, not surprisingly, Seneca's tragedies, which mirror an age almost as corrupt and irrational as the present, are coming back into their own. The best example is Ted Hughes's version of *Oedipus,* where startling staging and the hammerblows of Hughes's language combined to make shattering and controversial live theatre of an anthology-piece. My translation is another approach to Seneca; it aims at recreating the deadly exuberance of his rhetorical karate in (to let the metaphor go where it will) full dress. If any specific diction has been felt as a pattern, it is the English which some scholars still believe to be Cyril Tourneur's.

This version is dedicated doubly: both to John Herington, who long ago convinced me that it could be done, and to Charles Doria, who not so long ago convinced me that it should be finished.

Douglass Parker

A NOTE ON STAGING

Whether or not *Thyestes* was written to be staged, its *mise-en-scène* rests, conceptually at least, on the classic Athenian tragic spectacle: A building, in this case the palace of Atreus, fronting on an area whose imagined locale is quite fluid, but may be adequately embraced by the hyphenated term "Argos-and-environs." Thus, in Act One, the Ghost and the Fury see the palace from somewhere outside the city; in Act Two, Atreus and his Attendant probably enter from the palace and are considered to be immediately outside it; both these areas are jammed together without apparent difficulty in Act Three, where Thyestes and his sons view the city from afar at the Act's beginning, but at its end are very likely conducted into the palace by Atreus. In Act Four, the Messenger emerges from the palace to confront the Chorus somewhere outside. Act Five begins like Act Two, but then adds an interior view of the palace when the double doors are thrown open, disclosing Thyestes at dinner—a fairly standard bit of traditional staging, recalling the Athenian use of the *ekkyklêma*.

But not all is Greek: None of the Chorus' odes or speeches argues physical motion by the group, whether entrance, exit, or dance. Nor does anything in the structure of the lyrics show the least hint of antiphonal orientation such as might reflect the usual Athenian division into semichoruses. And the play's sudden end, where Atreus and Thyestes are cut off in the middle of a bitter argument, certainly evokes no remembrance of the Greek *exodos,* with its leisured departure of characters and chorus from the stage. The effect here is rather one which (if it is based on any physical staging at all) would have been that produced by the Roman stage-curtain, the *aulaeum.*

As to stage-directions: The original text, of course, contained none. I have tried to be sparing in their addition, inserting only those which (1) are necessary for the action's understanding and (2) cannot be immediately inferred or deduced from the text itself. The putative producer is of course at perfect liberty to supply such scenery and business as he chooses. Given that the play was probably not written for full production, 'authenticity'—whatever that might be here—is scarcely the criterion to observe.

DRAMATIS PERSONAE

THE GHOST OF TANTALUS, grandfather of Atreus and Thyestes

THE FURY

ATREUS, king of Argos, brother of Thyestes

ATTENDANT to Atreus

THYESTES, exiled brother of Atreus

YOUNG TANTALUS

PLISTNENES* } sons of Thyestes

ANOTHER BOY†

THE MESSENGER

CHORUS of aged citizens of Argos

* Mute part.

† Mute part—so effaced, in fact, that a good case can be made, and has been made, for its complete non-existence. This version follows the traditional interpretation of the pertinent lines [730-742, 1023].

525

ACT ONE

TANTALUS' GHOST:
Where am I?
          Extracted from my hapless home in hell,
My mouth no longer snaps at fugitive meals. . . .
Who did this?

          Before dead Tantalus the living earth
pulses again in display. . . .
                    What brutal god
conceived this?
          Have they devised some new,
improved-on agony, sure to surpass the blistered
thirst of a waterlogged ghost, guaranteed to better
the empty swallows of a shade at table?
                              I know,
there's been a switch: My shoulders are set to assume
the massive slickness of Sisyphus' boulder . . .
                                        or else
my spoked extremities will spin in Ixion's giddy
rotations . . .
          or perhaps I'm due to take on Tityos'
torture:
          splayed in a monstrous cave, I'll offer
black birds lunch on my guts, be careful to grow
them back at night, supply a fresh and full
repast for the next day's horror to pick at . . .
                                        I'm slated
for a change in pain—what is it?

                    To the underworld judge
in charge of requital, you who assign new anguish
to those who have already paid, I tender a word
of advice:

If you can swell the tale of affliction,
can find an increment of torment to frighten death's warden,
to freeze the waves of Acheron solid in mid-sob—
in fine, sufficient to terrify Tantalus, set me
shaking in fright:
                        You'd better get it ready,
prepared for my posterity:
                        Down they come,
descending in droves, jostling hordes predestined
to outperform their origins, to mould new shapes
of sin, to reduce my rank to purest innocence.
Does hell have any vacant wicked nooks?
I'll stuff them up with lodgers:
                        While Pelops' issue
lasts, no recess holds in Minos' court.

(The Fury suddenly appears.)

FURY:
MOVE, you loathesome phantom!
                        Put handle to madness
and whip your household gods to loss of faith.
There's a contest in crime to open, no evils barred,
swords unsheathing in ceaseless to-and-fro.
Shame is abolished. Erase the limits of rage.
Send mania stabbing and spurring at blotted minds.
Stiffen the limp ancestral frenzy, stretch on
horror through time till it fetches up in grandsons.
Squeeze out repentance, stack fresh crime on old:
Each single sin's avenging spawns a new
profusion.
                        Let power slip from brothers in pride,
to hunt them out again in despair. The fate
of a rabid dynasty wobbles unsure between
unstable kings, where rule grovels, and groveller
rules, chance tumbling power in its churning pulse.

527

Expelled for crime, to crime restored, make them
sicken mankind as much as they sicken each other.
Let anger open every approach to action:
brother shivers at brother, father at son
and son at father, children go foully to death
but worse to birth, wife lies in menacing wait
for husband, war takes ship beyond the sea,
blood saturates the ultimate inch of earth,
lust runs riot in triumph above the beds
of the wide world's greatest leaders.
                                                    Incest?
A mild domestic slip in a house like this,
a fitting terminus to right, and trust, and law.

And while you're about these evils, why should heaven
remain exempt? In its dome, the stars shine still,
and still the sun spreads over the earth its weary
glory:
              You'll change all that, supplant the night
with newer, blacker night, and drop the day
from the sky.
                      Shuffle and fumble the family gods,
furnish your kin with hatred, slaughter, final
rites, swell up and cram the house to bursting
with Tantalus.
                        Deck the soaring columns, let doors
grin wide and sprout with laurel, set the torches
ablaze in proper welcome at your return:
Restage the Thracian horror with an increased cast. . . .
Why, look. The wicked uncle's hand hangs limp;
that shouldn't occur till the final act, until
Thyestes begins to mourn his sons. That hand
should be raised. In action. See that it is.
Now fires be set and cauldrons seethe, disjointed
limbs be split twice over, blood of sons
spatter and smirch the hearth in their pedigreed kitchen . . .

528

Then let the table be set and sit you down
to a banquet of quite familiar crime. For you,
we powers that be in hell herewith decree
a day of rest and lift your imposed starvation.
For this one feast.
                    So, Tantalus, *bon appetit.*
See to the mixing and drinking of wine, full-bodied,
full-blooded wine. My own invention: a dinner
where Tantalus tantalizes.

(The Ghost attempts to exit.)

                    STOP! Not so fast!
Where do you think you're going?

TANTALUS' GHOST:

                    To pools and streams,
to water that ebbs away when I bend, to a fruit-filled
tree that jerks out of reach when I purse my lips.
All that I ask is permission to crouch again
in the murk and gloom of my cage. If Acheron's waves
are weak in torture, find me another river:
Phlegethon, let them moor me fast in your channel,
a burned-out hulk swathed in your fiery swell.
—I call on all my fellow-sufferers, fixed
by fate to undergo endless torment in hell:
You, who quiver and lie in a gouged-out cave
and wait for the mountain to fall, as it surely shall;
You, who struggle against unbreakable bonds
to shake off the savage maws of starving lions,
the awful troops of Furies; You, who fight
and writhe to escape the torches that set you alight,
Tantalus rushes to bring you advice:
                    Believe
this expert:
          Adore your pain; embrace your torture.
—When comes my chance to escape the pangs of heaven?

FURY:

First burst into your house and spread convulsion,
infect the kings with strife and love of steel,
embroil the brutal beasts in their breasts with madness.

TANTALUS' GHOST:

My proper sphere is suffering, not infliction.
But now you launch me like some noxious gas
that swirls from a crack in the ground, a rank miasma
that drips decay on mankind—a doting grandfather
handing down unwilled his shares in sin
to grandsons.
            —Jupiter, great begetter of gods!
(Of Tantalus, too, to use a disgusting distinction.)
Pierce my jabbering tongue and hang it up
a hideous example . . . still I will not keep
my peace, not here, not now.
               —Descendants, a warning!
Keep your hands inviolate, clean of murder's
rot! Don't soil your altars with hellish crime!
Here will I take my stand to stop you. . . .

(The Fury whips the Ghost.)

               —Your whip:
I can't look for sheer terror. Those twisted snakes:
They're vicious, writhing threats. One sign from you,
and famine eats my bones from the inside out,
sparks stud the smouldering ash in my entrails. . . .

Lead me! Lead me!

FURY:

           That's it. Precisely the frenzy.
Dispense it throughout the household. Plenty for all.
You'll be their pattern: Out of control they'll veer,

each crazy to slake his dryness on the other's
blood.

   Now enter; the house responds to your nearness;
it flinches in total shock at your loathesome touch.

(The Ghost exits into the palace.)

(Calling to the house.)

—Done! Overdone!
              Turn your steps to the caves
of hell, to the river you can't forget. At last
the earth, in nausea, frets at the load of your tread.

Look there! All moisture goes into hiding, seeking
its underground sources, forsaking springs.

And there! The banks and channels lie bare. The hot
and dessicant wind sweeps free the sky of the last
sparse clouds. The trees are blanched and bleached of leaf,
their branches denuded of runaway fruit.
                                 Where once
the Isthmus boomed and rumbled as neighbor waves
slapped and crashed at the slender slip of land
that sunders them, now the shoreline strains to hear
a distant whisper. Lake Lerna shrinks to its center,
the streams of Inachus empty in full retreat,
holy Alpheos refuses to forward his flood,
Cithaeron's crests stand bald, nowhere topped off
by caps of white—the snows are fled away.

The highborn lords of Argos fear the return
of a thirst that blazed when Phaethon dipped too near.

And there! The Titan himself, uncertain of action:
Should he order the day to follow along in course. . . .

And drive it on full tilt to its final end?

(Exit.)

    Presume there exists at least one god
    with kindly concern for Achaean Argos,
    with love for the houses of Pisa
    where the famous race took rise,
    for the goal in Corinth, the Isthmus
    flanked by harbors,
                            splitting the sea. . . .

    Presume there exists at least one god
    to dote on the drifts that shroud Taÿgetus
    when winter's norther down from Sarmatia
    drops them atop the crests
    to grip the faraway glance
    until the summer trades sprout sails
    and the spectacle drips, gushes away. . . .

    Presume there exists at least one god
    who responds to the icy lapping
    of clear Alpheos flowing in fame
    along the Olympic course. . . .

To him we make our prayer:

    For his godhead's attention
    and gentle inclination
            that is our peace,
    for his cessation
            of crime's unceasing seesaw
            where grandson outweighs grandsir,
    for his abolition
            of guilt that mounts
            to delight a declining line.
    May he exhaust at last

                the lawless strain
                of waterless Tantalus,
            strip it of its vicious thirst.

Sin has reached satiety;
                                Right, futility;
            the limits of Wrong
            have lost all definition.

Murderer Myrtilus, his lord's defrauder,
dies a dupe from too much trust
in chariots, flung by Pelops
to grace the sea he fell in,
            change its name to his:
No other tale
is so much told
on Ionian ships.

Pelops the boy hops happily
for his daddy's kiss, is greeted
not by love but a sword,
and carved by your hand, Tantalus,
a dainty dish for gods at dinner.
Upon that meal follows
endless hunger, eternal thirst—
fitting and right reward
for such a monstrous menu.

Spent and empty Tantalus stands,
coddles the void inside him.
In mad profusion above
his culpable brow there hovers,
heavily, edible plunder,
at escape more apt than harpies.
Bowed in a ring around him
by branches' tonnage, the trees,
bowbent, flick their fruit,

teasing return his trembles,
play games with his greed's gape.

Repeated unfulfilment, nothing's *Then*
frustrating craving's *Now! Right Now!*
make Tantalus sly: stolidly
willing his arms to stillness
he squinnies his sight aside,
clamps his lips together,
pens the glutton inside him
sealed up behind his teeth. . . .

No use.

The whole grove turns enticement,
sets its treasures bobbing
nearer, nearer by.

Ripe and perfect the apples
fan his insatiable famine,
at whose bidding his hands
wriggle and clutch on air,
happy at even a foredoomed reach. . . .
as all the crop leaps up and away,
        as trees retreat.

And then descends a withering
thirst to match the hunger,
flash of torchbearing drought
scorching his boiling blood.
Harrowed, hapless he stands
pursing his lips for ripples. . . .

But renegade water, shunted,
shrinks away into shoals
and shuns its parched pursuer.

Nothing daunted, he bends,
inserts his mouth in the maelstrom,
and drinks,
      drinks deep,
          all dust.

ACT TWO

(Atreus and his Attendant enter from the palace.)

ATREUS:

Vapid Atreus, torpid Atreus, flaccid
Atreus—not to forget your most disgusting
imperial failing—tepid Atreus, sitting
unavenged, poor tyrant stuck in your moment of wrath:
Your brother intrigues, his crimes cheat number, Right's body
lies ruptured . . . and you mouth empty complaints
and are . . . upset.
                Already creation should crack
beneath your ordnance; already your fleets should harry
the isthmus; already the fields and towns should bristle
with flame, flecked with the glints of unsheathed steel.
Commit your cavalry till this land groans with hooves,
flush out the enemy from every sylvan pleasance
and crest-perched mountain stronghold, void Mycenae,
pour out its populace screaming to war.
                          Whoever
helps or harbors that most detested Thyestes
goes down in appropriate slaughter.
                          From the top of its power
the house of Pelops may crash on me, provided
it crashes upon my brother. I cry for courage
to make the future catch its breath but never
hold its tongue.
                A horror is what I need,
a vengeance so bloody and vicious my brother might well
choose it for *me*:
                Crimes not outdone are not
avenged.
            But what? Where can I find some outrage
to overbid his brutality?

Will he continue
in abject exile? Hardly; a calm defeat
is as much his nature as was a moderate triumph.
I know the man; I know his soul . . . it's proof
against teaching, immune to change. Pliable, no . . .
but brittle, yes. And so, while still he slumps
and wobbles, break him; if I nod, he'll break me.
It's crush or crumple; the crime is poised between us,
grab it who can.

ATTENDANT:
                    Would adverse public opinion
give you any pause?

ATREUS:
                    The principal profit of power
is this: A ruler's actions compel his public
to applause no less than compliance.

ATTENDANT:
                              The fear that drives
a people to praise drives that same people to hate.
The man who seeks the glory of sincere goodwill
prefers his praise from the heart . . . not from the tongue.

ATREUS:
True praise is for peasants. False praise is a king's preserve,
when the will of the people is forced to deny itself.

ATTENDANT:
The king's one wish should be for honor; then all
his people will wish the same.

ATREUS:
                         You show me a king
whose only choice is honor, and I'll show you

a king who rules by begging.

ATTENDANT:
>   A kingdom void
> of shame and law, of piety, duty, and trust,
> will surely fall.

ATREUS:
>   Piety, duty, and trust—
> all lower-class baggage. Nothing should keep a king
> from going wherever he pleases.

ATTENDANT:
> To harm the vilest brother is still a sin.

ATREUS:
> Against my brother, any sin is virtue.
> Run down a list of possible crimes: Which, please,
> has my brother missed? Or where has his hand disdained
> to deposit its daub?
>   *Item*, my wife in whoredom.
> *Item*, my looted kingdom.
>   *Item*, the theft
> of our ancient symbol of power—
>   a theft which, *item*,
> purloined our line and left it in chaos.
>   Yes:
> Hidden in Pelops' royal stalls is a pedigreed
> animal, a ram who commands a sumptuous herd.
> Its body supports a fleece shot through with gold—
> the gold which goes to gild the scepter of each
> new Tantalid king.
>   Possess this ram, and rule:
> It controls our dynasty's luck; the power follows.
> So, safe in isolation, it feeds unmolested, pent
> in a meadow where one huge stone plugs walls of rock
> and guards our destiny. This is a holy beast . . .

and one which Thyestes—summoning up his gall,
spoiling my marriage bed, enrolling the aid
of my noble spouse—one which Thyestes stole.
That theft was the single source for broadcast disaster:
Me, skulking, a snivelling exile, through my own kingdom
and finding no place in the nation safe from ambush;
my wife, polluted; my power's confidence, shattered;
my house in dubious health; its blood uncertain;
no trust . . . except in my brother's hate.
                                                    Enough
of this stunned inertia. The time has come to begin,
to call up courage. Let Tantalus serve as your model;
pattern yourself on Pelops. Enlist your hands
in deeds that deserve your forbears' grand example.

—Suggest a method to use in his destruction.

ATTENDANT:
A chop from a sword should make him spit out his soul.

ATREUS:
You mention revenge's result; I want the process.
Any nervous usurper can murder; I am
a king, and here in my kingdom they grovel for death.

ATTENDANT:
But surely a sense of family duty. . . .

ATREUS:
                                                    Oh, *that*:
Duty—if ever you've entered this household—we'll do
without you. Goodbye.
                            And welcome, you atrocious troops
of Furies:
            Good day, Erinys. Sow your strife here.
Come in, Megaera. Shake those smoky torches . . .
and heat my soul, whose natural rage burns far

too cool. I need some mad monstrosity in me.

ATTENDANT:
And what new plan does this new madness plot?

ATREUS:
Nothing defined by the usual outlines of pain.
No crime can be omitted.
                              No crime is enough.

ATTENDANT:
Cold steel?

ATREUS:
                    Petty.

ATTENDANT:
                              Fire, then?

ATREUS:
                                        Petty again.

ATTENDANT:
I fail to see what possible weapon a hate
like yours can employ.

ATREUS:
                              Of course: Thyestes himself.

ATTENDANT:
That revenge transcends mere anger.

ATREUS:
                                        I quite agree.
A cyclone twists and turns inside my chest,
flailing at my heart, driving me out of control
I don't know where. I only know I'm driven.
The ground sends groans from its deep foundation, the clear-skied
day erupts in thunder, the palace cracks and creaks

540

to argue the roof is smashed, the household gods
are shaken, shudder, and turn their faces away.

—You gods, my choice is made: I'll execute the horror
that makes you afraid.

ATTENDANT:
                              What course of action is this?

ATREUS:
No name to give it—an act too big for thought,
too large for formula. It swells beyond the bounds
of human practice and bumps at my sluggish hands.
I don't know what it is; I know its hugeness.
This shall be done. Oh, soul, grasp hard at this:
A crime Thyestes deserves, deserving of Atreus—
a crime for both to perform.
                              That Thracian business—
the palace feast's unspeakable bill of fare—
I must admit that has the required scope,
but it's been taken. An anger like mine should discover
some marked improvement.
                              Procne, be my inspiration:
Sister and mother warred in you. Our motives
are like. Stand by me; push my hand to the deed:
I'll have the father—my brother—hungry, ripping
his sons with a joyful air, and eating meat
from himself.
                              Oh, this is grand in abundance. This
is a mode of revenge that fits my mood exactly.
—But where is Atreus now? Uncommitted, pure,
spinning out time in pros and cons.
                              A vision
of slaughter wavers *in toto* before my eyes:
A father's bereavement chewed to bits in his jaws. . . .
What is it, Atreus? Afraid again? Do scruples
slack you before you begin?

                    Do show some courage;
get on with it. The principal part in this
atrocity, now, is set to be performed
by brother Thyestes.

ATTENDANT:

                    But what device is certain
to draw him this way, sure to snare his foot?
He lives in suspicion, trusts in nothing.

ATREUS:

                                        True.
He couldn't be taken unless he wanted to take.
And that he does. He hopes to take my kingdom. . . .
This hope will make him meet Jove, clubbing with thunder;
this hope will make him suffer the swollen threats
of the gulf, the shifting flux of the Libyan Shoals;
this hope will make him greet what is to him
disaster incarnate—his brother, face to face.

ATTENDANT:

But who can make a truce convincing? Who
can elicit so much trust?

ATREUS:

                    Corrupted hope
is overly prone to belief. However, I'll have
my sons deliver their uncle a royal message:
        Give up that unbearable life you lead with strangers,
trade in those rags for power. You, wretched exile,
are hereby begged to share the throne of Argos,
a master again.
                    —His stubbornness may resist,
may spurn his earnest offer. No worry. His sons
are naive, exhausted with strange misfortune, fair game
for any entreaty. the offer will win them over.

And then the long-standing lust for power will fester,
combine with eroding poverty and wearing labor
to undermine his spirit, stiff as it is with hardship,
till he says Yes.

ATTENDANT:

By now, he's used to suffering.
His troubles are trifles.

ATREUS:

No. The sense of hardship
accumulates day by day. Adversity is easy
to bear for a bit; drawn out, it presses down.

ATTENDANT:

But delegate others to do this terrible task.

ATREUS:

Youth is corruptible. All it needs is direction.

ATTENDANT:

The lessons they learn to use against their uncle
they'll turn against their father. Taught crimes have often
returned on the teacher.

ATREUS:

My boys are princes. They'll trace
the routes of crime and deceit without a tutor:
Power is instructive. You worry that they'll turn evil?
Heredity's seen to that already. In fact,
what you see fit to describe as viciousness here,
as harshness, stubborn to act, as compulsive neglect
of family duty—this is, no doubt under way
in that quarter now.

ATTENDANT:

And are your sons to know

543

the snare you're setting?

ATREUS:

Scarcely. Too immature
for the art of secrecy. They might expose the plan.
Silence is a virtue born of many reversals.

ATTENDANT:
You mean to deceive your very means of deceit?

ATREUS:
I'll keep them guiltless, clean of crime. No need
to soil my boys with a sin that's solely mine.
My actions alone will enroll my hate to its end.

—You're faltering Atreus, botching the job! You spare
your sons, and you'll spare *his*. Young Agamemnon
should understand fully the plot he furthers, and young
Menelaus should share his possession of all the facts.
In fact, their criminal conduct should declare
their still-disputed parentage. If they decline,
if they refuse to engage in revenge, if they
protest, "Not Uncle Thyestes!"—then he's not Uncle
Thyestes, he's their father. So let's get to it.

—But no. It's a fact that timid expressions expose
too much too often; mighty projects betray
agents with the best of motives. We'll have them help
in this affair, but hide its nature, its importance
from them. I've made a beginning; bury it deep.

ATTENDANT:
I hardly need the advice. Loyalty and fear
shut up the secret in me; loyalty locks it.

(Exeunt into palace.)

CHORUS:
Peace at last in the highborn court:
The line of longdead Inachus
brings brotherly backbiting
to rights and rest.

What madness flogs you,
drives you to give-and-take of blood,
to underhand clutch for the scepter?
You go wrong in rut for the High Place,
mistake true kingship's hidden home.

A king is not treasure's issue;
he is not to be found beneath
the mantle dyed in Tyrian purple,
the sign of royalty cradling the brow,
the sheen of gilded beams.

To define the TRUE KING:
He has purged his soul
of fright from evil,
of urge to evil.

   A King is
FIXED—
   never shifted or stirred
   by weak, splayed frenzy for power,
   by the always retractable love
   of the mob in its pell-mell career

UNMOVED
   by all the gouged-out gold from the West,
   by every nugget that dyes
   the yellow wave that tumbles
   it over in Tagus' bed,

by the total of wheat trod out
in burning threshing from Libyan stalks

UNFELLED, UNSTRUCK
by the skewed vector
of thunder's downbound bolt,
by the mistral's grab
and rip at the sea,
by the rabid heave
the Adriatic upthrusts
to the sky's mad blast

STRAIGHT, UNBENT
by footman's spear,
by sheatheless steel.

STEADY, SAFE,
The True King views
the sum of things beneath him,
welcomes and meets his fate,
gives no whimper to death.

Hold a convention of Kings:
Assemble those who flail
the North for the thinspread Scyths;
bring those whose widespread clutches
embrace the red shore's shallows
and bloody deeps where pearls wink light;
call those who release their borders' crags
to the rush of the rough Sarmatians;
add to their number the ruler
who dares to foot the Danube,
plus all the noble Serians,
born to the silk they spin . . .
        No Contest:
True title to Kingship true
resides in the righteous mind,

where
horses are useless
and weapons worthless,
pointless the craven shafts
the far-off Parthian shoots
to counterfeit rout,
needless the cunning machines
heaved into place to whirl
their rocks away and strew
      tall cities flat.

THE KING: No present fear.
THE KING: No future desire.
  This is the kingdom
        that each man gives himself.

All wouldbe men of might
may choose to test their footing
    on the court's slick peak;
I choose suffusion with
the sweetness of inner peace,
set down in a hidden spot
to know retreat's unwavering joy
as life—a life no Roman knows—
meanders its course in stillness,
until my days run out
unstrained and undisturbed
and,
      ordinary,
           old,
              I die.

Death is a heavy load
for the famous, the man
distinct to all
but blurred to himself.

ACT THREE

(Enter Thyestes and his sons.)

THYESTES:

At last the long-missed vista:

                My homeland's housetops,
Argos' splendid abundance . . . and there the end
and goal of all expatriate study: to see
the ground I sprang from spread before me, tended
by ancestral gods. (Presuming, of course, that gods
exist.) The holy towers, heaved up by the hands
of one-eyed giants, majesty not to be matched
by human strain or labor. And there, the racetrack
thick with boys . . .

                On father's chariot, more
than once I carried off the palm in glory.
All Argos will rush to welcome me home, the people
will jostle and shove to see me . . .

                and so will Atreus.
Better turn back again to the forest cloister,
the shuttered glades; learn life from animals there,
and share it with them. Power's radiance, for all
its bogus glimmer, cannot misguide my eyes:
inspect the gift . . . and then inspect the giver.

A moment ago, in what the world calls hardship,
I lived in joy and courage. But now I shy
and make my way back to terror. My spirit stumbles,
begs my body's retreat. I drag ahead
against my will.

YOUNG TANTALUS:

                What's happened? Father staggers
confused, his stride is sluggish, he won't look where

he's going . . . or worse, he doesn't seem to know.

THYESTES:
O Soul, why the suspense? Why spend this long
and tortuous agony on such a simple decision?
Do you really trust those uncertain items, your brother
and his power? Are you afraid of adversity mastered
already, familiarized? Do you run from troubles
long since put in their place? Exile's discomfort
is joy.
      Go back while you can, and save yourself.

YOUNG TANTALUS:
Father, you see your homeland. What makes you turn
your steps away? Blessings rain down upon you—
why pull yourself aside and refuse to catch them?
Your brother, minus his anger, is yours again.
He returns your share of the kingdom. It's yours again.
He binds up the cuts and breaks of your wounded house,
he restores you whole to yourself.

THYESTES:
                  You ask the cause
of my disquiet. I do not know its name.
I see no reason for fear, and yet I fear.
My mind says go ahead, but my knees refuse
and my legs give way, and I am carried off hostage
to some other destination than I intend,
a ship plying oar and sail to keep on course,
while tide fights oar and sail to drive it back.

YOUNG TANTALUS:
Reduce and rout the obstructions that block your will.
Think of the prizes that await only your return.
Father, you can rule!

THYESTES:

        Since I can die.

YOUNG TANTALUS:

  The greatest power . . .

THYESTES:

          . . . is worthless, if you want nothing.

YOUNG TANTALUS:

  To leave to your sons.

THYESTES:

        The throne seats one, not two.

YOUNG TANTALUS:

  Who with a choice would rather be sad than happy?

THYESTES:

  Greatness derives its charm from bogus labels.
It's needless to fear bad fortune. I know, I assure you.
When I stood poised on the topmost spot, I trembled
endlessly, never free from fear of the very
sword that swung at my side. The genuine blessing
is this:
       Provoke no person. Dine in freedom
carelessly sprawled on the ground.
                     Sin is a snob
who visits no hovels. The safety of dinner increases
as the table shrinks. And poison is served in gold cups.

I know quite well what I say. I have the option
of choosing bad luck over luxury. So I choose.

I have not pitched a lowering dwelling high
on a mountain's peak to frighten the lowly folk
down in the valley. No ivory flashes high

on the beams of my roof. No guard patrols my sleep.
I have no need to take the navy fishing,
or stack up mighty jetties to pen the sea
sternly in place. I do not appease my glutton
belly with morsels extorted from farflung subjects.
The earth's last field, beyond the wildest tribes,
will yield no crop for me. For me no incense
curls in smoky reverence. I have no altars
daily adored and adorned with finery stripped
from Jupiter's shrine. No transplanted forest quivers
in giddy balance above my ramparts. No pools
are stoked by gangs to bring me smoke and steam.
My day is not consigned to sleep, my night
is not awarded to wide-eyed Bacchus's orgies . . .
Add one more negative, please:
I am not feared:
My unarmed home secures me safe asylum;
my sparse estate is rich, endowed with peace.

The vastest domain is never to need dominion.

YOUNG TANTALUS:
Do not decline dominion if god presents it,
but don't pursue it: your brother entreats you to take it.

THYESTES:
I should take fright. Deceit is loose nearby.

YOUNG TANTALUS:
The castoff family tie returns again;
true love, misplaced, restores itself in force.

THYESTES:
Thyestes loved by his brother? Not until ocean
soaks the heavenly Bears, and the restless surge
that rips along the Sicilian strait stands still,

until ripe wheat breaks through the Ionian Sea,
and black night breaks in radiance over the world,
till water comes to terms with fire, till death
makes up with life, till wind and wave conjoin
in trust and truce.

YOUNG TANTALUS:

But still, what trick do you fear?

THYESTES:

All tricks. I cannot keep my terror fenced.
His power and hate co-extend.

YOUNG TANTALUS:

What? Power over you?

THYESTES:

I cause myself no worry. You and your brothers
make me afraid of Atreus.

YOUNG TANTALUS:

Exercise caution.
No need to be afraid then.

THYESTES:

When evil surrounds you,
the time for precautions is long since past. We should
proceed. But witness this one paternal fact:
You lead me on; I follow.

YOUNG TANTALUS:

God will favor
a good design. Step out, then, bold and firm.

(Enter Atreus.)

ATREUS *(Aside)*:

The spread snare snaps and clips the animal fast.
I spy! The despised species: full-grown male,

attended by litter of young.

From this point on,
my hatred has room to maneuver. A trip and a fall
at last deliver to a brother's grip Thyestes,
supply Thyestes complete.

But self-control
comes hard; my rancor grudges the least restraint.
Compare the Umbrian hound, pat on the beast's track,
snout bent down to sniff out the trails, his senses
keenly and loosely leashed:

As long as he scents
the boar from afar by a spent spoor, he will obey
his handler and inspect the tract with muzzle mute . . .
but when his prey is nigh, he bucks and struggles
with all the force of his neck to slip his collar,
breaks into a bay to hurry his hangdog master,
and rips away from the hand that holds him back.
There is no hiding the hatred that pants for blood . . .
but hide it must.

—Look how his unshorn locks
entomb his gloomy looks in squalor; the beard
hangs down in filth . . .

And now to fulfil a promise:

(To Thyestes.)

—How grand to see my brother! Clasp me close,
and serve my yearning. Let us jettison every
scrap of antipathy, consign it to oblivion.
From this day forward, the mutual ties of blood
and family rise, solemn objects of our worship.
And from our souls all hatred, banned and banished,
vanishes.

THYESTES:

To any other response except
such greatness of heart, a thorough defense is possible:

I could and would absolve my actions, wash
all guilt away. But now I confess, dear Atreus,
I must confess. Whatever you think I did,
that have I done. Today's fraternal affection
exhausts my best defense. If such a greathearted
brother decrees me guilty, guilty I am.
Tears must be my advocates. You are the first
to see me beg; these hands never touched
another's foot before; they implore you now.
Let hatred abate; the angry swelling, scraped out
of the soul, deflate. To secure my pledges, these:
Your pure and guiltless nephews.

ATREUS:

                                Away with your hand
from my knees, and come to my arms instead.
—And you, boys, all of you, fit barricades
to save old men, come, hang about my neck.
—Take pity, brother, on my suffering eyes:
Off with this grubby apparel, and deck yourself
in finery equal to mine. An end to gloom:
Rejoice to take a brother's share of empire.
With this, a grander honor accrues to me:
I keep my brother safe and restore him to glory.
Power's possession is luck; its bestowal, virtue.

THYESTES:

Brother, I pray that the gods will tender you payment
for all you deserve. The wretched filth I live in
shuns the royal symbol circling the brow.
My luckless hand rejects the scepter. I prefer
to hide in the ranks of the many, curtained in crowd.

ATREUS:

A kingdom as spacious as this accommodates two.

THYESTES:
The belief that yours is mine is enough for me.

ATREUS:
But who refuses the gifts of luck at its flood?

THYESTES:
The man who knows how lightly they ebb away.

ATREUS:
Do you forbid your brother to win great honor?

THYESTES:
Your honor is already won; mine, still to win.
And I am firmly resolved to refuse all power.

ATREUS:
Accept your share, or I abandon mine.

THYESTES:
Very well. Endow me with power and call me king . . .
but you will be master of law, and might, and me.

ATREUS:
Then wear this band I set on your noble head,
while I purvey to the gods their appointed victims.

(Exeunt into palace.)

CHORUS:
Such a scenario beggars belief:
Unbridled Atreus, acknowledged brute,
ever vicious in ferocious motion,
took one look at his longlost brother
and stuck,
        stockstill,
                stunned,

numb.

No force in nature can breach the family tie.
Between outsiders the gap of rancor abides,
but true love bonds together, once and forever.

Reasons of state have stirred up strife
to rupture accord, to blare forth war.
Flickers spray from the jerking sword
as mad Mars jabs his way through a medley
of thrusts to supply his gourmet bloodthirst . . .
    No matter:
  The family tie will hobble the steel,
  will bring protesting parties
  to clasp their hands in peace.

       A god devised
       this implausible pause,
       this quick sharp stop
       to turmoil's uproar:
         Which god?

Only a moment ago in Mycenae:
  The rasp and scrape of weapons whetted
  a war turned in on itself.
  Bloodless mothers gripped fast
  at foredoomed sons.
  Alarmed, wife fretted
  for husband in arms,
       whose wayward blade,
       corroded with peace,
       sulked but obeyed
       his hand's command.

Rivalry rife:
  One struggled to prop the sagging walls,
  another to batten down uprooted towers,
  another to stop the gates with rods,

while tense on the ramparts
the sentinel shivers,
awake, on watch
of the worried night.
The fear of war is worse than war itself.

But Now:
the menace of savage steel lies collapsed.
Now:
the boding rumble of bombardons goes mute.
Now:
The shriek of the piercing trumpet shrinks and stills.

Deep peace returns,
recalled to make
the city glad.

Even so on water:
When billows belly and surge on the deep
as the mistral pummels the Bruttian Sea;
When Scylla barks at the sea-slap
knocking against her cave,
When sailors huddle in harbor, afraid
of the sea Charybdis gulps
and vomits back again,
When bestial Cyclops crouches high
on a crag of seething Etna,
fearing his father might loose
the waves to ravage the flame
that crackles in endless stoves,
When Ithaca quivers and shakes,
and indigent ancient Laertes
forecasts his kingdom's death by drowning . . .

Even then, even there, if the winds' force fails:
the sea relaxes,
blander than pond;

the deep tracts,
                    out where the ship feared
                    to furrow a path,
          go smooth, now here, now there,
                    spangled with set sails,
                    open to pleasure boat's play;
and you can count the fish down there
          where only now
          beneath the giant gale
          the Clashing Rocks worked loose
          and shook in shock at the deep.

No lot lasts long:
     Pain and Pleasure
change and change about,
Pleasure the briefer.
          The moment's whim trades high for low.

Consider Him
     Who gives the crown to the brow,
at Whom the nations trembling bend the knee,
at Whose least nod
                    The Medes,
                    the Indians
                              whose lands lie near the sun,
                    the Dahae
                              whose horsemen make Parthia shake,
                    put away war,

Consider Him:
          in worry he holds his scepter,
          in frightened foresight
                    of Chance that overturns all,
                              that transforms fortune,
          of Time so fixed in its looseness.

You, to whom the ruler of sea and lands
   has granted death and life's great rule,
put off that inflated arrogant air:

   All an inferior fears from you
   a superior threatens against you:
   Every rule is ruled by a greater rule.

        Arriving day beholds a man in pride;
        departing day beholds that man cast down.
          No one should trust in good times,
          no one despair in bad.

Clotho merges all extremes,
prevents the persistence of fortune,
twirls each fate round and round.

        No one is so fixed
        in the gods' good graces
        that he can promise himself tomorrow.
        God spurs and spins
        our lots and lives
        at a whirlwind's speed.

ACT FOUR

(The Messenger enters from the palace.)

MESSENGER:
Where can I find a whirlwind to spin me away
through the upper air? And where a dark black cloud
to swathe my eyes and rob my sight of such
abomination? A house to make Tantalus blush,
at home at which even Pelops would feel ashamed!

CHORUS:
What news do you bring?

MESSENGER:
But where on earth can I be?
Is this land Argos? Sparta, perhaps—the shared
allotment of brothers who love each other? Or Corinth,
sprawled on a narrow spit that parts two seas?
The frozen Danube, furnishing savage tribes
a swift retreat? Is this the Hyrcanian tundra,
under meltless snow? Are these the restless Scyths
who stay nowhere for long? What place is this
that plays accomplice in such a monstrous crime?

CHORUS:
Speak out: Expose the nature of this disaster,
whatever it is.

MESSENGER:
First let my soul regroup
and my fearstiff body loosen its limbs a little;
that savage image is pasted tight to my eyes.
—Blow, you lunatic cyclones, blow me away
to the dead day's burial ground, and dump me over
the edge!

You make our confusion even worse.
Disclose the cause of your terror; speak his name:
Not *who*, but *which* one did it? Tell us now.

MESSENGER:
At its farther face on top of the stronghold's peak,
the south elevation of Pelops' palace sweeps
to a height that matches a mountain. It presses down
on the town below and keeps the sullen citizens,
for all their resistance to absolute rulers, in line.
A dazzling gleam goes out from its highroofed hall
whose colossal compass can swallow the mob entire
beneath the gilded beams raised up and exalted
by marble columns spotted and streaked to glory.
Beyond the public section (thronged by the lowly,
known to the mass), this home so rich in room
fans out in a widespread sprawl of suites and chambers.
Now make your way to the inmost remove, and there
a hidden zone lies open, fettering fast
an ageold wood inside a deep defile.
This is the palace's holy of holies. Here
never a tree that supplies delightful shade
or offers a branch to the billhook's bite; instead,
the yew and the cypress nod, the lightless ilex
dims this dismal forest, and high above
an oak looks down on the grove in gloomy triumph.
From here the newmade Tantalid kings take omens;
from here they sue to be saved from ruin or doubt.
Outdated votive offerings stud the oak:
Here deeptoned trumpets hang, and chariot wrecks,
and wheels that lost to the slippery axles' ploy—
salvage dredged up out of Myrto's sea.
Trophies of every crime this race has committed:
Pinned to this spot is Pelops' Phrygian turban;

561

here, plunder from enemies; here, an embroidered barbarian
cape depicts the triumph in which it was won.

Deep in the shade a spring congeals; its water
dawdles slack and blackly in a sluggish marsh,
aping the misshapen waves of the ominous Styx,
by which the gods are sworn. Here, they say,
the lower gods lament, the grove resounds
with shaken chains, and specters blubber and moan.
Here all the gruesome ghost-tales come to life:
A moldering mob bursts out of their antique tombs
and walks abroad. There, monsters beyond all myth
parade their oddity. There, a restless flame
flickers throughout the forest, while highbuilt beams
blaze without fire. Again and again the grove
re-echoes to three-part barking; again and again
the household gapes at the onset of giant shapes.
The break of day does not diminish this terror:
Night makes its home in this wood; the horror of hell,
the dread of the dead keep full control at high noon.
Here are sure answers pronounced to oracle-seekers,
fate is disclosed in the shrine with a clamorous din,
and the god, to the cave's resounding, launches his voice.

Here enters Atreus, raving, hauling his brother's sons
behind him. The altars are fitted out . . .
                                        but who
can tell the deed as it deserves? He ties
his nephews' fine white hands behind their backs
and binds their sorrowful brows with purple bands.
All the essentials are there:
                              The incense burns,
the wine is poured to the gods, the knife applied
to the victims, the salted meal dusted around.
In each and every particular point, the order
of service is kept. A crime of this importance

proceeds, as it must, by the rules.

CHORUS:
                                        Who sets his hand
to the knife?

MESSENGER:
                    Who else? Himself. He acts the priest . . .
himself. He prays the pitiless prayer, he sings
the deadly dirge, he cracks his vicious voice . . .
himself. He stands at the altar, strokes those doomed
to slaughter, puts them in place, and sets to the knife . . .
himself. Himself, he directs; himself, he performs. . . .
No tiniest bit of the ritual goes undone.
A shiver runs through the grove, the ground beneath
the palace jerks, from top to base the structure
sways in doubt, the picture of indecision:
where should it collapse? Across the sky's left quarter
a racing star drags a gloomy track in its wake.
The wine poured out in libation changed to blood
as it streamed on the fire. The crown fell down and slid
from the king's head twice, three times. The ivory statues
wept in their temples.
                            These prodigies shook us all . . .
but Atreus. He, unswervingly bent on his job,
refused to be swayed . . . indeed, he turned the omen around
and daunted the threatening gods.
                                        And now, delay
dismissed, he springs to the altar, fiercely flicking
his eyes from side to side. As a ravenous tiger
in the jungles that line the Ganges pads madly back
and forth between two bullocks, guided by equal
greed for each, perplexed at where to bite first,
now flashing its teeth at the one, and now the other,
delaying its hunger's appeasement till choice is made . . .
so Atreus, void of feeling, inspects the quarry

563

appointed to fall before his vicious revenge:
Which should he slaughter first? He checks. Then, which
to sacrifice with a second cut? The question makes
no difference; still, he checks again and takes
wild joy in setting sin's priorities straight.

CHORUS:
And, then, which one did he fall on first with the sword?

MESSENGER:
Mindful of family duty—as you must admit—
he grants the pride of place to his grandsir, whose namesake
is sacrifice number one: Young Tantalus.

CHORUS:
How did the boy meet murder? What was his manner?
How did he carry himself?

MESSENGER:
Upright he stood,
serene, unworried. He would not let himself
indulge in fruitless begging. But the maniac uncle
hid his sword up to the hilt in the wound he opened
then pushed, fusing his hand with his nephew's throat.
And when the sword was drawn from its second scabbard,
the corpse stayed up for an endless moment, weighing
in which direction it should fall, then fell . . .
directly on its uncle. At this, the monster dragged
young Plisthenes to the altar to double the sum
of his brother:
The boy's neck parted at a single stroke;
as the spine was severed, the cropped cadaver pitched
straight forward; the head, with a mumbled, mournful murmur,
bounded swiftly away.

CHORUS:
That made two murders:

What was his next performance? Extending mercy
to the boy remaining, or piling crime on crime?

MESSENGER:

In the far-off Armenian forests, a lion bristles
its mane and settles down to destroy a herd.
It conquers quickly, but, crouched in carnge, its maw
flooded with blood, its hunger sated and glutted,
still it persists in frenzy on murder's momentum,
sluggishly rushing bulls now here, now there,
roaring at calves through teeth that can barely open.
So goes Atreus, raging in sheer compulsion,
irreducibly swollen in anger, his sword sunk doubly
deep in butchery. He forgets what it is he hates;
his madness drives the sword into and through
the little body: The point no sooner pierces
the breast of the boy than out it explodes through his back.
And the victim falls, life quenched and altar doused
by the blood that gushes from holes both front and back.

CHORUS:
Hideous ferocity!

MESSENGER:
               Does *that* much frighten you so?
If this is where horror stops, we can call it love.

CHORUS:
Does nature have room left for a greater atrocity?

MESSENGER:
You think this is evil's outmost limit? A baby
step.

CHORUS:
           But what was there left for him to do?
Dump the bodies out to be mangled by beasts?

Prohibit pyres for the boys' cremation?

MESSENGER:
                                       Oh,
for such prohibitions!
                     Let no earth bury the dead!
Let no fire burn the dead!
                   Or possibly these:
The father may drag out the bodies for birds to feast on!
The father may set them out as a shocking fodder
for famished beasts!
               Or, given this new disaster,
let's earnestly pray for what was a penalty once:
Grant that the father may gaze on his unburied sons!

This crime would strain belief in any age;
the future will flatly deny it:
                   The innards, ripped
from the living breast, still throb with life; the veins
still pulse with blood; in shock, the heart still beats.
But Atreus thumbs the entrails over, checks
the fate their disorder ordains, observes and notes
the temperature of the vessels that serve the viscera.

At length he declares the victims proper and good,
and thus is free to prepare his brother's banquet:
Shunning assistance, he quarters each body himself,
disjointing the outspread shoulders close to the trunk,
removing the forearms—which tend to get in the way—
stripping the joints in a quite unfeeling fashion,
and boning the rest. The only parts he reserves
are the heads, and of course the hands, given him in trust.
Some inner parts he spits, and sets to drip
on a gentle fire. Others bob up and down
in boiling water in moaning copper pots.
The fire revolts, skips over the flesh placed on it,
must be remade again and again on a shaky

hearth and sternly commanded to stay in place.
It obeys, but burns reluctantly. Stuck on a spit,
the liver screams. I cannot easily tell you
which uttered louder complaints, the flesh or the flames.
The fire subsides in smoke, gummy and black.
The smoke, a heavy, threatening haze, moves slowly,
refuses to rise: Compressed in a misshaped cloud,
it smudges the household gods. It will not leave.
—Phoebus, sun-god, you suffer much too long!
I know that you ran away, broke off the day,
and drowned it at noon . . . but still you set too late.
Already:
            The father tears his sons to bits,
chews and swallows meat that is flesh of his flesh.
A glistening sight to behold as the ointment melts
and runs down his hair, he sinks in a stupor from all
the wine he must needs drink to force the morsels
down his protesting, contracting throat.
                                    In all
your afflictions, Thyestes, one single blessing remains:
You don't know what your afflictions are.
                                    But this
will pass away, and soon:
                        Let Titan, the Sun,
turn 'round his car and reverse his course; let Night,
deep Night, rise up at another's hour and bury
your monstrous act away beneath new shadows . . .
still you must see it.
                    All evil will be made clear.

(Exit the Messenger.)

CHORUS:
    Sir,
        Sun,
            source

of all material, all establishment,
stern chucker-out of every spangled charm
that trims the night's round corners,
                    a query:

        Whither, we ask, and why?

            Too soon for the voice of Vesper,
                harbinger of tardiness,
                to beckon the beacons of dark,
            Too soon for the occident wheelspin
                to order its car
                unhitched from a job well done,
            Too soon for the scheduled trump
                to blat the onset
                of night-bent day's third third.
            The plowboy gawks in his tracks:
                So sudden supper,
                too soon for bulls to tire?

    What grounds have engendered this sharp decline
                from your lofty causeway?
    What assignable cause has spilled your team
                from its curb's enclosure?

        To advance a few unthinkable wherefores:

            From Hell's ruptured jail
                do the Giants, down and now out,
                try war once more?
            In Tityos' shivered breast
                does the inchoate wound
                renew his outdated hatred?
            Out from under his shucked-off Alp,
                does Typhoeus unfold his cramp?
            Through monstrous, rimy troops
                does a high road rise,

from Thessaly transfer Pelion
to dump it on Ossa in Thrace?

The world's appointed periodicitis: Dead.
Rise and set will cancel out.

Dawn's jaw hangs down:
Dainty, dewspent mother of first light,
trained to tender the god his reins
in bon voyage—
and now her kingdom's doorway
muddled beyond all housekeeping:

How wash down a weary wagon?
How slosh in sea the manes that smoke with sweat?

A freakish welcome to stranger Sun,
the very same: Set for setting,
he stares at Aurora, makes to muster
the rising murk . . .
too soon for Night to be dressed.

No stars proceed to their places,
no twinkle flicks over the pole,
no moon detaches the shadows.

AWAY with all conjecture:
mere night this is,
and night may it remain.

Here is the thud,
the thud of dread
that hammers the heart:

The coming totter and glide of the sum of things
in destiny's wreck,
The returning crush and press of gods and men
by shapeless chaos,

Till Nature again clasps earth and sea together
            and paves the footloose stars
                that stipple the sky.

No more at thrust of deathless torch
        will the astral conductor, ages' lord,
            inscribe his brand on winter and summer.
No more intercepting the blaze of Sun
        will Moon purge Night of panic, and rout
            her brother's horsemanship,
                whizzing quick her truncated track.
                    The mob of gods
                    will roll in a lump
                        and drop
                        to one
                        sole
                        pit.

Watch them:

            The sanctified Throughway of sainted stars
            cuts slant its track across the zones.
            star-studded, bends trudging years to end. . . .

                slip, Throughway,
                watch your stars slip ahead.

            The Ram, before the gentle spring is come,
            spreads sail to genial westwind. . . .

                dive, Ram,
                down to the waves,
                Where once you bore up Helle's tremor.

            The Bull shakes five damp sisters
            at his shiny horntip. . . .

                pull down the Twins, Bull,
                drag along the claws of crooked Crab.

The Lion, once the game of Hercules,
seething with fervid glow. . . .

    fall, Lion,
        down from heaven again;
    fall, Virgin,
        back to the earth you left;
    fall, Scales,
        weighty with Justice,
        draw down Scorpion's sting.

Old gaffer Sagittarius,
        feathered shaft nocked to Thessalian string . . .

    snap string, Centaur,
    snuff your shaft.

Chilly Capricorn, usher of sluggish winter . . .

    fall, Goat, fall,
    and fracture whatshisname's jug,
    and Fish, last stars in heaven,
    go share his fall,
    and Wagon, never damped by the sea,
    sink down out of sight in the gulf,
    and slippery Snake, you replica river,
    who keeps the Bears apart.
    and monster Dragon's minuscule yokemate,
    Dogtail frozen hard and stiff,
    and barely mobile wagon-watcher,
    Boötes, Bearward,
    now not half so steady,
        fall all,
            fall all,
                fall all. . . .

So many candidates,
    and the honor falls on us,

to be crushed when the universe slips its hinge?

Has the final stage of creation
fixed on us as its target?

Oh, at our birth we got
a most sad lot
in a most hard draw.

Did we let the sun fall down,
or did we push?

Laments leave us, and dread depart:

The universe is ending.
Unseemly greed for life
has one who refuses to die
among such company.

ACT FIVE

(Enter Atreus from the palace.)

ATREUS:

One stretch, and I match the stars; I tread humanity;
away aloft I feel my head's pride knock
against heaven's peak. Now that I own the trappings
of power and my father's throne, I'll allow the gods
to go about their business; I've struck upon
the apogee of all my desires. Ah, this is excellence
in abundance, swelling into sufficiency. Even for me,
this is enough.
                    And not enough. The simple
gorging of a father on his sons' cadavers demands
an encore. And the time is right: The coward daylight,
for fear its finer feelings might be offended,
has gone to bed too early. It's clearly my office
to fill the void in the unemployed sky.
                                        It would
be nice, of course, to grab the craven gods
and force the pantheon to sit in attendance on all
these courses of edible vengeance . . . but the father himself
is audience enough for me.
                          —See here, brother:
Since natural light is reluctant, I shall shatter
and disperse the murk that masks your anguish in such
obscurity. Too long have you played the happy guest
and toyed at your food with a worriless face. An end
to dawdling over dinner, an end to sopping up wine—
ruin of this rank requires Thyestes sober.
—You slaves, undo the doors, and let the scene
of cozy domestic cheer lie open. What
a feast of visual delight awaits me now:
The subtle shifts of complexion when he beholds
his sons' heads, the sudden expulsion of words impelled

573

by the shock of recognition, the stiffening, stupefied sigh
that heralds corporeal rigor. This is the rich
reward for all my efforts:
                    Not to see
a destroyed Thyestes; to see Thyestes destroyed.

(The doors are opened, revealing Thyestes within.)

. . . And here's a clear view of the dining room, starkly
alight with torch upon torch.
                    And there he is,
the grand seigneur, taking his ease on his back,
cuddled on scarlet and gold. He needs his left hand
to prop up his head . . . sooo heavy . . . must be the wine.
And there's a belch, a spot of vomit. . . .
                                    Oh, this
is joy. I transcend the loftiest god in heaven,
overrule all kings on earth. My wildest wish
lies far below me now.
                    He's eaten his fill,
so now for the wine. A large cup, please—that's good—
and straight.
                    No need to stint on drink; there's plenty—
so many victims, so much blood . . . and just
the shade to mix and match that noble vintage. . . .
Yes. A generous draught of that should be
the perfect finishing touch to a lovely meal.
It's only fitting for the father to imbibe the blended
blood of his boys; he'd have drunk mine soon enough.
—I do believe we're about to be favored with holiday
noises. A happy song, of all things, from Thyestes,
of all people. Lamentable lack of self-control

THYESTES *(Sings.):*
                    Heart numbed under long duress,
                        cast away anxiety.
                    Farewell, grief and fearfulness,

farewell, grinding poverty,
    comrade in your lone distress.
Forget defeat and shame; recall
the height you fell from, not your fall.

    Power crashed and might was wrecked
        when your loftiness was downed.
    But your headlong plunge was checked:
        You refused to bend to ground,
    took the shock with head erect.
Affliction sat in ruinous weight,
and you stood firm, unconquered, great.

    Put that by, now, and dispel
        all these vicious clouds of fate.
    Now dismiss the frowns that tell
        wretched tales of low estate
    where the old Thyestes fell.
Turn face and soul to smiles, and then
create Thyestes new again.

A special flaw attends the walking wounded:
Utter absence of trust in happiness.
When luck turns round and long distress is ended,
the truly injured man makes pain from bliss.
Causeless agony bubbles and bursts with a cry,
as I try keeping this feast, to warn and forbid . . .
Why do you order me to weep? And why
unbind the flowered wreath from around my head?
I cannot keep it on. The springtime roses
slip down my neck and decay, turned by my hair:
Plastered and fixed with perfumed unguent, it rises
to stand abruptly surrounded by circles of fear.
Rainstorms rake my face, straining to be fair;
my normal speech is studded with sudden groans.
Sorrow, the lover, squeezes her usual tears;
lust stays long with the wounded, who burn to whine.

This happy time, what joy to mourn,
what joy to rend these robes that drip
with Tyre's purple, what joy to weep,
what joy to grieve, to keen, to moan.

My mind makes signs of sadness due,
    divines the future evil;
so coming storms let sailors know
    when out upon the level
    the billows swell all windless.
    —Give up inventing endless
    concocted sadness, mindless
    swelling evil, *STOP*! . . . .

    Your heart must trust your brother;
    this fear is something other,
    displaced, irrational, late:
    It is a thing I hate
    and would not do. But down
    beneath the skin there run
    shapeless lumps of dread
    and from my eyes there bleed
    sudden, unbidden tears
    and who can find their cause?

Pain or panic, grief or fright?
Or does excessive joy delight
    in weeping, weeping, weeping?

ATREUS:
No depression, now. Show your brotherhood; match
my mood. We have a festal occasion here—
the day that sets my scepter upright and clamps it
straight, with unshaking trust in contention's end.
Indulge to oblige me; keep the feast.

THYESTES:

                                        Can't move.
Too glutted with food, and wine, and joy. No room
for more—except this final cap to my happiness:
You've served me royally; serve my sons as well.

ATREUS:

It's done. Consider them here, already within
this body. With you they are, and with you they stay.
Your family lies so close to your heart that nothing
can come between you. And soon I'll see that you feast
your eyes upon those beloved faces—in fact,
I'll effect a total reunion of father and sons.
You'll have your fill, never fear. I've put the boys
together . . . a children's feast, peculiarly theirs . . .
but everyone's eaten now. They'll be called out.
So here, take up this brimming heirloom and drink.
Be careful; lots of family in that cup.

THYESTES:

                                        I accept.
And, since a banquet of brothers demands some ceremony,
first I pour to the gods of our fathers, and then
I drain the cup to the . . . .
                                        Something's wrong. The cup's
turned heavy . . . . I need two hands . . . and both refuse
my orders. I open my mouth, I lift the wine
to my lips . . .
                                        and down it skitters in fear, defrauding
my jaws. It spills on the table, which jumps in answer;
the floor jerks up beneath.
                                        The torches blot.
Air droops confused somewhere between the edges
of light and dark.
                                        What's happened?

577

The sky is squirming,
slumping its dome down, down where gloom and shadow
stiffen and clot. The last lorn star departs.
Night falls on night.
                              Some storm is gathering forces.
—I don't know what you are, but spare my brother,
leave my sons alone. I'm worthless; burst
and vent on me.
                    —Now give me back my boys.

ATREUS:

Oh, I'll return them, never again to be parted
by time or effort.

THYESTES:

                        What's happened to me? My innards
are pitching, my guts go churning into panic, spasm
on spasm. I feel an oppression beyond all feeling.
And from my lungs moans push while I hold my breath.
Boys, listen, wherever you are. Come here and relieve
your father's worry. One glimpse of you will cure
this torture.
                    —They say it won't . . . but where are their voices
coming from?

ATREUS:

                    Prepare the paternal embrace.
They're here.

(Uncovers a dish, exposing the boys' heads and limbs.)

                    You know your sons, I believe?

THYESTES:

                                                  I know
my brother.

O Earth,
how can you shore yourself up
beneath this overload of horror? Split and sink
to the murky Styx, tumble kingdom and king
down that huge highway to the empty matter of chaos,
root out these deepset towers and capsize Mycenae.
Now is the time:
We both have earned our stations
on Tantalus' flank. . . .
Or rip up the floor of Hell
below our ancestors, deposit us in the unplumbed
gulf of your womb, and seal us over with all
the howling waters of Acheron. Send the souls
of the guilty to stumble above our heads, and let
blazing Phlegethon rage its length and roof
our exile with dunes of burning sand. . . .
Earth!
I'm talking to you!. . . . You lie there, unmoved, unmoving,
senseless, imperceptive stuff.
The gods are gone;
they've run away.

ATREUS:
Such protracted longing decrees
that you shouldn't delay your reunion. Receive the members
of your family. Surely no brother stands in your way.
Kiss and embrace each one, and multiply your joy
by three. At least.

THYESTES:
Is this our reconciliation,
our trust, a brother's sworn word? Contention's end?
To restore my sons intact is a father's request
I will not make. But, brother to brother, I seek

579

to preserve your hatred whole: Let me bury them.
Return what's left and watch me burn it now.
I only wish to end what I begot.

ATREUS:

You're in possession of all your sons' remainders.
And, as for the balance . . . well, you hold that, too.

THYESTES:

Where are they? Spread out as fodder for carrion birds?
Reserved as feed for fishes? Shredded and torn
to nourish the beasts of the field?

ATREUS:

                      They've served as a dainty
dish for you. A most immoral meal.

THYESTES:

This is what blackened the gods; this rolled day backward
toward its beginnings. There's nothing at all to say:
No grunts, no cries. . . . No names contain my ruin.
I can only look at severed heads, and wrenched-off
hands, and soles ripped away from shattered legs . . .
the scraps not even a greedy father could stomach.
Inside, my guts revolve; the pent-up horror
wrestles in confinement, fights to find an exit.
Brother, hand me that sword. It knows my flesh
and blood quite monstrously well: I'll take the iron
and make way, make way for my children.
                            You refuse the sword?
I'll beat my fists against my chest until
it booms and breaks and. . . .
                     Madness! Stop it!
Show some respect for the dead.
                      And who can ever
have seen such horror before? The Caucasian savage
who gelds his guests? The Athenian thug who cuts

his victim to fit? Have they seen a father who cramps
his sons while they cramp him?

                              This evil must have
some ending.

ATREUS:

                    Evil committed is allotted a limit;
evil requited, none. I find this tiny,
puny. For full satisfaction I should have funneled
the hot blood straight to your gullet, let you
imbibe the vital juices from living sources.
My revenge was undone by hurry; I *would* do it all
myself.
                    Who raised the knife and gave the cuts?
Who chopped them down at the altar? Who sliced the thighs
and placed the bits on the flames to appease the gods?
Who quartered and boned the corpses, split the limbs
and diced them finely, set the smaller chunks
in a kettle to boil and spitted the rest to roast
and drip on a medium fire?
                              I did, of course.
But all this—not to mention the jointing, the drawing
of tendons tense with life, the delicate hiss
produced when spleens are skewered, the constant worry
of feeding the fire—it missed a father's touch,
which shrank the resultant guilt. To eat one's sons
was surely immoral, but lacked the taste of intent:
Eater and meat had not really been introduced.

THYESTES:

Oceans, pause in your restless prisons and listen.
Runaway gods, pop out of your holes—give ear
to evil in all its hugeness.
                              Earth, attend me.
Hear me, Hell.
                    And you, Night, shrouded and squeezed

581

to the pit's opaqueness, give my ravings space.
I'm abandoned to you, my ruin's only spectator;
we're two of a kind, our stars gone out.
                                        I pray
with all decorum, seeking no personal profit—
I'm proof against all profit. My prayers are made
to benefit you.
                        To the Ruler who sits on high
to manage creation, who holds unbending court.
in the fire beyond the sky:
                                Swaddle and swathe
the earth in dirty weather, rush all the winds
together in war, clap thunder around the world,
then raise your hand—but not the hand whose petty
weapon disposes of innocent human structures . . .
the hand, the hand which flattened triplicate mountains
to level a range of Giants—raise up that hand
to heave your armory, fling your fires. Avenge
the departed day with flaring, flaming volleys,
replenish the burnt-out, looted heavens with lightning.
Expedite justice: Find both brothers guilty . . .
or if that fails, put all the guilt on me.
Now hunt me down, let fly the three-pronged shaft
to riddle this breast and put it to the torch. I am
a pious father, who burns to see his sons
decently buried, delivered to the ultimate flame . . .
so burn me. Burn me!
                        Does nothing budge the gods?
Does not divinity arm to seek out sin?
Then last, Night! Last till time wears out, and swallow
these sweeping crimes in endless dark.
                                O Sun,
stay set, and earn my thanks.

ATREUS:
                        Now I commend
my hands for a job well done. Now I bow
to these midwives of glory. Without your agony, brother,
my crime would have been stillborn. But now I am in
at the birth. Of sons. I now can vouch for the honor
of the conjugal couch.

THYESTES:
                        But what had the children done?

ATREUS:
    Been yours.

THYESTES:
                    You gave a father his sons to. . . .

ATREUS:
                                        Precisely.
And further—a fact which affords me special delight—
legitimate sons.

THYESTES:
                    O gods who save our loved ones. . . .

ATREUS:
    Try "Marriage Gods." It has a pertinent ring.

THYESTES:
    Evil cannot repay evil.

ATREUS:
                    You seem upset—
and I know why: Not because of internal disorder
brought on by a monstrous gluttonous meal . . . oh, no.
You grieve at your own delay—I acted first.

You felt the identical impulse, to set out similar
food for an unaware brother, to enlist a mother's
aid in approaching and stretching out *my* sons
in similar slaughter . . . but worry stayed your hand:
My sons just might have been yours.

THYESTES:

                                Vengeance is coming.
To punish you, my prayers call down the gods.

ATREUS:

To punish you, I pass you on to your sons.

(By curtain, or blackness, or whatever, the scene disappears.)

Notes on Contributors

RICHARD CALDWELL has taught Classics at the Universities of Minnesota, Texas, and Colorado. Also, many years ago, at a small Catholic college from which he was fired for "scandalous conduct." Most recently he has been affiliated with the Center for the Psychological Study of the Arts at SUNY/Buffalo and with the Denver Psychoanalytic Institute. He has published a dozen articles on psychoanalysis, Greek literature, and Greek mythology; at present he is completing a psychoanalytic commentary on the *Library* of Apollodorus.

CHARLES DORIA, classicist at large, is co-editor and translator of *Origins, Creation Stories from the Ancient Mediterranean* (Doubleday, 1976) and associate editor for Jerome Rothenberg's *A Big Jewish Book* (Doubleday, 1978). Books of poetry include: *The Game of Europe* (Membrane Press, Milwaukee) and *Austin Flaco* (Swallow Press). His other recent publications include "The Dolphin Rider" in *Mind in the Waters* (Scribner's/Sierra Club, 1974), and "Pound, Olson and the Classical Tradition" (in the Olson issue of *Boundary 2,* 1973–74). Presently he is a CETA artist living in New York City.

GEORGE ECONOMOU was born in Great Falls, Montana, on September 24, 1934. He was educated at Colgate and Columbia Universities and is a Professor of English and Comparative Literature at the Brooklyn Center of Long Island University. He founded and edited *Trobar* with Robert Kelly from 1960–64. His poems, translations from modern Greek and other languages and criticism have appeared in many magazines, journals, and anthologies. He has been married to poet/playwright Rochelle Owens since 1962.

Books by George Economou:

The Georgics, Black Sparrow, 1968.
Landed Natures, Black Sparrow, 1969.
Poems for Self Therapy, The Perishable Press, 1972.
The Goddess Natura in Medieval Literature, Harvard University Press, 1972.
In Pursuit of Perfection: A Study of the Literature of Courtly Love, Kennikat Press, 1974 (co-editor and contributor).

EMILY E. HILBURN, a 1972 graduate of The University of Texas at Austin, is currently Promotion and Advertising Manager for the University of Texas Press. Her translation of lines 1–87 of *Prometheus Bound* was published in *Arion,* Winter 1970.

W. THOMAS MacCARY was born in Atlanta, Georgia (July 19, 1941), educated at Dartmouth College (B.A., 1963), Cambridge University (M.A., 1965) and Stanford University (Ph.D., 1969). He has taught Greek and Latin literature—mostly comedy—at the University of Minnesota (1967–1971), the University of Michigan (Summer, 1969), and the University of Texas (1971–1975). His publications include articles on Diphilos, Menander, Plautus and Beaumarchais; an edition with introduction and commentary, of Plautus' *Casina* (in collaboration with M. M. Willcock); and a collection of essays entitled *Woman in Bondage: Sexual Patterns in Ancient and Modern Comedy.* He is currently involved in research on Aeschylus' *Oresteia* and its modern adaptations by O'Neill, Eliot and Sartre.

DOUGLASS PARKER (b. 1927), an itinerant rhetorician and sometime trombonist best known for his versions of Aristophanes, makes his living teaching Classics at the University of Texas at Austin. He also acts in Elizabethan-Jacobean drama as the occasion offers, and has been type-cast as Casca, Pandarus, and Morose. If he survives, he may yet fill the gap in near-English letters left by Abraham Cowley on his death in 1667. Failing that, he will be remembered for his work-in-progress, *Guidelines for Epigonoi.*

TIM REYNOLDS (Isshin, b. 1936), studied at Antioch, Wisconsin, Tufts, and Texas. His books include: *Ryoanji, Halflife, Slocum, Que, The Women Poem, Qarrtsiluni,* and *Ertanax* (the last two not yet published) and an unpublished translation of the works of Mencius. He is now living in Yellow Springs, Ohio, and writing *Epistles* for his friends.

ARMAND SCHWERNER. 7 books of poetry, among them *Seaweed,* Black Sparrow, 1969; *The Tablets I–XV,* Grossman, 1971; *The Bacchae Sonnets,* Cummington, 1974. Workings from oral traditions of North American Indians, Eskimos, Hawaiians in various collections. Work represented in 22 anthologies. Now Professor of English at Staten Island Community College of City University of New York. NEA Fellow in Creative Writing 1973. CAPs-New York State Council on the Arts Creative Artists Public Service Grant 1973. Musician—mainly bass clarinet—and working recently with Charles Morrow's New Wilderness Preservation Band: improvisational chanting, music, with poetry. Translations from Tibetan medieval sacred texts for about two years. Lives in Victorian house overlooking the Narrows in Staten Island with artist wife Doloris Holmes, two sons Adam and Ari.